Praise for
The Twelve Steps: A Modern Hero's Journey

"And although the author's underlying assertion that the recovery process is itself heroic, which is certainly true, the book's main attraction throughout is the wonderfully sharp and knowing reflections on the nature of addiction and recovery writ more broadly. The device of mapping this onto Campbell is thought-provoking, but it's the author's deeply felt plumbing of the 'abyss of self' through which every addict must journey that makes the book so unexpectedly gripping. Recovering addicts and alcoholics in particular should read this book, not because they consider themselves heroes (far from it; humility is built into the Twelve Steps), but to find their struggles very eloquently described."

—*Kirkus Reviews*

"*The Twelve Steps: A Modern Hero's Journey* is a stirring read. It's smart and hopeful. I'd recommend it to anyone in recovery, especially those looking for something more soulful than standard fare. It's also great for folks outside recovery who are curious about transformation, or anyone who loves myth and wants to apply it to real life. You don't need to be a wizard or Jedi to take this journey, you just need to be willing."

—*Literary Titan*

"Drawing a parallel between the classic Twelve Step recovery program—originally founded by Bill Wilson of Alcoholics Anonymous—and Joseph Campbell's iconic hero's journey from his *Hero with a Thousand Faces* makes this an imaginative read, offering a fresh, accessible framework for those navigating the difficult path of recovery from addiction. Readers will find the guidance gentle but insightful…"

—*Booklife Reviews*

"Libraries interested in adding more Twelve Step surveys to their collections will especially appreciate the intellectual and psychological approach that sets *The Twelve Steps: A Modern Hero's Journey* apart from most others on the subject. Accessible to a wide audience, (this book) will especially appeal to book clubs looking at Twelve Step memoirs and books which take the next step into better understanding and appreciation of the promise and delivery of the Twelve Step program."

—**D. Donovan**, senior reviewer, *Midwest Book Review*

"Recovery is indeed a heroic journey, and the author shines a light on the transformative power of Twelve Step programs through this fascinating exploration of the relationship between the Steps and Joseph's Campbell's most celebrated work. In doing so, the author honors the undertaking of sobriety and abstinence, providing invaluable encouragement to those who have the courage to let go of who they have known themselves to be for the possibility of who they might become. Beautifully written and deeply inspiring."

—**Katherine Woodward Thomas,** *New York Times* bestselling author of *Calling in "The One": 7 Weeks to Attract the Love of Your Life*

"*The Twelve Steps: A Modern Hero's Journey* offers a fresh and engaging perspective on recovery, even for those with decades of experience in the field or in personal recovery. The author provides a valuable service by using heroes from familiar myths and stories to illuminate the milestones, processes, and mechanisms of the recovery journey—insights that even seasoned professionals may overlook. Highly recommended for those seeking a fresh and intriguing perspective on the journey of recovery."

—**Jason Schwartz, LMSW,** director, social work and spiritual care, Michigan Medicine

"*The Twelve Steps: A Modern Hero's Journey* offers great insight into the Twelve Step journey, and it does so with unusual scope, enchanting detail, and breathtaking clarity. Academics, clinical addiction professionals, researchers, and the lay public will all be drawn into this book. Its stories and its revelations, and its elegant, real, and compelling handling of our shared and ancient all-too-human nature will surely win many readers over. Highly recommended!"

—**Brian Coon,** chief clinical officer, Pavillon Addiction Treatment Center

"In *The Twelve Steps, A Modern Hero's Journey*, the author intertwines the time-tested Twelve Steps with the hero's journey developed by Joseph Campbell. Wonderfully illustrated with examples from *Harry Potter, Star Wars, The Wizard of Oz,* and more, the author reveals and interprets the complex layers of the recovery journey. We are reminded that transformation is the ultimate goal of both journeys, and that it cannot happen in isolation. We gain a deepened appreciation for the role of a mentor/sponsor, the collective wisdom of community and, in turn, the necessity to give back to others. As a result, the hero savors hope, expansiveness, and a newfound territory of true belonging."

—**Andrew Susskind, LCSW, SEP, CGP,** author of *It's Not About the Sex: Moving from Isolation to Intimacy After Sexual Addiction*

"This amazing book combines all the skills I use as both a mental health counselor and certified addictions professional, particularly integrating the original concepts of recovery with the well-known hero's journey as shown in movies and modern storytelling. Fascinating and inspiring, I highly recommend this book to all those who are searching for ways to both deepen and expand their understanding of the recovery journey and move closer to the person they were always meant to be."

—**Jill Haire, LMHC, CAP, NCC,** Free Flow Counseling, author

"*The Twelve Steps: A Modern Hero's Journey* guides the reader through the transformative path of the Twelve Step journey of recovery in a thrilling and inventive new way. Using examples drawn from modern and ancient stories alike, the author illustrates the variety of pathways offered throughout cultures and across the millennia that have been navigated by heroes to achieve both redemption and self-actualization. This book's relevance extends beyond those with substance use disorders and offers hope, direction, and encouragement to individuals at any stage in their lives and with their own hero's journey. An important addition to both the recovery literature and self-help genres."

—**Chris Budnick,** executive director, Healing Transitions

"In *The Twelve Steps: A Modern Hero's Journey*, the author reframes addiction recovery as a heroic transformation, drawing from Joseph Campbell's *The Hero with a Thousand Faces*. Like every mythic hero, those in recovery face a call to change, go through trials, and rely on the help of mentors, ultimately emerging from their journey transformed. While the author beautifully ties recovery to universal storytelling, the book draws many of its references from A.A. Those who travel the Twelve Step journey through other fellowships, however, will find it inspiring and validating as well. Its message of growth and renewal is universal, reminding us that true recovery is about more than just abstinence—it's about transformation, purpose, and finding a new way to live. Highly recommended for all those on a spiritual path."

—**Lesley Pregenzer,** CEO, FAVOR Upstate

"*The Twelve Steps: A Modern Hero's Journey* transforms the ancient archetype of the hero's journey into an insightful interpretation of the Twelve Steps. This contemporary telling unveils the practical magic of recovery amulets like sobriety chips and the Serenity Prayer, while doubling as a masterclass in the history of Alcoholics Anonymous and the origin of the Twelve Steps. The familiar recovery structure —'what it was like, what happened, and what it's like now'—is reimagined as Joseph Campbell's monomyth: The recovering hero moves from a state of separation into initiation and then returns, ready to be of service to the community. Secular examples, too, thread through the discussion: Dorothy in *The Wizard of Oz*, Luke Skywalker, and an exploration of improbable heroism in *Groundhog Day* serve as examples that make the hero's journey accessible. Readers, whether in recovery or not, will feel the pull inward, called to reflect on their own mythic path toward transfiguration. These pages recount an age-old adventure that promises to edify all, while validating those modern heroes who tread the Twelve Steps today. A worthy, enlightening read."

—**Quincy Gray McMichael,** poet, adventurer, and director, Healing Appalachia

"*The Twelve Steps: A Modern Hero's Journey* is a vital contribution to the recovery literature. Over the decades, critics of the Twelve Step process have sometimes called it 'simplistic.' This book offers a deeper look at recovery by interpreting it through the lens of the transformational process of the spiritual journey as revealed by the age-old pattern of the hero's journey. This new understanding of recovery is a gift to us all. Thank you!"
—**Stephanie S. Covington, PhD, LCSW,** author of *A Woman's Way Through the Twelve Steps; Helping Women Recover; Helping Men Recover, Healing Trauma+*; and *Exploring Trauma+*

"*The Twelve Steps: A Modern Hero's Journey* takes us on an exhilarating tour of the recovery process through the lens of Jungian mythology and the quest through the long, dark night of the soul and into the light of a renewed life. This is a fascinating read and an important interpretation of the journey of recovery."

—**Bill Stauffer,** executive director, Pennsylvania Recovery Organizations Alliance (Pro-A)

"*The Twelve Steps: A Modern Hero's Journey* creatively, clearly, and intelligently deepens our understanding of the Twelve Step path of recovery and enhances our journey, whether we're currently engaged in this path or any other. I wholeheartedly recommend this wonderful book—for the novice and the experienced alike."

—**Phillip Stephen Mitchell, MA, MFT, MAC,** psychotherapist (ret.), author

the TWELVE STEPS
A Modern Hero's Journey

the TWELVE STEPS

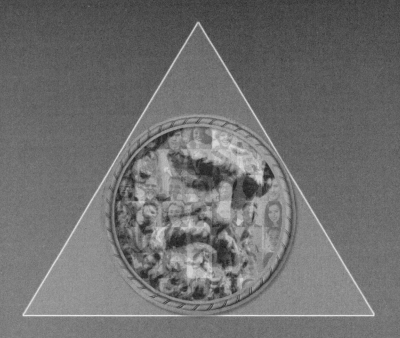

A Modern Hero's Journey

anonymous

Health Communications, Inc.
Mt. Pleasant, South Carolina

www.hcibooks.com

Library of Congress Cataloging-in-Publication Data
is available through the Library of Congress

©2025 Anonymous

ISBN-13: 978-07573-2600-4 (Paperback)
ISBN-10: 07573-2600-5 (Paperback)
ISBN-13: 978-07573-2601-1 (ePub)
ISBN-10: 07573-2601-3 (ePub)

All rights reserved. Printed in the United States of America. No part of this publication may be reproduced, stored in a retrieval system, or transmitted in any form or by any means, electronic, mechanical, photocopying, recording, or otherwise, without the written permission of the publisher.

HCI, its logos, and marks are trademarks of Health Communications, Inc.

Publisher: Health Communications, Inc.
1240 Winnowing Way, Suite 102
Mt. Pleasant, SC 29466

Cover, interior design, and formatting by Larissa Hise Henoch

To all the heroes, past and present,
who have come before me

Contents

Preface — xv
Introduction — 1

Part One: SEPARATION — 15

Step One: **The Call to Recovery** — 17
Step Two: **Meeting the Mentor** — 37
Step Three: **Crossing the First Threshold** — 71

Part Two: INITIATION — 93

Step Four: **Into the Abyss** — 95
Step Five: **Initiation** — 125
Steps Six and Seven: **Revelation** — 147
Steps Eight and Nine: **Atonement** — 177

Step Nine: **Making Amends**   191

Steps Ten and Eleven: **Attunement**   201

Step Eleven: **Apotheosis**   217

Part Three: RETURN   227

Step Twelve: The Return   229

Appendix   259

Preface

> It would not be too much to say that myth is the secret opening through which the inexhaustible energies of the cosmos pour into human cultural manifestation.[1]
>
> —Joseph Campbell, *The Hero with a Thousand Faces*

JOSEPH CAMPBELL (1904–1987) was the world's foremost authority on comparative mythology and religion, and in his many books, lectures, and television documentary interviews, he revealed the power and purpose of storytelling over the millennia. Using tales, myths,[2] and modern stories, he showed the significance of these stories and the true impact they have had, and continue to have, in our consciousness and in the world today. In the work that established the theme for his life and future work, *The Hero with a Thousand Faces* (1949), he introduced the world to the enduring, universal themes and archetypes that appear in both mythical storytelling across cultures and history, and the motifs in these stories that continue to inform, direct, and delight us today. Central among these motifs is the archetype of the hero's journey, a universal framework for personal transformation, which leads to a rebirth of the individual, resulting in the renewal of the world.

The hero's journey represents the universal spiritual journey of man, a journey from immaturity and isolation to unity and freedom—from birth to spiritual rebirth. It is a story told a thousand times, by hundreds of different cultures across history, yet its pattern and purpose remain the same. This one story, or "monomyth"[3] as Campbell called it, serves to free spiritual energy by transforming a person's separate sense of self, thus allowing pent-up spiritual energy to flow from the individual into the community, healing them both.

The structure of the hero's journey follows the ancient rituals and ceremonies that tribes, societies, and cultures have used to mark the transition of the child into an adult. Known as the rite of passage,[4] these rituals serve as a symbolic death and rebirth: the death of the dependent, ego-centered child and the rebirth of a responsible adult member of the community. The hero's journey follows the same three stages of the rite of passage: separation, initiation, and return. It serves the same purpose: to transform, through a series of trials and tests, an independent, often childish personality structure and then to return the hero to his or her community, where they can contribute the experience, strength, and hope they learned on the journey.

As we will see, the hero's journey is present, not only in myths, stories, and tales from the world's disparate cultures, but it is also the same journey a modern hero takes through the recovery program of the Twelve Steps. We will discover that the journey of recovery is the modern retelling of this timeless pattern that heroes have taken throughout the ages. The Twelve Step program follows the classic stages of the hero's journey, starting with a call to adventure where the newcomer separates from their known world of drinking or using, and enters the new landscape of recovery, wherein the great change in their psyche will take place. The next phase of the hero's journey in recovery involves an intensive phase of initiation, whereby the newcomer undergoes a series of steps that plunge them into the secret depths of themselves, the only place where a fundamental shift in attitude and self can occur; finally, once transformed, the newly reborn hero returns to their community, bringing with him the boon—the lessons, insights, and new ways of dealing with life in a spiritual way. We will see that Bill Wilson, the cofounder of Alcoholics Anonymous and creator of the Twelve Steps, reached into the collective unconscious and drew out this archetypal pattern of transformation, thus creating the modern map of recovery.

For this book and the examples of the Twelve Steps, we focus on the recovery a person working the Twelve Steps (as originally created by Bill Wilson) used in the program of Alcoholics Anonymous. It's important to note that the Twelve Steps—as a modern interpretation of the universal hero's journey archetype—are just as effective for treating addictions to a variety of substances, behaviors, and obsessions. This is because recovery from any compulsive behavior is the result of a transformation of thoughts and attitudes, all of which lead to a spiritual experience: the same goal and purpose of the hero's journey itself. Therefore, this is the universal journey a compulsive overeater takes to recover in the program of OA—Overeaters Anonymous—or a codependent person takes in Al-Anon, or a sex and love addict takes in the program of Sex and Love Addicts Anonymous, S.L.A.A. Thousands of modern heroes have traveled the path of recovery. Despite their differences, the programs follow the same order and methods of working the Twelve Steps, including the rituals of meetings, the importance of a sponsor as mentor, reliance on a Power greater than oneself, and more. We see that the path of recovery, like the hero's journey itself, is thoroughly known, and so the stories of recovery share a deep and remarkable resemblance. That resemblance is the power of the spiritual journey of humankind and the unlocking of and pouring back into humanity the spiritual energy of the universe.

The hero pattern, as translated into the Twelve Steps, retains the power to heal and transform, to destroy the old and give birth to the new. The program of recovery is filled with stories of pain turned into promise, of fear turned into faith, and of isolation turned into a feeling of community. The experience, strength, and hope of all the heroes who have gone before show, time and again, how this universal archetype has the power to turn desperate, and seemingly hopeless, situations into miraculous journeys of healing and hope.

I quote the fourth edition of the "Big Book," as it is known in the program, of Alcoholics Anonymous (A.A.), as well as the *Twelve Steps and Twelve Traditions*, nineteenth printing, 1995. Both books are the fundamental texts of the A.A. program, are the original source of the Twelve Steps, and represent the journey of recovery across all programs. Both of these books are filled with strikingly similar examples of every stage of the hero's journey, as we will see, one that has changed millions of lives around the world. It is a journey that you, or someone you know, may be on at this very moment.

Additionally, I use examples of myths, legends, and modern stories from films to show how the archetype of the hero's journey has been used to both entertain and teach us the universal meaning and importance of this journey. Films such as the Star Wars series, the Harry Potter series, *Groundhog Day,* and *The Wizard of Oz*, among others, have enduring popularity precisely because the pattern they reveal of the hero's journey resonates deeply within us all. As a side note, George Lucas was a great admirer of Joesph Campbell, and when writing the original Star Wars trilogy, he used as his outline for the series Campbell's book *The Hero with a Thousand Faces* (he referred to Campbell as "my Yoda"). As we will see, Luke Skywalker's journey follows each stage of the hero's journey perfectly, as well as the substages within the pattern (as do the other stories, films, and recovery programs).

Also, in the appendix for each chapter, you'll find illustrative examples from numerous stories and myths of the various stages in the hero's journey. I hope you'll take some time to read this additional material to gain even more insight. When you do, you'll soon find that this universal journey of transformation has been with us as long as storytelling has, and these tales serve a lasting and fundamental purpose in helping us discover our true purpose.

One final note on the use of gender throughout this book: I use the term *hero* to refer to both the male and female in the hero's journey and in recovery. The word *heroine* is a derivative of hero and takes something away from the female's journey and importance. To me, both males and females who set out upon the hero's path are equal and should be referred to as such. Therefore, I will randomly use both *his* and *her* as it best suits the text.

There is a saying in the rooms of recovery that there is a miracle waiting for you in the Twelve Step program. As you will see, all you have to do is answer your call and begin the journey to have that miracle happen for you—and for the world.

Introduction

THE FIRST MODERN HERO to take the journey into recovery, which would ultimately result in the Twelve Step journey of today, was a man who was at a jumping off point in his life. In the early 1930s, Rowland Hazzard III had hit a physical, emotional, and spiritual bottom. A prominent member of one of the most well-respected families in the Rhode Island textile industry, Rowland enjoyed the privileges of a Yale University education, served briefly in the Rhode Island state senate, and initially worked in the family's business. During the Roaring Twenties, he held a position in a New York banking firm, and whoopee parties, flowing alcohol, and limitless optimism filled Rowland's days and nights. Married with four children, Rowland seemed to have it all, yet he also had a problem as old as humanity: He was an alcoholic, who, by himself, couldn't stop drinking himself to death. Rowland had sought out the best American psychiatrists of the day and struggled through one sanitarium after another. Finally, on the verge of losing not only his position and reputation but also his life, he called out for help from a distant doctor and boarded an ocean liner for Zurich, Switzerland, where he placed himself under the care of the renowned psychiatrist Dr. Carl

Jung. In the archetype of the hero's journey, Jung would serve the role of mentor to Rowland, and through Dr. Jung's encouragement, Rowland would find a power greater than himself that would restore him to sanity.

Carl Jung's philosophy and the focus of his life's work was based on a spiritual understanding of a patient's consciousness, as well as what lies beneath it. For Jung, just below our observable consciousness sits a pool of unconscious wisdom that the psyche is longing to plunge into in order to complete its thirst for unity and wholeness. Jung calls this pool "the collective unconscious" and says that while individual consciousness contains the sum of all personal experiences, the collective unconscious contains the vast collective wisdom, symbols, and images shared with people across all time and cultures. Merging the self with the unconscious is the goal of psychological growth Jung calls the *individuation process*. And it is from this collective well of material that the narratives of myth are created and re-created.

To Jung, the collective unconscious holds the very life force itself, the instinctual energy that shapes and drives our development, behavior, and our desire to connect back with it. This raw energy is always seeking expression, and the vehicles it uses are primordial images called *archetypes*. Archetypes are raw forms into which the molten energy of the life force is poured. Archetypes—the original, deep, and abiding patterns in the human psyche—are structure-forming elements without content themselves. Once activated with spiritual energy, however, they become alive with the tremendous energy of spirit, and their expression can be at once awesome and terrifying. The archetype of the hero's journey is the vehicle spiritual energy uses to transform the individual and the world, allowing the energy to flow from the separate self back into the larger whole, uniting and thus awakening both.

Jung had seen alcoholic cases as bad as Rowland's before, but he hadn't had much success treating them. In Jung's experience, alcoholics tended to be ego-driven in the extreme, and almost childish in their grandiosity and denial. Furthermore, when someone was as far given in to alcohol as Rowland was, the hope was slim that any kind of long-term sobriety would take place. Despite this, Jung worked with Rowland for months, and he did recover for a time. Filled with relief and confidence that his new understanding of himself would enable him to resist the lure of alcohol for good, he returned to the United States.

Within no time, however, Rowland started drinking again, and this time it was worse than ever before. Commitment to an insane asylum, which was common for alcoholics of his kind in those days, seemed his next probable destination. Broken and deflated, Rowland returned to Dr. Jung and pleaded with him to give it to him straight: Would he ever recover? What he heard back sounded like a death sentence. Jung told him that he was utterly hopeless and would have to be locked up or hire a bodyguard if he wanted to live much longer, as this seemed the only way to prevent him from drinking himself to death. When Rowland begged for some sort of solution, Jung briefly considered and told him that his only hope was for a life-changing "vital spiritual experience"—the kind he had been working with him to produce.

Jung had observed these experiences and believed that they had been occurring since ancient times; they always involved a dismantling of the psyche and a complete rearrangement of emotions, ideas, and attitudes. It required the death of the old man and the birth of a new man, a spiritually different person in every way. Only with the complete transformation of the personality structure, and the development of a new set of intentions and motivations, did the new man have a chance. Jung was describing the work that is done during the initiation phase of the hero's journey, a time of tests and trials that challenge the hero's conceptions of himself and that ultimately result in a complete rearrangement of motivations and convictions. Rowland grew hopeful again and told Jung that perhaps he could achieve this change through his church. Jung deflated this idea by revealing that, while strong and useful, religious convictions were seldom enough on their own to bring about this vital spiritual experience.

Dejected, Rowland returned to the United States and soon faced another jumping off point. His drinking spiraled out of control, and by 1933, he had lost the ability to keep up with even simple, everyday living. It was at this dark bottom of despair and hopelessness that he reached out to a local therapist who convinced him to seek the kind of spiritual experience that Jung had mentioned. Rowland answered yet another call in his journey and joined a Christian fellowship movement called the Oxford Group, setting in motion the next chain of events that continue to transform millions of lives around the world even today.

The Oxford Group was a popular Christian organization started by Dr. Frank Buchman, an American Christian missionary, who received a spiritual awakening in a chapel in Keswick, England, in 1908. The movement was first called A First Century Christian Fellowship in 1921; however, in 1928, when a group of members from Oxford, England, were traveling to South Africa, a railway porter wrote the name Oxford Group on the windows of the compartments to identify them. By 1931, the name had stuck and the group was thereafter known simply as the Oxford Group. The goal of the organization was to help its members become spiritually reborn by having a conversion experience, which it achieved through following a four-step spiritual practice.

To begin this process, a person first shared his sins and temptations honestly with another member of the group. Second, they were directed to make restitution to those they had wronged either directly or indirectly. Third, they surrendered their past, present, and future life to God. Finally, they were instructed to listen to and follow God's guidance from then on in their lives. These four spiritual practices would later become the basis for the Twelve Steps in the program of Alcoholics Anonymous.

Rowland began attending Oxford Group meetings in New York and surrendered himself completely to its precepts. With the help of many companions in the group, he had a spiritual conversion that soon relieved him of the compulsion to drink. True to Jung's prescription of having a vital spiritual experience, the four-step process helped break down Rowland's personality structure and gave him a new set of conceptions and motives by which he ran his life. Rowland's initiation phase of his hero's journey was now complete, and the last part of the journey, the return, began. Rowland strengthened his reborn self by returning to Oxford Group meetings, where he shared the boon—his experience, strength, and his spiritual awakening—with other members. It was through this classic return that Rowland passed on to other alcoholics the solution he had found and, in doing so, formed another link in the direct lineage of the A.A. program.

Rowland developed a wide support circle of "groupers," as they were called, and one of these members, Shep Cornell, introduced

Rowland to another alcoholic, Ebby Thacher. Ebby was a serious alcoholic who had been visited by two sober members of the Oxford Group who were his former drinking buddies. Though Ebby was impressed by what they said, it was Rowland's visit with him that had the biggest impact. Ebby was impressed with Rowland's prominent background, with his outrageous drinking career—his drinking sprees often included cross-country travel and carousing on a high level—and the fact that despite his high professional position he was still a regular, genuinely nice guy who was willing to help Ebby get clean and straighten out his life.

Rowland stuck by Ebby from the beginning, and when Ebby appeared in court for being intoxicated and firing his double-barreled shotgun in his neighborhood, Rowland convinced the judge to release Ebby into his care. Rowland then helped Ebby move from Manchester down to New York City, where Ebby began living at the Calvary Rescue Mission run by Reverend Sam Shoemaker. Sam was a staunch supporter of the Oxford Group's philosophy, and his fifty-seven-bed mission on Twenty-Third Street was the home of last resort to down-and-out drunks. It was there in the crowded and smoky meeting rooms that Ebby learned a crucial lesson from his new mentor, Sam, who worked with many of the drunks who attended the Oxford Group meetings. He taught Ebby that if he had a problem with the God concept, he could simply surrender to God as he understood Him to be at the time.[1] It was this lesson that would later have a profound impact on Bill Wilson (Bill W.), the founder of A.A.

Ebby experienced his own hero's journey in recovery, first by answering his call to get sober through the Oxford Group meetings, by going through the initiation process of the four-step spiritual practice, by having a spiritual experience through which he attained sobriety, and then by returning to work with and help other alcoholics. In keeping with the Oxford principles, Ebby knew to reach out and help others was a way of keeping and maintaining his own conversion experience. That's when Ebby heard of an old drinking buddy's desperate battle with alcoholism, and he decided to pay his old friend a visit.

Bill W. and the Twelve Steps

Bill W. was born on November 26, 1895, in East Dorset, Vermont. He started drinking as a young officer during his military training, while serving at the end of World War I as a second lieutenant. After the war, Bill's drinking continued and nearly ruined a promising career on Wall Street. The stock market crash of 1929 took care of that, but nothing could stop his drinking. In and out of hospitals because of his alcohol addiction, Bill was at his own jumping off point, when one morning in November 1934, his old friend Ebby called and asked whether he could come by for a visit. Bill hadn't seen his old drinking buddy in a couple of years and didn't know Ebby was sober. For Bill, Ebby's visit seemed like a great opportunity to relive old times and drink with someone who enjoyed and needed a drink as much as he did.

Bill thought back to the shenanigans he and Ebby had gotten into over the years, especially in 1929 when they persuaded a barnstormer pilot, Ted Burke, to fly them to Manchester, Vermont. They learned that the Manchester Airport was due to open and decided it would be great fun to be the first to land there. They called the local press to make sure their landing was recorded, and then drank themselves into a stupor the night before. When they finally landed and stumbled out of the plane onto the ground, still drunk from the night before, the crowd, press, and even the town band was dumbfounded. Bill spent the next day writing apologies.

In the kitchen waiting for Ebby that evening, though, he smiled to himself: Yes, a visit from his old pal was exactly what he needed at this low point in his life. When Ebby arrived, Bill immediately knew something was wrong. Ebby glowed with a quiet excitement, and his eyes were bright, clear, and alive. Ebby followed Bill into the small kitchen, where Bill produced a pitcher of gin and pineapple juice with two glasses. Bill poured Ebby a drink and pushed the glass toward him. Ebby pushed the glass back. Bill was now officially worried and asked his old friend what was wrong, and that's when Ebby beamed and said he was sober and had found religion. Bill was aghast, but he comforted himself with the thought that his gin would last longer than the evening of preaching he was sure he was about to endure. To his surprise, though, Ebby didn't preach. Instead, he described how he had found a solution to his drinking problem and that solution was a new belief in God.

With the mention of God, Bill, an agnostic, felt his chest tighten. Ebby shared openly and honestly about his own reservations over the concept of God and suggested that if Bill had a problem with God, then he could choose his own conception of God. Ebby described the experience he had had at the Oxford Group and invited Bill to join him sometime. Bill didn't let on, but as the evening unfolded, he felt a sense of hope by seeing the obvious transformation that had happened to his friend. In time, Bill would concede that if Ebby could get help for his drinking, then there might be hope for himself as well.

One afternoon in early December after Ebby's visit, a very drunk Bill W. stumbled into the Calvary Rescue Mission looking for his friend Ebby. He attended his first Oxford Group meeting there and, in a somewhat belligerent mood, got up and surrendered himself to God. Unfortunately, this experience at the altar in the mission did little to slow his drinking, and a couple of days later, a drunk and broken-down Bill W. was admitted to Towns Hospital in Manhattan for the fourth and final time. It was here that Bill finally and completely surrendered, and something miraculous happened. Here, in the abyss of self, Bill humbly offered himself to God and unreservedly placed himself under His care and direction. At this moment, Bill had a spiritual experience that came to him in what he described as an intensity of light and ecstasy. He told his physician, Dr. William Silkworth, that he saw an all-encompassing white light, and that his room had suddenly been filled with an indescribable presence. At first Bill was afraid that he was hallucinating or insane, but Dr. Silkworth saw that his patient had experienced something powerful and real, and he advised Bill to trust and hang on to that experience.

Indeed, he did, and Bill never drank again. When he was released from the hospital, he attended Oxford Group meetings and focused on carrying his experience to other alcoholic members of the meetings. Although unable to keep anyone else sober, Bill learned that working diligently with others ensured his own sobriety. It was this experience of continuing to work with others that brought Bill, while on a business trip in Akron, Ohio, in contact with Dr. Bob Smith in 1935.

Dr. Bob, as he is simply known in the program of Alcoholics Anonymous, was the first person Bill worked with who was able to achieve and maintain sobriety. In fact, the official date of the beginning of the fellowship of A.A., which Bill W. and Dr. Bob would soon begin, corresponds to the first day of Dr. Bob's sobriety, June

10, 1935. For the next two years, Bill and Dr. Bob attended Oxford Group meetings and expanded its four-step process to six steps in an attempt to help other alcoholics achieve the conversion or spiritual experience needed to attain sobriety. These first six steps constituted the very "word of mouth" program and varied from person to person in the early fellowship. They can be summarized as:

1. We admitted we were licked.
2. We got honest with ourselves.
3. We got honest with someone else.
4. We made amends for the harm we'd done.
5. We tried to help others with no thought of return.
6. We prayed to whatever God we thought there was for the power to take these actions.

By the fall of 1937, Bill and Dr. Bob had been able to help over forty alcoholics in Akron, Ohio, and New York stay sober—a success rate of about 5 percent. By this time, Bill had separated from the Oxford Group and was holding his own recovery meetings in his home. Bill burned with the passion of making his program of spiritual principles more accessible, and with a one-vote margin by the original eighteen members of the Akron group, he was given the approval to write the book that has come to be known simply as the Big Book of Alcoholics Anonymous.

The Big Book is the official book of recovery for the program of A.A. Until it was published, the program of recovery was largely carried by one member to another. While writing it, Bill discovered that a more detailed approach needed to be developed, and this was when he expanded the original six steps to twelve. The Twelve Steps came easily for Bill, over the course of just one night, as if they flowed from the very source zones of spiritual energy itself. The Twelve Steps represent the official program of recovery. They are:

1. We admitted we were powerless over alcohol—that our lives had become unmanageable.
2. Came to believe that a Power greater than ourselves could restore us to sanity.
3. Made a decision to turn our will and our lives over to the care of God *as we understood Him.*
4. Made a searching and fearless moral inventory of ourselves.
5. Admitted to God, to ourselves, and to another human being the exact nature of our wrongs.
6. Were entirely ready to have God remove all these defects of character.
7. Humbly asked Him to remove our shortcomings.
8. Made a list of all persons we had harmed, and became willing to make amends to them all.
9. Made direct amends to such people wherever possible, except when to do so would injure them or others.
10. Continued to take personal inventory and when we were wrong promptly admitted it.
11. Sought through prayer and meditation to improve our conscious contact with God *as we understood Him,* praying only for knowledge of His will for us and the power to carry that out.
12. Having had a spiritual awakening as the result of these steps, we tried to carry this message to alcoholics, and to practice these principles in all our affairs.

Bill's journey of transformation had come full circle. To help others achieve recovery, he reached into the collective unconscious and intuitively pulled out the map of this modern journey, the map called the Twelve Steps.

The Twelve Steps are a modern retelling of the hero's journey, and they fit perfectly into the three broad categories of the hero pattern: (1) Separation: Steps One through Three, (2) Initiation: Steps Four through Eleven, and (3) Return: Step Twelve. Looking deeper, each of the Steps also represents clearly defined substages in the archetype of the hero's journey, including answering the call, getting a mentor, crossing the threshold, and plunging into the abyss of the Fourth Step. The journey unfolds perfectly, step-by-step, leading to the final transfiguration and return with the boon.

Once again, healing comes as the result of having a spiritual experience as the initiate dies to the old, isolated self and is reborn as a larger, more inclusive self. The transformed person then rejoins his community and releases spiritual energy back into the world. In this way, millions of lives have been and continue to be healed.

Years later, Bill wrote what he called a long overdue letter to Dr. Carl Jung expressing his gratitude for Jung's involvement in the chain of events that led to the formation of the A.A. program. Dr. Jung commented on his work with Rowland in this way:

> [Rowland H.'s] craving for alcohol was the equivalent, on a low level, of the spiritual thirst of our being for wholeness, expressed in the medieval language: the union with God....
>
> I am strongly convinced that the evil principle prevailing in this world leads the unrecognized spiritual need into perdition, if it is not counteracted either by real religious insight or by the protective wall of human community....
>
> You see, alcohol in Latin is *spiritus* and you use the same word for the highest religious experience as well as for the most depraving poison.

This was the first time the obsessive craving for alcohol was put in the context of the soul's yearning for connection with God, and as such it defined alcoholism as a sickness of the soul, which could only be remedied by achieving a spiritual experience and merging with the fellowship of community. Moreover, alcoholism—once seen as a scourge and near-certain death sentence—could now be seen as a crossroads offering two diverging paths: one leading to spiritual transformation and union, and the other to perdition. For the alcoholic, the doorway to this path is hitting bottom, and choosing the path of recovery then becomes the heroic choice.

When Bill W. answered his call to get sober and embarked on the modern hero's journey of recovery, it seemed at first that he was entering uncharted territory, but his spirit knew the journey well. The map he used is found deep within us all—the abiding, enduring pattern of the archetype of the hero's journey.

Today, a person facing recovery is someone who clearly has the hero's choice in front of him. Does he choose to respond to his soul's call for freedom and transformation by answering the call of his rock-bottom experience, and entering what at first seems like the dark road of recovery? Or does he refuse his call, take flight from the call of his spirit, and keep drinking or indulging in old behaviors and face the certain physical, emotional, and psychological deterioration of that path? The modern hero stands at a jumping off point, but he need not be reluctant nor afraid. The path of recovery is clearly laid out, and the journey has been successfully navigated by both ancient and modern heroes alike. To start this journey requires only the willingness to answer the call to adventure and follow the Twelve Steps of the modern hero's journey. If you are ready, you can begin the journey today.

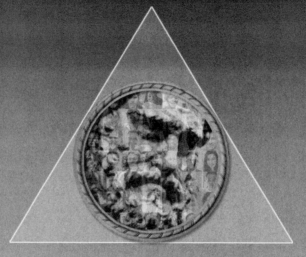

PART ONE
SEPARATION

STEP ONE
The Call to Recovery

THE HERO'S JOURNEY always begins with a call that signals a great change is coming. The call invites us, or sometimes pushes us, into a journey of discovery and transformation, pulling us away from our ordinary world and into the deeper reaches of ourselves. For it is here, in the inner chasms of our psyche, that the real causes and difficulties reside, and it is also here, in the very source zones of ourselves, that we will find the primordial power that allows us to transcend the feared and repressed parts of ourselves, to meet them head-on, and to finally integrate them and to heal. The call beckons the hero into an unknown landscape, both internal and external, to a strange new place where a great rebirth is possible. Sometimes we willingly choose to answer this call; other times we blunder into it or we are dragged. The call can come as an inner or outer need for change and it serves as the gateway to a great awakening, to a dying of the old and a rebirth of something entirely new. It is both a beginning and an end, the start of a great adventure leading to a transformation that will change both the hero and the world.

The call to recovery is heralded by what is known in the Twelve Step program as *hitting bottom*. This is defined by Step One as: "We admitted we were powerless over alcohol—that our lives had become unmanageable." This refers to when an alcoholic (or food addict or sex addict, etc.) has hit either an emotional, physical, or spiritual (often all three) bottom and an event—either internal or external—has brought him or her to a jumping off point. This is often defined as when the alcoholic can no longer imagine a life of continued drinking, yet cannot imagine a life without drinking either. The hero answers this call by admitting to his innermost self that he is an alcoholic, and the path to recovery begins once he has entered the program and has a sincere desire to stay sober. Taking Step One represents the loosening grip of the ego, and this first crack in the shield of self-reliance and self-deception is the key that opens the door through which the hero begins the journey of recovery.

The call often comes in the form of an external crisis or event that exposes a growing inner dissatisfaction or sense of discontent and restlessness with the life the hero is living. For some alcoholics, this bottoming out can be heralded by a drunk driving accident or arrest, and depending on whether there were injuries or deaths, or how traumatic the circumstances were, this outer event, coupled with the necessary inner conditions, can lead an alcoholic into recovery. Sometimes the alcoholic will voluntarily enter recovery, while at other times a judge may require him to attend A.A. meetings. Numerous other outer circumstances caused by alcoholic drinking or compulsive behaviors can also serve as external calls that motivate the hero to enter recovery as well: disintegration of or pressure from a relationship or family; loss of a job, career, or reputation; or a variety of physical ailments, etc., can all serve to signal the opening to a destiny that can no longer be denied.

Whatever the outer events or circumstances are that lead the alcoholic to a bottom, they always combine with or reveal an existing inner state of restlessness and discontent: feelings that result in emotional crises or ongoing turmoil that lead to a spiritual bottoming out. This internal catalyst awakens the sense that something is vitally missing—either exposing a deep unhappiness or incongruity with the lives they are living, or by uncovering a feeling that they have outgrown their old life. This internal restlessness signals an awakening of a new self, offering a chance for growth and new insights, and it leads the hero to the portal of a new world where this essential change is possible. This inner state, described in the rooms of recovery as a *state of spiritual bankruptcy*, is often so profound that it alone can be the call that the hero answers, and it is this state of perdition, along with other growing problems, that force, or allow, the newcomer to surrender to the journey.

Examples of the call to adventure in stories and films abound. Luke Skywalker, in the film *Star Wars: Episode IV—A New Hope*, for example, also has a deep internal restlessness that responds to an external call. Luke feels trapped working as a moisture farmer on the desolate planet of Tatooine, and he is bitter and frustrated as his step-uncle repeatedly delays his departure for another growing season. Luke spends his days moping around, dreaming, and longing to leave his isolated planet but feels there is no way out. The external events that trigger this inner yearning start first with R2-D2's holograph of Princess Leia's message—a classic princess in distress. Obi-Wan Kenobi then urges Luke to set off to help, but Luke refuses this first call and heads for home. Luke's next external call comes when he finds his home was destroyed and his step-uncle and -aunt were killed by stormtroopers. Luke is at a bottom at this point, and this final catalyst propels him to answer his inner call to the journey.

Harry Potter in *The Sorcerer's Stone* is also awakened from a familiar yet unsatisfying life when he has a conversation with a boa constrictor at the zoo. This external event triggers a series of unspoken and disturbing questions that contribute to his growing inner sense of uneasiness. Soon, the external call intensifies as mysterious letters begin flooding his home, overwhelming him and the family he lives with, the Dursleys. The truth inside Harry—that he has powers that make him very different from his adopted family, and that he has outgrown his known world—is his inner call. The escalating external events literally force Harry to answer this call and begin the journey.

Dorothy in *The Wizard of Oz* also starts off with an internal call to change and grow. She has outgrown her small life on the farm and longs to see and live a life larger than the one she's living in Kansas. The song "Over the Rainbow" gives voice to her need for transformation as she sings of a place where "skies are blue and the dreams that you dare to dream really do come true." The external event that heralds Dorothy to the adventure is Toto being captured by Miss Gulch, and Dorothy subsequently rescuing Toto and running away with him. The traumatic external event of the tornado then literally launches Dorothy into her adventure.

While external events often motivate a hero to answer a corresponding internal call, sometimes the internal call actually causes the external event to occur. Luke's whole adventure is caused by his carelessness in removing the restraining pin from R2-D2 that allows the droid to go off into the wilderness looking for Ben.

The same carelessness is present in Dorothy in *The Wizard of Oz*. The reason Dorothy is locked out of the tornado shelter to begin with is because of her own immature and stubborn refusal to comply with the rules of society. It begins when she neglects minding Toto, who repeatedly runs to her neighbor's yard, digging up the plants and flowers and chasing Almira Gulch's cat. Her self-centeredness and childish refusal to care about the needs and wants of others (part of her internal call), in addition to now needing to save Toto from the consequences of this behavior, is what motivates her to run away from home and to later become locked out of the storm shelter in the first place.

The crisis of hitting bottom exposes this underlying emotional immaturity that underscores the classic hero's character defects of self-centeredness, unrestrained egotism, and selfish immaturity. Most alcoholics enter recovery selfish and self-serving, bitter, and filled with childish grandiosity. It has been suggested that an alcoholic's emotional development is halted at the age they began drinking or using, and since many alcoholics start drinking in their early teens or younger, almost all alcoholics share the childish characteristics of deep selfishness and immaturity. For years they've acted like children, looking out for their own interests only, caring little for how their behavior affects others, the community, or even their own family. They come in as children who haven't grown up and matured to take their place among society or to assume the responsibilities of an adult. This excerpt from one of the stories from the Big Book is indicative of this lack of emotional development:

> Apparently I'd grown physically at the customary rate of speed, and I had acquired an average amount of intellectual training in the intervening years, but there had been no emotional maturity at all. I realize now that this phase of my development had been arrested by my obsession with self, and my egocentricity had reached such proportions that adjustment to anything outside my personal control was impossible for me.[1]

Dr. Harry Tiebout, a psychiatrist who studied and wrote about alcoholism and alcoholics' emotional state from a psychoanalytic perspective in the 1940s, noted how alcoholics uniformly displayed a grandiosity that was consistent with this lack of emotional development and not usually found in the general population. He characterized alcoholics as being ego driven to the extreme and used Freud's phrase "His Majesty the Baby" to describe the alcoholic's demanding feelings of entitlement and superiority. Dr. Tiebout further characterized the alcoholic's infantile psyche as having trouble dealing with frustration and as being in a hurry to get things done and to have his needs satisfied. When getting sober, this impulsivity can be evidenced by newcomers wanting to rush through the Steps, to be recovered already, and by their need for instant approval or redemption by wanting to make amends to family or friends before doing the necessary internal work. They often feel they deserve a medal because they are now "being good" and that everything should be forgiven now that they are sober.

Dealing with these unbridled defects of character often proves to be an arduous task, and the bravado of the newcomer can be a high hurdle to overcome. Many newcomers whose lives are often coming apart, for example, aren't convinced they even need to attain long-term sobriety; rather, they think they just need to slow down a bit, and that they can resume drinking again once things are back under control. They come into the rooms of recovery with their old ideas in place and with "back pocket" plans of how they are still going to have and do things their way. To underline their narcissism and sense of self-delusion, old-timers in the program have a saying that the easy way to tell whether a newcomer is lying is if his lips are moving. Getting them to slow down and examine themselves and the effects of their behaviors, and helping them uncover the real causes and conditions in their lives, is the great challenge facing the newcomer and all those who set out to help him.

Childishness and self-centeredness are just some of the characteristics that make up many heroes' inner need for growth and change. Luke also starts off immature, reckless, and self-centered. Early in the adventure, when Ben warns Luke to "watch your step" before they enter the cantina because "this place can be a little rough," Luke responds with the naivete and bravado of many would-be heroes. "I'm ready for anything," he brashly claims, but clearly he isn't. He repeatedly has to be saved—first from the stormtroopers outside the cantina, then from the intergalactic bully in the bar, then from his own recklessness in the Millennium Falcon when he wants Han Solo to rush into light speed. This immaturity is characteristic of the hero's early emotional state and contributes to the imbalance that oftentimes pushes the hero onto the hero's path.

The immature inner state of the alcoholic before recovery is often evidenced by the state of the ordinary world she is about to leave. The alcoholic's pre-heroic life is often a tangle of dysfunctional relationships and situations that can range from unmanageable to incomprehensibly demoralizing, and sometimes even dangerous—all either caused or made worse by her drinking or compulsive behavior. All these situations, both internal and external, make up the call of recovery, pushing the hero to separate from the known or ordinary world, and draw them into an unknown world where a great transformation can take place. This process starts once the hero separates from her known world of drinking—the familiar behaviors, routines, old companions—and enters the mysterious, confusing, and unknown world of recovery. Either through an A.A. meeting or a prolonged stay in a treatment facility, recovery is a strange place indeed, filled with many unfamiliar sights, sayings, and rituals. To start with, recovery meetings are often filled with smiling, healthy-looking people who are actually happy to see the down-and-out-newcomer. This is usually a much different reaction from what a low-bottom drunk is used to receiving, for by the time she has hit bottom there are few people—except perhaps a group of lower companions—who are happy to see her. In addition to this unexpected welcome, there are many strange customs and rituals to be found here: meeting directories and phone lists, recovery pamphlets and literature, sponsors and sponsees, various prayers and meditations, readings both before and after the meeting, recovery and Twelve Step sayings, and much more.

Examples in myth, stories, and film abound with the hero leaving their known world and venturing into a strange new world as well. When Dorothy is torn from her small farm in Kansas and thrust into the enchanting and colorful world of Oz, she looks around in amazement and utters the memorable phrase, "Toto, I have a feeling we're not in Kansas anymore." Here she finds a new world filled with Munchkins, talking lions, both evil witches and protective witches, and a pathway that is a literal Yellow Brick Road. It is only in this unknown world, far away from the familiar and safe one she is used to, that a magical transformation can take place.

Luke Skywalker also leaves his familiar and humdrum life on Tatooine once he answers his call and sets off with Ben to find a way to Aldernaan. Everything is different in the unknown world Luke enters, starting with the cantina filled with beings as different and diverse as the universe itself. When Luke begins his lightsaber training in the new environment of the Millennium Falcon, he is introduced to new ways of fighting—blindfolded for one—as he tries to avoid the stun blasts of the remotes that buzz and swarm around him. When he finally arrives at the Death Star to rescue Leia, he gets trapped in a trash compactor with walls that threaten to crush him and his companions. In the unknown world of this adventure, Luke is challenged to adapt, grow, and change, and is given the help and resources that weren't available to him in the known world he left behind.

Harry Potter is also separated from his ordinary and dreary life with the Dursleys when he answers his call. Separated from the non-magical people, the Muggles, Harry enters the unknown wizarding world, where everything, including the laws of gravity and physics, is different. Harry spends the majority of his time in and around a magical castle that houses the Hogwarts School of Magic, where everything is new to him, starting with the sorting ritual that determines the house of Gryffindor he is to become a part of. As Harry explores the castle, he finds paintings that talk and staircases that twist and turn while he's on them. Even the grounds around Hogwarts, the Forbidden Forest, are different and dangerous, and Harry needs to learn many spells and charms just to survive. From owls that bring mail and messages, to the game of Quidditch played on flying broomsticks, this is clearly a new world to Harry.

Yet help is always offered in this unknown world, and for the person in recovery, rituals and procedures that meetings and the program adhere to help the newcomer make sense of this new place and help her discover her role within it. Rituals have a strong transformative effect, and the most effective ones start by putting us in a state of mind to do what we must do next for our development. Twelve Step meetings do this by following a uniformly structured format that both guides and reinforces the newcomer's recovery. Meetings generally start with selected readings from the same sections of the Big Book, usually with the beginning of chapter five, "How It Works," and then either the Twelve Traditions or another section from the book. This is routinely followed by acknowledging sober anniversaries as well as giving commemorative chips or medallions to newcomers to celebrate various lengths of sobriety—usually a welcome chip, a thirty-, sixty-, or ninety-day chip, and six- or nine-month chips. The chips and anniversaries acknowledge the changes that are already taking place for the newcomers and signify acceptance and validation by the group and the recovery community. Meetings also follow specific formats and end with participants rising, holding hands, and saying either the Lord's Prayer or the Serenity Prayer. This closing practice prepares the initiate to leave this separate world and return to the everyday world. All these rituals give a shared meaning to the experience by celebrating the work being done and the transformation taking place.

Another important function of meetings is to teach people in recovery how to integrate and function as part of a group. People new to recovery have often become isolated or self-consumed, and by joining a meeting, they are now taught how to be part of a community again. Meetings require people to plan and act together, to show up on time, and to participate in the various readings, and members are encouraged to take commitments and actively engage in one of the roles necessary for putting a meeting on. Indeed, the members of the group themselves are responsible for meetings to take place. One member is elected by the group to become the secretary, and it is their job to take or assign the key to the meeting room to open up the space and to allow the setting up of chairs and tables before beginning. Various members volunteer to take other commitments, such as bringing food or making coffee, and still others are responsible for bringing the anniversary cakes and chips, bringing and setting up the recovery literature, making A.A.-related announcements, etc. At the close of the meeting, members once again act as a group to clean the meeting space and restore the room. In this coordinated way, members learn by participating with others, and through the structure and rituals of meetings, they learn how to commit to and become part of a community again.

Members are also encouraged to open up in meetings, to let themselves be known by sharing their feelings and experiences with their new community. This is often hard at first as most newcomers, after years of heavy drinking or drugging, have become defensive and secretive. The thought of opening up to a group of strangers and letting them know what is really going on can be terrifying. Many newcomers balk at participating at first, but after hearing many other people in meetings share openly and honestly about their experiences, newcomers do finally begin disclosing parts of themselves and letting others in. Many meetings offer open participation formats for this kind of sharing, and this structure helps normalize the bewildering feelings and fears newcomers have, and helps provide them the chance to step outside their isolated self and become a part of their new recovery community. Like all good rituals, meetings act as transitional spaces teaching, supporting, and helping to transform the newcomer's attitudes and actions and, ultimately, provide an environment where the essential work will be done and the great change can take place.

In this unknown world of sobriety and meetings, there is also a new language—the language of recovery. Sayings such as "Let go and let God," and "One day at a time," the Serenity Prayer, and many other prayers and sayings are ritualistically repeated or hung on the walls to emphasize and facilitate the spiritual changes taking place. "It's an inside job" is a saying that heralds the work the hero will undergo and helps prepare him for the onslaught of unfamiliar and often threatening feelings this inner journey is about to uncover. Another saying helps make light of this experience when it says: "The good news in recovery is that you get your feelings back; the bad news is that you get your feelings back." Early recovery is a dizzying place indeed, an emotional roller coaster as years of suppressed feelings surge their way to the surface. Many of these feelings lie on top of volcanoes of anger that soon explode into a rage as old as time itself—a rage manifested as the self-loathing that almost caused the alcoholic to drink himself to death. The new language of recovery gives a voice to these unacknowledged and often threatening feelings, and helps provide the tools to decipher and deal with them.

All of the transformational elements are here for the hero in this unknown world of recovery, and it is a place that indeed holds great treasures. Ahead await wondrous experiences of redemption, connection, and growth—miraculous changes that cannot be anticipated nor imagined. If the hero has the courage to enter the journey path, a great healing for himself and the world will result. But, like all new worlds, it is also a place of troubles. Ahead lie challenges that will push the hero past his limits and force him to grow in ways never anticipated. Ahead there will be dragons and monsters long forgotten and buried memories and emotions too scary to face. While the call to the adventure will entreat and promise, it will also threaten and challenge and call out fierce resistance from the old self. The dangers on the path ahead are real, and the greatest danger of the journey will come here at the entrance to this unknown world—the danger of refusing the call itself.

Refusal of the Call

> "Aldernaan? I'm not going to Aldernaan. It's late, I have to get home. I'm in for it as it is."
> —*Luke Skywalker,* Star Wars: Episode IV—A New Hope

While the world has been changed by heroes who have answered their call and fulfilled the quest, and while myth, literature, and tales old and new tell of the deeds and of the boon of the hero's journey completed, the world's stories also tell a different tale. This is the cautionary tale of the tragic hero—the hero who refuses to answer the call of his soul and indeed of destiny itself. The tragic hero instead chooses to remain in his ordinary world and consequently endures the eventual dull decline or tragic consequences of refusing to grow and change.

While the call offers to transfer spiritual energy from the individual to society, the refusal to accept this call leads to the hording of this energy. It is essentially a refusal to give up the seeming advantages of getting one's own way. The tragic hero chooses instead to keep this energy locked within his own twisted consciousness where it unleashes unmanageable and sometimes gravely pitiful consequences. The power that would have transformed the hero and the world is now imprisoned by the inflated ego tyrant, which, having turned inward, becomes the opposite of its true nature: a dark, terrorizing monster that threatens and tortures the would-be hero. By damning up this vital energy of the spirit as it seeks expression—a way of connecting with and helping others—the hero prevents its release and thus renewal. The refusal to let go of this energy leads to a life that is powered by self-centered fear and tormented by the perceived threats of a rapacious ego.

The alcoholic who refuses the call of recovery is truly the tragic hero. For the alcoholic or addict, selfish and self-centered in the extreme, refusing the call to stop drinking and using—and so refusing the call to shed his childish and demanding ego state—means the twisting of spiritual energy to serve only himself. He becomes physically and emotionally sick, relationships suffer and are broken, and in time the alcoholic becomes unable to save even himself. This condemned state of the alcoholic/addict who has refused his call is one of complete spiritual bankruptcy. When spiritual energy is trapped in the prison of self, it becomes the darkest shadow of its true nature, ultimately destroying the alcoholic and the lives of those closest to him. Like the Minotaur (from the Greek myth of King Minos[2]) ravaging the countryside of Crete, the alcoholic is, as the Big Book says, "like a tornado roaring his way through the lives of others."[3] The energy that had the power to save the alcoholic becomes the monster that now destroys him, and as he clings to his perceived advantages, the very gates of a living hell clang shut around him. The hero turns away from the joys of life, the challenges and surprises of ever-changing situations, the endless cycle of deaths and births, and instead demands that his rigid system of values, beliefs, and goals be protected and maintained.

This refusal can have consequences both big and small. For many, the unanswered call leads merely to a dull and boring life of unrealized potentials, hopes, and dreams. Think of the kind of life Luke Skywalker would have had if Ben had left on the adventure without him and Luke went back to moisture farming. Or think of the kind of life Indiana Jones would have had if he had refused the call to go after the Ark of the Covenant and instead chosen to stay and teach archaeology in the dull and dusty classroom. If Dorothy had made it into the storm shelter, imagine her living the rest of her life on the farm in Kansas. To refuse the call and wait life out is to live the life of quiet desperation Thoreau wrote about.

At its unresolved worst, the refusal becomes the demon that destroys from the inside out, leading to the kind of emptiness and misery that is never sated or eased and can easily lead to years of depression and even suicide. By rejecting their own innate need to grow and change, the hero is rejecting both the power and the freedom that comes with rebirth. Rejection turns situations that would have been empowering into their opposites—into their shadows. The journey, which would have liberated, instead enslaves, and the hero turns himself from potential savior to a victim needing to be saved.

This refusal to transform from the child state to the adult stifles not only the growth of the individual but the whole of society as well. His Majesty the Baby becomes the tyrant monster—forever vigilant to resentfully avenge any threat (real or imaged) to his selfish demands. The consequences of the refusal of the call can run the gamut from a perpetual state of discontent and anxiety to an unmanageable physical, emotional, or spiritual state to an existence that can be described as "pitiful and incomprehensible demoralization."[4] Alcoholics who have deteriorated to this state live lives trapped in situations that continue to spiral out of control, each situation or result seemingly worse than the one that came before it. Losing homes, families, and careers is just the start down this dismal road, and it is said in the program that there are only three final destinations for alcoholics who continue to refuse their call: jail, institutions, or death.

Alcoholism is a cunning disease, however, and the consequences of the refusal may appear at first—and from the outside—mild for some alcoholics, as some "high-functioning" alcoholics are able to maintain high levels of activities and careers and even achievement. Closer inspection, though, often reveals convoluted behaviors: lying to bosses, family members, or friends; manipulating and taking advantage of others; hiding bottles or their drug use from spouses; or indulging in increasingly selfish and often risky behaviors in order to keep drinking and acting out. This labyrinth of deception grows more complex as the disease of addiction progresses and the alcoholic continues to charge through people's lives, lying, stealing, cheating, and telling more lies to cover things up. Behaviors and situations deteriorate as the unrecovered hero continues to deny his problem and defends his right to drink. Horrific wreckage is often just "inches and seconds" away and becomes the sad reality for many antiheroes as overdoses, fatal car wrecks, and other accidents can result in the ultimate, life-changing disaster.

There are common stories, for example, in the recovery program when someone answers the call to get sober but then is either unable or unwilling to take the Steps required to get and maintain sobriety. Many heroes come into the program but refuse to take the suggestions to get a sponsor or to begin working the Steps, and they soon start showing up late to meetings, leaving early, and then stop going altogether. Many a sad tale can be recounted by A.A. members of people who were deeply in need of sobriety but who just couldn't humble themselves enough to get sober. Their fates are recounted in newspapers seemingly weekly. One article told the tale of a woman who didn't stop drinking between meetings and instead got behind the wheel of her car one more time while intoxicated. When she came out of her blackout, the police were knocking at her door, looking for answers to her broken fender and asking questions about a hit-and-run fatality just blocks from her home. Unable to remember the incident, an eyewitness identified her fleeing the scene, and today this woman is serving a long jail sentence in prison for manslaughter. Countless tales such as these can be recounted, and new stories just like this one are the ongoing, tragic result of the call refused.

While the refusal of the call is bad enough and causes untold negative consequences, the real problem of refusing the call is that, despite the resulting wreckage and pain, the situations that generated the call don't simply go away. Instead, they taunt and haunt the hero and often become a horrible mirror reflecting back to him his character defects and fears. By refusing to change and grow, the antihero loses the ability to save himself. Nothing he does helps. As he sinks deeper and deeper into isolation, desperation, and frustration, the opportunity for growth and discovery is lost. Now his energy is spent on self-defense and the protection of his ego, values, and perceived advantages. And that's just the start. If the call to adventure is not answered, the hero continues to find himself facing similar situations that attack the same weaknesses and character defects again and again. He continually creates and then gets locked into his own labyrinths filled with greed, self-centered fears, and obsessions. You may have heard that the definition of insanity is doing the same things over and over again and expecting different results. By refusing the call and not changing, it's easy to find himself in the same relationship over and over, only with different people, or in the same job, only at different companies. The self-replicating situations that once offered a chance for redemption and freedom become a recurring nightmare keeping the hero enchained in the prison of refusal.

A modern example of the call refused and how the hero faces the same situations—in this case the exact same situations—until he resolves his weaknesses and character defects is in the wonderful film *Groundhog Day*. In the beginning of the film we see that the main character, Phil Connors, has already refused his call to grow beyond his childish, ego-driven self. Phil appears smug, self-serving, demanding, intolerant, self-pitying, bitter, and defensive. He is the antihero taken to the extreme, and he is quick to exploit others and situations without a care for the welfare of others or the community. Phil is immaturity and refusal of the call personified, and he shows no interest in changing. As a result of this stubborn refusal to change, Phil gets trapped in the same day over and over. Each morning, he wakes up in the same motel room in Punxsutawney, Pennsylvania, to the Sonny and Cher song "I've Got You, Babe" blaring from his bedside alarm clock, and he finds his inner refusal to change mirrored by his outer world not changing either. Each new day is exactly the same as the previous day: all the people, situations, and events occur exactly the same as the day before.

The first half of the film reflects the consequences of not answering the call. Still refusing to change, Phil spends the next weeks, months, or even years (it's hard to tell just how long this goes on) manipulating people and situations as his childish, immature self tries to run the show. Each day offers a new call to change his reactions and grow, yet he chooses instead to do as he pleases and to push his advantage: He repeatedly punches Ned Ryerson, sets up Nancy Taylor, robs an armored car, etc. Phil is locked in the labyrinth of his refusal and goes through each day trying to change things through self-will and manipulation. This is the tragedy of all antiheroes because the only thing they can truly change is themselves, and this is exactly what they refuse to do. Phil's situation represents the virtual prison the refusal of the call ultimately brings: He is frozen emotionally, incapable of helping himself, and tortured by a seemingly endless future that includes all the same people, situations, and outcomes from the day before. He wakes each day to a living hell, and the only way out is to answer the call of that new day, which he slowly, eventually does.

Ultimately, the refusal of the alcoholic to get sober is the same as all antiheroes' refusal to pass on to the next stage of life. The tyrant child's refusal to grow up and accept the responsibilities and freedoms of adulthood stifles both his own growth and that of his family and community. Though the unknown world of recovery offers a path to freedom and transformation, the troubles for the immature, selfish, and fear-based alcoholic, often burdened with financial, physical, and emotional wreckage, frequently outweigh the treasures. Mired in their own living nightmare, and driven by an insidious need to get their own way, the "Hideous Four Horsemen—Terror, Bewilderment, Frustration, Despair"[5]—stand as powerful threshold guardians barring the path to a new way of life. For many in this desperate situation, it often takes a severe bottom before they are willing to finally admit to their innermost self that they are powerless over alcohol (or other substances) and that their lives are truly unmanageable. While many may hear the call, it takes the courage of surrender to submit to and choose the hero's journey.

The call that beckons, pushes, entices, or drags the hero into the adventure signals that a great change, a new awakening or spiritual transfiguration, is about to take place. The hero is soon to leave behind not only his ordinary world but also the essential parts of himself, which he once relied on to make his way through that world. These immense changes don't occur in the ordinary world, so the hero is drawn out to a new land, either physically or metaphysically. New rules, new insights, and new ways of knowing are acquired, and new ways of acting must be learned to survive here. In this unknown land a source of magnified Power will be accessed, a Power that, once aligned with and surrendered to, will make possible the transfiguration needed to transform and heal. The hero will be made new again by this wondrous, mysterious, and threatening journey, and if he answers the call, both he and the community to which he returns will benefit from the lessons learned and risks taken.

Joseph Campbell said that "the hero is a man of self-achieved submission,"[6] and for the alcoholic, this submission is achieved through a great willingness to surrender his old way of life and take the First Step of recovery. Once the alcoholic/addict has answered his call by admitting to his innermost self that he is powerless over alcohol (or other substances) and that his life has become unmanageable, he becomes ready to be introduced to a Power greater than himself. This is the Power that will at first save him and eventually transform him as he works the rest of the Steps. Meeting a mentor who will introduce the hero to a Higher Power and lend his experience, strength, and hope to help him prepare for the obstacles ahead is the next step of the hero's journey and the purpose of Step Two.

STEP TWO
Meeting the Mentor

"Furthermore, we have not even to risk the adventure alone; for the heroes of all time have gone before us; the labyrinth is thoroughly known; we have only to follow the thread of the hero-path."

—*Joseph Campbell,* The Hero with a Thousand Faces[1]

ONCE THE HERO has answered his call and embarked on the hero's path, he is introduced to a mentor,[2] who will shepherd him through the challenges and trials ahead and prepare him to cross the threshold that is coming up. The mentor is a protective figure who has traveled the hero's path before, knows the obstacles well, and has the experience of surviving and overcoming them. The mentor offers the hero guidance and support during the journey, providing him with amulets, skills, and the knowledge he needs to defeat and survive the tests and troubles he is about to face.

Mentors appear in fairy tales and legends in many forms, including that of the Fairy Godmother, the Wizard, and the Wise Old

Man, or as magical creatures (think of Yoda, from the Star Wars movies). Mentors can also be companions or helpers or other heroes traveling the hero's path. These characters fill the crucial role of reminding or helping the hero both answer his call and stay the course of the journey, of guiding and steering the hero along the path, by saving or rescuing him, and most important of all, by introducing the hero to a supernatural Power. The wisdom and protective advice mentors offer, along with the amulets, tools, and skills they give the hero, help shield him from the dangers and trials of the adventure.[3] The mentor appears over and over again in the world's stories and tales, and his or her role is always to support and shepherd the hero along the path of the adventure.

When the hero in recovery has answered her call, entered the unknown world of meetings, and become aware of the Twelve Step program, she is encouraged to get a sponsor. The sponsor guides the hero through the work of the Steps and helps her navigate the tests and trials ahead while also preparing her for the threshold that is coming up in Step Three. In recovery, the sponsor serves as the protective figure of the mentor, and, having worked the Steps of the program before, she offers the hero suggestions during the journey, providing her with guidance, support, and the experience needed to overcome the challenges, resistance, and obstacles she is about to face. In addition, the sponsor fulfills the vital task of introducing the newcomer to a supernatural source of unlimited power. This is summed up by Step Two: "Came to believe that a Power greater than ourselves could restore us to sanity."

In the beginning of the journey, one of the sponsor's first goals is to help the newcomer acclimate to the strange new world of recovery and help her feel comfortable in Twelve Step meetings. The sponsor's early suggestions provide the first tools the hero needs, things such as taking commitments at meetings so the newcomer feels she belongs, and encourage the hero to join in fellowship before and after meetings and to share openly with others so she can become known and feel a part of the group. The siren call of many sponsors begins with "ninety and ninety"—a suggestion that the newcomer go to ninety meetings in ninety days. If the newcomer balks at attending so many meetings, the sponsor simply asks how many days in the week she used to drink or engage in other compulsive behavior. Most newcomers' answer is "every day." The sponsor then says that she should simply replace the daily routine of drinking or using with the daily routine of recovery. This rigorous meeting schedule not only helps replace the destructive habits most newcomers are used to but it also introduces the hero to a wide variety of recovery formats—speaker meetings, book study meetings, participation meetings—and so exposes her to many different personal stories. By attending these meetings, newcomers begin hearing parts of their own stories from others' shares, and this helps them feel as if they belong and encourages them to keep coming back. This early direction also serves the crucial role of changing the newcomer's awareness of herself, her habits, and the way she sees both herself and her world. It introduces an opening in the self-sufficient ego, a crack through which the power of spirit will soon enter.

The sponsor provides other important guidance on how to get the most out of Twelve Step meetings, such as getting to meetings early and interacting with others before the meeting begins. Going to unfamiliar meeting rooms filled with unknown people can be daunting, but there are often greeters whose sole purpose is to introduce themselves and make others feel comfortable. When a newcomer or stranger shows up, the greeter will introduce them to others, who then make it their job to make the newcomer feel a part of the group. Also, by arriving early, typically "regulars" approach newcomers and make sincere attempts to help them feel welcome. Other meeting advice includes things such as sitting in the front of the room rather than at the back, where it's easy to get distracted by others or where it's easy to sneak out early or right at the end of meetings. Another way to feel a part of the group is for the newcomer to stand in line to thank the speaker at the end of meetings, or by helping clean up the meeting space by putting chairs away or washing coffee cups in the kitchen. By staying after meetings and participating with others, the newcomer begins integrating with the group. By talking and interacting with others, she begins feeling a part of her new community, and it becomes easier for her to begin opening up and begin sharing part of her story. Little steps and actions such as these help dissolve the isolation she has become encased in, helps her feel safe, and allows her to begin making sense of this strange new world of recovery.

The next task of the sponsor/mentor is to lead the hero on the journey of recovery by guiding her through the rite of passage known as the Twelve Steps. As with all mentors, the sponsor has the benefit of having already navigated the journey herself, and the experience, strength, and hope she shares are invaluable in helping the newcomer work through each Step and deal with the multitude of feelings—from apprehension and misunderstanding to resistance and resentment through fear to faith—they bring up. This one-on-one guidance is crucial for the newcomer to whom the program often seems like a direct and threatening challenge to her immature and often rebellious ego. An early pitfall, for example, occurs during

Step One when the newcomer answers her call by admitting she is powerless over alcohol and that her life has become unmanageable. While this may have been true in the first few days or weeks when she was beaten down enough to come to meetings, soon any immediate trouble or pressure from family or bosses may have passed, and as she begins feeling better, the old bravado and ego can quickly return. It is the sponsor's role at this point to keep the newcomer focused on the hero's path by helping her thoroughly work Step One, thus reminding her of the reasons she entered the program to begin with. Getting a selfish, self-seeking alcoholic to remain humbled and surrendered long enough to stay on the journey of early recovery, especially once the initial threat or trouble that drove her into the rooms is relieved, takes all the experience, guidance, and patience the sponsor possesses.

In addition to providing the guidance and support the hero needs to navigate this new and strange world, the mentor also provides the hero with amulets, talismans, and the magical incantations she will need to survive parts of the journey for which she has no defense or experience yet. This kind of help can be found in stories and myths, both old and new. For example, in the movie *The Wizard of Oz,* Glinda, the Good Witch of the North, helps Dorothy on her journey by providing her with the most powerful and protective of all talismans when she transfers to Dorothy the magic ruby slippers from the Wicked Witch of the East. Like Cinderella's glass slippers, these magical slippers protect Dorothy from the unknown dangers ahead, and ultimately help her survive the supreme ordeal with the Wicked Witch. Later, Glinda gives Dorothy a talisman in the form of a mantra, "There's no place like home," which is the secret to unlocking the power of her return to her farm in Kansas.

Albus Dumbledore, Harry Potter's mentor,[4] who guides him through his journey, provides Harry with a variety of amulets as well, including the cloak of invisibility that used to belong to his father. Harry uses this valuable tool to first explore Hogwarts castle and gather knowledge, and later to escape threatening and dangerous situations such as hiding in Hagrid's cabin when Cornelius Fudge comes to take Hagrid to Azkaban. The mentor provides the hero with these amulets and magical potions because he knows that he cannot travel the path for the hero, only assist him in making his way through it.

The various tools, charms, and talismans the mentor provides allow the hero to not only make his way through the journey but also develop the skills and resources he will need to face the supreme ordeal coming up and to complete the transformation later on.

To help the hero avoid the pitfalls of early sobriety, and to help the newcomer navigate the tests and trials coming up, the sponsor also provides her with a set of amulets and talismans—in the form of spiritual tools, suggestions, and support—that the newcomer can begin using to make sense of and to survive the journey. Taken together, this unique set of tools is often referred to in the program as a "spiritual tool kit." These spiritual tools include a variety of new ways of dealing with the onslaught of feelings that come up; the complexity of situations, both old and new, she faces; and making sense of the mysterious realm of the spirit she is about to enter that will help her achieve the spiritual experience needed both to save and transform her life. The sponsor, who was given and has used these very tools herself, knows that the spiritual tool kit contains the necessary coping strategies that act as the amulets and talismans that will not only protect the hero but also allow her to develop the new reactions and perceptions, such as acceptance and surrender, and the willingness needed to trudge the road ahead. As each new spiritual tool is provided and practiced, the hero grows in competence, becoming better able to handle the increasing difficulties and challenges as they come up.

One of the first amulets the hero is given when he enters the rooms of recovery is a welcome chip used to acknowledge that he is new to recovery or, during the first twelve months, that he has achieved various lengths of time sober or recovered. These chips are often inscribed with recovery sayings such as "To thine own self be true" or "Keep coming back," and they act as symbols to help protect the hero from the evil disease of alcoholism and addiction. The newcomer is often told that if he feels the need to have a drink, he should put the chip in his mouth, and as soon as it dissolves, then he can drink. Or he is instructed to return the chip to the nearest meeting first, explain what he is about to do, and then he can act out on his addiction. This last practice of returning the chip before taking a drink was started by Sister Ignatia (often referred to as the Angel of Alcoholics Anonymous) who would give a Sacred Heart badge to newly sober patients upon their discharge from the hospital. Ignatia made each person solemnly promise to return the badge to her personally before they decided to pick up the first drink. This amulet protected many an alcoholic from the imperious urge to recklessly throw away their sobriety on the impulsive and often short-lived compulsion to take a drink. Many stories are also related in meetings of newcomers keeping these chips in their pockets, and when searching for money to buy a drink—at a bar or at an airport, for example—they pull out the chip instead and are immediately reminded of the meetings, of the sobriety they have, and what they are trying to accomplish. In that instant, many slips back into drinking have been averted as the chips restore the hero to sanity just long enough for the compulsion to pass.

Another powerful amulet the hero is given in early recovery is the charm of laughter. Oftentimes, after years of drinking and using and the demoralizing behavior it brings, the laughter and lightness has long gone out of a newcomer's life. The hero, filled with the shame and secrets of unexplainable and incomprehensible actions he has engaged in, enters recovery feeling alone and alienated. At meetings, however, he begins hearing others share similar things they went through or put others through (demoralizing or even illegal), and he is surprised to hear others laugh over these episodes. Hearing others share openly and honestly secrets and behaviors of which he himself is deeply ashamed of and terrified of being found out for is a hugely freeing experience. The walls begin to come down a little, and the crack widens into which recovery begins to seep.

In the Big Book, it says, "We are not a glum lot" and "We absolutely insist on enjoying life,"[5] and the laughter he hears in meetings creates an environment of acceptance and tolerance where the hero learns that it is safe to begin sharing himself and his feelings. Learning to be honest is a key to getting and staying sober, and he soon learns that no matter how far he has fallen, or what he has gone through, he, too, has something special, unique, and important to share and ultimately contribute. He learns that his experience, regardless of what it is, has value. This is a lesson the hero will soon come to cherish.

An additional tool the sponsor provides the newcomer with is encouraging him to get commitments at meetings, which is a key to ending his sense of loneliness and isolation. The unfamiliarity of meetings can be intimidating at first, as there are unknown rules and rituals and many established relationships, which seem like "cliques" and appear difficult to break into. The best and fastest way to become part of the meetings, the sponsor advises, is to jump into the middle and begin participating. Remaining on the outside of the group is dangerous, the sponsor warns, as there are still many temptations that can distract and lead the newcomer back out into his old world of drinking and using. The sponsor likens this to the dangers in nature, where the animals that get picked off by predators are usually the ones on the outside of the herd. To remain safe, the mentor urges the newcomer to get into the middle of the program and to surround himself with the protective shield of the recovery community. The way to do this, the sponsor suggests, is by volunteering for commitments.

Commitments can be little things such as getting to meetings early and helping set up the chairs and tables, make coffee, or stand at the door and greet people as they arrive. These types of commitments help get the newcomer to meetings early, get them involved with others, and get them out of themselves and their impending problems. There are also commitments needed during the meeting, such as being responsible for bringing literature or food, handing out chips to commemorate various lengths of sobriety, offering to read portions of the literature, or even serving as secretary or treasurer. These and other commitments help keep the newcomer on the hero's path, and by taking them he learns to keep showing up, since others rely on his participation each week at a specific time. By taking commitments, the hero learns to become accountable, gets introduced to others, and begins to shed his sense of separateness by integrating and becoming part of a group again.

There is natural resistance to this and other suggestions, but the mentor—having been through this early stage of recovery and having helped many others through it—is prepared for it. For example, once, when a newcomer questioned what the commitment of cleaning ashtrays after a meeting could possibly have to do with his staying sober, the sponsor calmly responded, "Recovery is found under the ashtrays." The newcomer took the commitment and only realized years later the wisdom in that statement. By spending time after the meeting out in the parking lot emptying ashtrays (instead of rushing off to isolate), he developed friendships with other heroes on the path and learned to share important parts of himself. Many of the people he met during that commitment became lifelong friends who helped him through other tough times later on in his adventure.

Another talisman the sponsor gives the hero at this point is the suggestion of taking contrary action. Initiates new to the path of recovery have many old behaviors that are maladaptive or destructive to themselves and others. In addition to drinking or other compulsive addictions, newcomers often cope with the stress of dealing with people, situations, and other activities by smoking too much or overeating, isolating, indulging in excessive spending, or acting out sexually to escape their feelings. Unfortunately, acting out in these old ways only leads to different kinds of problems, so the sponsor suggests to the newcomer that if he wants different results in his life, then he needs to become willing to take different actions. And this often requires doing the exact opposite of what his mind is telling him to do.

At first, this suggestion doesn't sit well with the alcoholic because he is used to doing whatever he wants, regardless of the consequences. The sponsor points out, however, that the source of most of his problems come from him listening to and acting on his "old ideas," and a simple inventory of cause and effect quickly prove the insanity of this behavior and its results. The solution, the sponsor suggests, is by listening to what his old best thinking is telling him to do, and then by doing the exact opposite: taking the contrary action. It's like going to the gym, the sponsor explains. At first you don't want to go, but once you've gotten off the couch, driven to the gym, and moved your body, you always feel better. It's the same thing in recovery. Acting contrary to what his mind tells him to do, for instance, getting off the couch and going to a meeting when he doesn't want to go, or raising his hand and sharing what he's thinking and feeling when he'd just as soon remain quiet, or joining a group after the meeting for coffee instead of isolating, all these contrary behaviors make the hero feel better and help teach him new ways of acting and behaving. It's often said in the program that you should always run your thinking by someone else before you act on it, and this not only helps the hero make better decisions but it also prevents the hero from creating more wreckage that he'll need to clean up later.

Other tools offered to the hero are the various quotes and sayings that are sprinkled around the rooms and freely shared during meetings. At first these slogans are like a foreign language without any significance to the newcomer. Sayings such as "Live and Let Live," "Let Go and Let God," and "One Day at a Time," which line the walls of meeting rooms, initially confuse the newcomer rather than help him. For example, the idea of tolerance and respect represented in the saying "Live and Let Live" doesn't resonate with an alcoholic who is fueled by resentment and self-righteous judgment. Slowly, however, as the fog clears and the hero becomes more open and willing, these simple sayings come to mean a great deal, and as the path grows more difficult, these and other sayings can act like Harry Potter's invisibility cloak, protecting and helping the hero navigate and make sense of the journey while also helping him through some challenging times.

For example, when the newcomer is experiencing a particularly rough time, the saying "When you're going through hell, keep going!" reminds him not to dwell but rather to stay busy and take action (often contrary action). If he is stuck on trying to figure out or explain the "God" thing, the saying "A God small enough for me to understand wouldn't be large enough for me to trust" teaches him that it is okay not to have a clear understanding of God yet, and that his own conception of a Higher Power will come with time. And when dealing with the tumultuous feelings brought up by the Fourth Step (made a searching and fearless moral inventory), the saying "When I did my Fourth Step it felt like the world was being turned upside down. What I found out later was that it was being turned right side up" helps him keep moving through the Fourth Step inventory with the faith that, in the end, it will lead to his recovery. There is a deep wisdom in the rooms, a wisdom that comes from all the heroes who have traveled the path before. This collective wisdom is passed on from one hero to the next and often comes just when the new hero needs to hear it the most.

As the hero begins accumulating the amulets, talismans, and tools of his spiritual tool kit, he begins building the foundation of his recovery. The bedrock of his sobriety is attending regular meetings, which introduces the hero to the mystery, magic, and message of this unknown world of recovery. Taking sobriety chips helps reinforce and acknowledge both his commitment and early progress, and taking commitments at these meetings helps him feel a part of this new world and encourages him to keep coming back. The valuable tools of sharing with others and of listening to their experience, strength, and hope help the message of recovery get through the hero's initial resistance during this early stage, and learning to take suggestions and different actions begins changing both the hero's thinking and his results. Becoming open to and looking for the deeper wisdom in the recovery sayings and quotes that at first don't seem to apply to him begin to slowly change his perception, and the constant laughter in the rooms helps to lessen the shame and secrets he's been carrying. These and other tools he acquires along the way strengthen and protect the hero, enabling him to successfully face the increasing challenges on the road ahead.

Companions and Helpers

Along with the mentor's guidance, and the amulets and talismans he provides, the hero also meets companions at this stage of the adventure that serve as important helpers during the journey. They have many functions, including helping keep the hero safe; providing other skills, guidance, or advice; and, by sharing their own experience on the hero path, providing lessons and examples of what might be needed or avoided for the hero to overcome or survive the tests and trials in the steps ahead. Helpers add or contribute something that the hero doesn't have yet, be it experience, maturity, knowledge, or other tools and skills the hero hasn't had the opportunity to develop. In addition, companions sometimes directly help the hero through some part of the adventure, as Minos's daughter, Ariadne, did with Theseus when she held one end of the golden thread while he worked his way into the labyrinth to slay the Minotaur. As the hero benefits from the assistance of helpers and companions and learns new skills, he integrates these lessons and becomes more and more competent and capable of handling the increasing challenges ahead.

The helper's role is more significant in the beginning than at the end of the journey, as the hero at this stage is unfamiliar with the unknown world and the hero's path and so lacks the requisite skills to survive the early part of the journey. Thus, the things experienced helpers provide can often mean the difference between successfully making it to the next stage in the journey or not. Heroes in the beginning of their adventures are frequently in need of being saved, such as when Nemo, in the film *Finding Nemo*, is captured by divers looking for exotic fish and needs to be saved by his father, or when Luke Skywalker is saved by the droids, R2-D2 and C-3PO, when he is trapped in the trash compacter on the Death Star. Along with getting critical help to survive the early part of the adventure, the hero also benefits by listening to and trusting his companions, and by accepting their help and guidance, the hero learns that he doesn't have to go it alone—indeed, he wouldn't survive the journey by himself. As he learns to reach out for and accept help, he also learns the value in becoming open, humble, and teachable. These new behaviors are the beginning of the personality change away from the egocentric know-it-all who entered the journey and represent the beginning of the hero's development and growth.

The sponsor in recovery makes the strong suggestion that the newcomer surround herself with the many available companions and helpers she finds in the fellowship. "Find someone you can tell the truth to; we don't do this alone" is a common saying in the program, and acting on this suggestion is one instance where contrary action will be put to the test. An early obstacle in recovery is that many years of drinking and using have led to behavior that has burned many bridges, so when the alcoholic does enter the program, she is often isolated and alone. In addition, alcoholics and addicts also enter recovery with deep shame and remorse—to say nothing of resounding resentment and anger—and this powerful mix of feelings makes the newcomer feel unworthy of the help she both needs and sees others getting in the rooms. Her old instincts are to turn to her former drinking companions who she knows will "understand," but this dangerous choice often leads to her drinking and using again and so refusing her call. Faced with the alcoholic dilemma of not being able to face life without a drink, but also not being able to envision a life of continuing drinking and using, the sponsor, once again, indicates she take contrary action by reaching out to others when she feels anxious, desperate, or alone. When she becomes willing to do so, she finds others who have experienced the same things she has, and these new companions offer solutions to the new and often scary situations she is facing.

Along with benefiting from other heroes' experience and suggestions, reaching out to others also helps the newcomer deal with the bewildering array of feelings that come up early in recovery. For many newcomers, who have in some cases been drinking and using since their early teens, dealing with feelings usually meant escaping through a drink or some other compulsive behavior. Now that the filter of alcohol has been removed, feelings come fast and furious, and learning to sort through and deal with them can be both threatening and deeply unsettling. One saying in the rooms that captures the roller coaster of emotions in early sobriety is "The good news about recovery is that you get your feelings back. The bad news is that you get your feelings back." The sponsor teaches the newcomer in the very beginning that "feelings are not facts" and that they don't have to run from them. The sponsor offers several tools she can use to deal with them, such as taking them to a meeting and sharing them, calling another person and discussing them, calling her sponsor and processing them, or meeting with others in the fellowship after meetings and getting an idea of how others have dealt with similar feelings during this part of the journey. Another saying in the rooms helps this process along as well. The newcomer is reminded that "a problem shared is a problem halved."

Luckily for the initiate, many other heroes on the path happily and enthusiastically give the newcomer their phone numbers and encourage them to call. Most meetings put together phone lists and suggest their members put their phone numbers and email addresses on them so others in the program can reach out to them if and when they need to talk. By calling and relying on one another, a strong fellowship develops with many other heroes all traveling the same path. The "protective wall of humanity," as Jung called it, has begun. Each member of the program may be at different stages of the journey; those who have the same amount of "time" in the program often mirror the same needs of the newcomer while those just a bit further down the road—or working on the next Step—can also lend their experience with that next step in recovery. Together, however, they all offer their knowledge and successful strategies to each of their fellows. In this way, the newcomer never has to travel the path alone, and by just attending a meeting or picking up the phone, she can receive assistance and guidance from many other helpers and companions. In the true spiritual tradition of giving, both people are helped when the newcomer calls, as the other person gets an opportunity to get out of their self-centered thinking and be of service to the person who is reaching out to them.

Harry Potter has many companions at various stages of his journey as well, and they all serve different functions, often mirroring his different levels of development and need. In the very beginning, it is Hagrid whom Dumbledore entrusts to rescue Harry after his parents are murdered by Lord Voldemort. Years later, it is Hagrid again who helps Harry answer his call when the Dursleys have taken him away to a lonely rock surrounded by the sea. Like Ben, who tells Luke that his father was a Jedi Knight, it is Hagrid who tells Harry that his parents were a witch and a wizard, and that Harry is a wizard as well. Hagrid introduces Harry to the concept of Muggles, "non-magical folk," and presents him with his letter of acceptance to Hogwarts School of Magic. Hagrid constantly watches out for Harry once they arrive at Hogwarts, and during frequent visits and conversations in his hut in the Forbidden Forest, Hagrid teaches him much about the unknown world of Hogwarts and reveals things to him about his next mentor, Dumbledore. Hagrid also provides various amulets that help Harry, such as the flute he uses to lull Fluffy to sleep in the first adventure, *Harry Potter and the Philosopher's Stone*, and it is Hagrid who is there with Harry in the end when he rescues Harry and carries him out of the forest in *Harry Potter and the Deathly Hallows*.

Harry's two closest companions, though, are Ron Weasley and Hermione Granger, and, as is so often the case with companions, they each have qualities the hero is lacking and must develop to survive, transform, and complete the journey. Harry meets both Ron and Hermione on the Hogwarts Express train as they begin their adventure together. Both Harry and Ron first consider Hermione arrogant, but it is soon revealed that she is a Muggle-born witch with a chip on her shoulder who is driven to be an overachiever and so overcome the label of being a Mudblood, an insulting term for a Muggle-born wizard. As such, Hermione studiously does all her homework, learns all the magical charms, and is then able to recall them just when they are needed most. She has the skills of discipline, logic, and studying that Harry lacks, and these are the skills he learns from her and needs to develop to become an accomplished wizard. Ron's family, the Weasleys, help launch Harry into his adventure when he is lost at King's Cross station, and they guide him through the barrier of Platform 9¾. Ron and Harry share similar qualities in the beginning, in that Ron is insecure and feels he needs to prove himself. But Ron has an inner courage that Harry needs to develop, and as with many companions and helpers, Ron saves both Harry and Hermione by helping them through the dangerous life-sized, animated chess men blocking their way on their quest to save the Philosopher's Stone. Ron uses his skill at chess and then his courage as he sacrifices himself to allow Harry and Hermione to pass through to the next chamber. By watching Ron grow throughout the adventure and act with courage in spite of many of the same handicaps he feels, Harry also learns to act with courage, to stand up for himself and others, and to sacrifice himself for the greater good.

Newcomers are also encouraged to surround themselves with companions who have similar amounts of time in recovery. The unique challenges of early recovery—such as dealing with family members, free time, old drinking friends, overwhelming feelings, and even how to do simple things without a drink or engaging in a compulsive behavior, such as overeating or overspending—can easily overwhelm the newcomer. Learning to rely on the experience of others who are dealing with the same things and learning how they are successfully coping with these situations help the newcomer find similar solutions. Reaching out to companions also helps the newcomer break down the walls of isolation and teaches her to begin trusting and letting others in. It is crucial at this stage that she begin listening to the solutions and experience of others rather than to the insanity of her old thinking. Newcomers, like most heroes new to the journey, are by nature stubborn, self-centered, and immature, and have been taking their own advice for far too long. In the Big Book, it says that "some of us have tried to hold on to our old ideas and the result was nil until we let go absolutely."[6] By reaching out to others and sharing her thoughts, feelings, and plans with them, the newcomer begins to let in new ideas, new perspectives, and new ways of acting and thinking. This is the beginning of the end of self-reliance, and this shift paves the way for reliance on a Power greater than herself.

Companions and helpers also serve as an external conscience for the newcomer. Before entering the program, many newcomers relied solely on their own judgment, often acting out of self-righteousness and self-centeredness rather than focusing on the right action. If something didn't go their way, it was easy for them to bend the rules or the truth to fit their will. Lying, cheating, and telling white or black lies to get what they want is old behavior for many newcomers, and this way of acting and thinking doesn't change overnight. Because of this, the sponsor suggests that the newcomer run their thinking by someone else before acting on it. She directs the newcomer to pick up the phone and let others know how she truly feels and what she is thinking, and to hang out with other companions in the fellowship and share the actions and decisions she is thinking of making. As the hero takes this direction, she is surprised to find that even embarrassing or self-centered thinking is not only tolerated by her companions but understood as well. Through a mutually open exchange, one where her companions share their own selfish and sometimes twisted thinking also, the newcomer soon finds that it is safe to begin revealing herself and her deepest thoughts, and this teaches her the invaluable lesson that it is safe to begin telling the truth again. Interacting with others in a sincere way teaches the hero initiate how to have relationships again, how to be honest, and how to think and act responsibly. In this way, slowly at first, the newcomer begins to "grow her own conscience," as it is called in the program. Developing and cultivating the ability to be open and honest with someone will turn out to be one of the most important tools in the hero's spiritual tool kit.

While most helpers are trusted companions with common goals that help the hero through the adventure, even adversarial companions with contrary goals provide the hero with important lessons, often with examples of what not to do. Draco Malfoy fills that role for Harry Potter, and his qualities of snobbish bigotry and intolerance of others immediately put them at odds with each other. When they meet for the first time at a clothing shop in Diagon Alley, Draco reveals his character defects as he speaks to Harry about "our kind," pure-blood wizards, and disparages "the other sort," Muggle-born, claiming they shouldn't be allowed to attend Hogwarts. As they both begin the school year, it is Draco's bullying and manipulating that teach Harry of the realities and dangers of the wizarding world. It is through Draco's behavior that Harry learns what he once thought of as a magical wonderland, the wizarding world, instead can be just as oppressive—and much more dangerous—as the life he left at the Dursleys. Draco's continuing refusal to grow and change during the journey helps keep Harry on the alert for danger, spurring him on to learn even more spells and magic, which help him prepare for the lethal trials ahead, especially for his battles with Voldemort. In the end, companions of this sort act as the hero's shadow, reflecting back to him the consequences of the opposite path, always reminding him that the dangers and struggles he endures are worth the sacrifices he is making.

In recovery, not all companions offer direct positive assistance either, and, as previously explained, some companions also provide examples of what not to do. Some would-be heroes, for example, remain stuck in self-will and refuse to follow direction. Instead, they insist on listening to and following their own advice, and this often leads to them remaining stuck in their old situations and feelings. Their resistance usually manifests as refusing to get a sponsor or trying to work the Steps alone, or not at all. Some antiheroes feel it's enough that they stopped drinking and using, and they remain stuck as a "dry drunk"—physically sober but mentally, emotionally, and spiritually still sick and uncomfortable. For many heroes unwilling to follow the path of recovery, the inevitable result is that they go back out and drink or use. The all too familiar progression of this sad fate starts when the newcomer (or old-timer) stops calling her sponsor, if she has one, and then it progresses to missing meetings and isolating and/or indulging in old behavior. Before long, the call of the insanity of alcoholism is too great to resist, and she experiences a slip or "goes out," as it is called when someone begins drinking or acting out compulsively again.

Newcomers, along with others who have longer-term sobriety, learn a lot from these slips. First, they learn what kinds of thinking and behavior precedes going out, thus reinforcing the importance of staying on the path of attending meetings, working the Steps, and of continuing to "do the things that got it good, rather the things that got good." In addition, the report from those who do go out and "do research," as they call it in the program, all reveal the same thing: They uniformly report that things immediately got worse as they couldn't control their drinking, were soon miserable, and lost most, if not all, of what they had gained (if they indeed had enough time in recovery to get anything back, i.e., career, family, material possessions). And most of all, before long, their drinking and using got even worse than it was before they got sober. In recovery they say that a person is never cured of the disease of alcoholism, and even though she may have stopped drinking or using, the disease is progressing daily, getting stronger and "doing push-ups each night while you're asleep." It pounces on heroes who let their spiritual condition lapse, and when they go out, they often pick up right where they would have been had they not stopped drinking at all. This fact has been borne out by the majority of heroes who have slipped and returned to the rooms to tell their tales. The experience of these companions, along with the positive experience of those who follow the Twelve Step path, all serve to guide the hero, helping her continue trudging the road of recovery and following the hero's journey.

An excellent example of both positive and negative companions can be found among the various helpers Luke Skywalker has in the film *Star Wars*, particularly Princess Leia and Han Solo. Although Princess Leia is portrayed as a focused, dedicated woman capable of fulfilling the woman warrior archetype, she often acts in a motherly way toward Luke (albeit a driven one) by constantly encouraging and supporting Luke's development. From prompting him to take a leap of faith by swinging over the Death Star's core to acting as Luke's external conscience by encouraging him to do the right thing and take the right action, Leia helps Luke fulfill his hero's journey of becoming a Jedi Knight by convincing him to join the resistance and fight as part of a community for a cause greater than himself.

Han Solo, on the other hand, displays the layers, contradictions, and uncertainty of the subconscious itself, and is both an example of what to do and, in many cases, what not to do. With the exception of his constant companion, Chewbacca, Han Solo is a loner (hence the last name "Solo") who refuses to join the resistance and is more concerned with himself than he is with others. He is driven more by money than by an intrinsic desire to be of help and only becomes interested in helping to save Princess Leia because of the likelihood of a large reward if he does. Reckless and self-seeking, he is detested by Princess Leia for his arrogance and is often held out to Luke as an example of how not to behave. Stubborn and self-seeking to the end, like many newcomers in recovery, Solo delivers Skywalker, Leia, and the droids to the Rebel Alliance, receives payment, and leaves. As Luke watches the solitary Solo depart, he intuitively knows he's made the right choice to stay and fight as part of the resistance. Throughout the film, Solo's behavior is one of refusing his call, but in the end we see him finally answer that call and return to save Luke's life during the last battle scene. Here, Solo's decision to answer his call proves to be the most important part of Luke's adventure, ultimately helping him destroy the Death Star.

In addition to providing help and guidance to heroes on the path, companions also provide qualities and strengths the hero has not yet developed, and they lend these qualities or skills to the hero or teach the hero how to develop or bring these latent qualities out in themselves. In *The Wizard of Oz*, Dorothy learns to develop the qualities that her helpers are in need of, such as intelligence, which is needed by the Scarecrow, love, which is sought after by the Tin Man, and courage, which the Lion seeks. As each of these characters discover these qualities in themselves, Dorothy also finds that she has them as well. Even her dog, Toto, who represents intuition, teaches her to look behind the mask put on by others when he pulls back the curtain on the Wizard. For Dorothy, as with all heroes, companions and helpers serve the important role of aiding, teaching, and assisting the hero as she enters the unknown world, and as they travel the adventure together, the hero is enriched, and sometimes saved, by the support they provide.

While amulets, tools, skills, and the experience of helpers and companions serve vital roles in helping the hero navigate the early part of his journey, it is the mentor who fulfills the most significant role at this early stage by introducing the hero to a supernatural source of Power that protects and eventually transforms him. Joseph Campbell calls the mentor figure the "protecting power of destiny,"[7] and, indeed, once the hero has answered his call, all the forces of the unconscious and the wisdom of infinite intelligence support the mighty task ahead. The problem for the hero at this point, though, is he is still tethered to his limited, rational thinking, and old, often childish, and selfish ways of behaving. The wise mentor knows that the challenges and trials of the road ahead cannot and will not be overcome by the old personality and limited consciousness of the hero initiate. Only by tapping into a zone of magnified power and learning to trust and have faith in something outside of—and yet curiously inclusive of—himself, will the hero be able to complete the journey. Moving the hero away from his old ways of thinking and acting, and toward this supernatural assistance and the unlimited power of destiny itself, is the main task of the mentor and signifies the beginning of the transformation the hero is about to undergo.

This is, of course, the role Ben plays with Luke Skywalker when he introduces him to the Force and encourages him throughout the adventure to listen to and use it to help him succeed.[8] Ben, being a mentor that has been in Luke's position before, knows that Luke can only go so far using his own limited skills and teaches him that becoming a Jedi Knight requires reliance on something outside of himself: something known as the Force. Throughout the journey, Luke slowly grows and changes, surrendering parts of his old self as he makes his way through the adventure to the supreme ordeal of battling with Darth Vader and the Death Star. During this crucial battle scene, however, Luke at first chooses to rely on his own skill (will) to outrun Darth Vader and the other Imperial fighters, and to use his ship's guidance system and his droid to maneuver his X-wing ship for his one shot at firing into the Death Star's core. As Luke comes under heavy attack, Han Solo returns and drives off the other fighters, allowing Luke to concentrate on the lethal shot. As the pressure mounts, however, Luke loses confidence when he sees that his droid has been disabled, and he soon realizes that by himself he may not be up to the task. It is at this crucial moment that he hears Ben's voice return from the void, reminding him that he is not alone, and urging him once again to "use the Force, Luke." In an ultimate leap of faith, Luke turns off his guidance system and surrenders to the Force, letting it guide him to fire the perfect shot into the belly of the Death Star.

Coming to Believe

The purpose of Step Two, and the ultimate role of the sponsor as mentor, is also to introduce the hero to a source of unlimited, supernatural power—indeed, to help him come to believe in a power greater than himself that can restore him to sanity. The sponsor—by introducing the newcomer to the Steps, helping him develop the tools in his spiritual tool kit, and encouraging him to seek help from companions—has been providing the initiate with the guidance, tools, and direction needed to successfully pass this early part of the adventure. But the sponsor knows that only faith and a working reliance on a Higher Power will give the hero the power and support needed to survive the trials and challenges of the Steps ahead and that only this Power can cause the total transformation that is required for the spiritual experience to come.

The great challenge of Step Two is guiding the hero to become humble and willing enough to believe that something outside of his own best thinking, outside of his all-powerful ego, a mysterious Power that he either doesn't believe in or, even worse, can't believe in yet is his only hope to regain his sanity around drinking and begin to truly live again. It is a challenge because most newcomers come into the program with many conflicting feelings and ideas around the concept of a supernatural power, and as soon as they hear the word "God,"—either in meetings or mentioned in the literature—their old ideas, conceptions, and prejudices trigger fierce resistance. Some people are confronted with an old notion of a Sunday school God, one that judged them relentlessly and stood ready to punish them for their sins, of which they're sure they have many. Others reject God out of intellectual superiority or scientific calculation, and consider themselves agnostic or atheist. Either way, they are unable to believe in a Power greater than themselves, and so are unwilling to even consider turning any control of their lives over to something other than themselves. The newcomer's complex feelings and experience with the "God" idea makes for a high hurdle in the beginning, and many feel frustrated and even angry when they learn that only by trusting and believing in a Power greater than themselves can they be rescued from their current state. This powerful mix of stubbornness, hopelessness, and resentment soon leads to a maddening paradox.

The Twelve Steps and Twelve Traditions sums this situation up best by saying that most newcomers at Step Two have arrived at an almost unbearable dilemma. Pointing out that in the First Step they were forced to admit they were powerless over alcohol and that their lives had become unmanageable, now, having found themselves in this vulnerable and helpless state, they are told that only by believing in a Power greater than themselves can they recover. But many, still driven by their old conception of this Power, remain unwilling or unable to do so. Backed into the proverbial corner, what are they to do?

Once again, the sponsor shares his own path through this seemingly impossible maze by providing even more tools and suggestions and by encouraging the newcomer to just remain willing and open to the idea at first. The most important point of this phase in the journey, the sponsor assures the newcomer, isn't that he comes to any conception of what that Power might be, but instead, that he only comes to accept that *he isn't it*. The point of this Step in the journey is to begin giving up reliance on self and to become open to the idea that there may just be something greater than himself that can restore some balance and sanity to his life. The sponsor does this by helping the newcomer see that, left to his own devices and best thinking, he has made a mess of his life. Directing the newcomer back to the First Step, he emphasizes that the unmanageability in his life was caused by his driving, self-serving ego and self-will. The sponsor suggests that maybe a different reliance, a Power greater than himself, can help to restore some order and sanity in his life. While this idea might make sense intellectually, practicing it can still be difficult. To turn an entire life of self-reliance and self-will around can not only still seem impossible to the newcomer but frankly unnecessary, too. Yet, if the hero can just remain open to the idea of an outside Power, then soon he may find that the door that has been shut for so long to any outside help or influence might begin to open just a little. As the hero grapples with this idea, the natural questions of what this Power might be and how much dependence to give it loom large.

To help the hero come to terms with the abstract idea of a Power greater than himself, the sponsor frequently points to a source of power that is undeniably more powerful than he is, and where proof of it exists at every meeting. He simply asks the initiate if the people in rooms who have been able to do something he hasn't—stay sober—might have more power than he has at this point. Even the most obstinate newcomer has to concede that this is indeed true. The sponsor's advice then is simply to make the Group of Drunks (G.O.D.) his Higher Power because they obviously have the power to do something together that he hasn't been able to do alone, and that is attain sobriety with a measure of peace and serenity. Becoming willing to turn his will and his life over to the program and group of sober alcoholics is sometimes easier at this point than accepting that some supernatural power exists, and it serves the important purpose of taking reliance off the old self and putting it on something outside of himself. In addition, this helps the hero concede a fundamental truth: that by himself, he lacks the power to get and maintain sobriety, that he is "power-less" on his own to do so.

Once the hero is willing to put faith in something other than himself, he becomes more willing to take direction from others and from his sponsor. The litmus test for this willingness is when the sponsor asks the hero if he is willing to go to any lengths to get and maintain sobriety. The newcomer, defiant and suspicious at first, is still mired in ego and self-will, and following direction often remains a challenge. The sponsor knows, however, that the hero's ability to develop faith in something outside of himself—and his ability to stay sober—is directly related to how much of his old ideas and self-will he is able to let go of and how willing he is to follow direction and make use of the new tools and suggestions he's being given. One of these tools is teaching the newcomer to begin praying and meditating at whatever level he can. A common suggestion at this point is for him to get on his knees in the morning and ask his Higher Power to keep him sober, and then to get on his knees again at night to thank Him for doing so. The goal here isn't to act with complete faith, which is usually difficult for the hero at this stage of the journey, but rather just to get him into the new habit of communicating with this new Power on whatever level he is able. Even if the newcomer is angry with his conception of a Higher Power or God, he is encouraged to let God know about it. It is said that even if you are yelling or cursing at God, you are still talking to Him. Following this and other directions from his sponsor and others in the program helps the hero divest himself of self and helps him swing the door open to a working faith even more.

The next tool the sponsor gives the newcomer to help him come to believe in a Higher Power is to read the literature, both *The Twelve Steps and Twelve Traditions* and the book of Alcoholics Anonymous, or the Big Book as it is called in the program. The first 164 pages of the Big Book contain the entire program of recovery in A.A., and the newcomer is directed to read this first. This section of the Big Book contains chapters such as "The Doctor's Opinion" and "More About Alcoholism," which demystify and explain what alcoholism is, and chapters such as "There Is a Solution" and "How It Works" explain how the program works. For Step Two, however, the most helpful chapter in breaking down the walls of self and coming to terms with the concept of a Higher Power is chapter four, "We Agnostics." The sponsor encourages the newcomer to read and reread this chapter to help him make sense of his current feelings about the concept of "God" and to help him become open to the idea of trusting and relying on a Power outside of himself. This part of the Big Book provides the newcomer with what is considered perhaps the most important ingredient in coming to believe in a Higher Power—the fact that he gets to determine and define what that Power means to him. This chapter, his sponsor, and the whole of the A.A. program encourage the hero to come up with his own conception of what this Power is and what to call it. No one forces his or her own conception onto the hero, and this one freedom has removed many hurdles in coming to believe in a Power greater than oneself.

The next part of the Big Book is made up of individual stories of how other people came into the program and recounts the various backgrounds, experiences, and adventures they have had with working the Twelve Steps. These stories follow the familiar format of what it was like for them before they discovered the program, what happened when they began working the Steps, and what has happened as a result. This section—more than half the book—is extremely helpful as it traces the many different paths other heroes have traveled, and, most importantly, it describes the many different ways people have come to believe in a Power greater than themselves, as well as the different ways a spiritual experience can manifest in other people's lives. By reading and identifying with the feelings and experiences of others, and by reading about how other heroes have dealt with or overcome the same kind of doubt or resistance in coming to believe in a Higher Power, the newcomer is given even more tools to help him deal with and begin building his own conception of this Power for himself.

The Twelve Steps and Twelve Traditions is an invaluable resource also, as this book further breaks down each of the Twelve Steps (and Twelve Traditions of the A.A. program) and details both the trials and obstacles of each Step while providing suggestions and solutions for working them. In discussing Step Two and coming to believe in a Power greater than himself, for example, it reminds the newcomer that the A.A. program does not demand that he believe in anything. All its Steps are but suggestions, and it encourages the hero to start by taking it easy when thinking about the "God" idea, and by suggesting he relax and "resign from the debating society"[9] when it comes to trying to figure out the deeper philosophical questions he may be struggling with. Taking it easy and developing an open mind are early suggestions in working Step Two. Reminding the newcomer that coming to believe is a process helps ease the pressure of what often can feel like a confusing, confounding, and seemingly impossible task at this early stage. By following these and other suggestions, *The Twelve and Twelve* promises that belief in a Higher Power will come as it has for countless heroes who have practiced these same techniques and followed the Twelve Step path. The transition from self-centered reliance to belief in and reliance on something unseen and untested can seem like the beginning of the end for the newcomer, and as *The Twelve and Twelve* says, "And so it is: the beginning of the end of his old life, and the beginning of his emergence into a new one."[10]

All the tools, suggestions, and guidance the newcomer has gathered to this point—from finding a mentor/sponsor, attending and participating in regular meetings, and getting commitments to learning to share openly and honestly, to building relationships with companions and helpers in the fellowship, to reading the literature and looking for the similarities in the stories rather than the differences, to learning to let go of his old ideas and reliance on self and to begin trusting that perhaps there is a Power greater than himself, a Power that has the ability to restore him to sanity and help him through the challenges ahead in this unknown world, and more—will be needed as the hero enters the road of trials ahead that will challenge and change him.

But first, the hero will face his greatest obstacle yet: a test of faith and resolve that regularly turns back those without the commitment and fortitude for the mighty journey ahead, for at this point the hero will meet the formidable threshold guardians whose duty it is to turn back those heroes who are not ready to brave the transformation by fire that is to come. To face and pass this first great test, the hero will not only rely on the spiritual tools he has developed so far but even more, he will be asked to deepen his nascent faith and make a decision to turn his will and his life over completely to the Power he has just begun to discover. The successful passing of this threshold will truly mark the end of his old life and the beginning of his new self.

The hero's surrender to this unlimited source of Power begins the transformative process of letting go of reliance on the rational, conscious mind and on his own limited and often self-serving will, and shows him there is a deeper source of Power to draw on outside of his old limited self and ego. It often takes repeated surrenders to connect with and trust this Power, and there are many painful lessons to be learned along the way as the hero insists on his stubborn ideas and selfish ways of getting his needs met and getting things done. Much growth and experience are needed before the hero, especially at this early stage, is willing to give up control and trust in this unseen source, but the supernatural power is patient and doesn't mind. Throughout the ages it has been ready to assist the hero with the powerful forces of the unconscious, the light of the spirit, and even the guardian angels of destiny itself. As the hero progresses through the journey and grows in acceptance, humility, and willingness, he learns to trust this Power more and more to help him through the adventure, and the first great test of this newfound dependence and developing faith comes with the crossing of the threshold that begins the next step of the journey: Step Three.

STEP THREE
Crossing the First Threshold

> "The adventure is always and everywhere a passage beyond the veil of the known into the unknown; the powers that watch at the boundary are dangerous; to deal with them is risky; yet for anyone with competence and courage the danger fades."[1]
> —*Joseph Campbell,* The Hero with a Thousand Faces

ARMED WITH THE TOOLS and guidance from his mentor and surrounded by companions and helpers, the first test the hero faces on his new adventure comes when he is challenged by the threshold guardians who block his way at the "entrance to the zone of magnified power."[2] The threshold guardians' task is to turn back those who are not yet ready to endure the trials and dangers ahead, and at this point the hero must make a decision to either decline the adventure or commit and have faith in the journey ahead. While the hero often meets many thresholds throughout the journey, this first and most important threshold symbolizes the crucial dividing line between the hero's ordinary world and the sacred world he is about to enter and be transformed by. Is the hero truly ready to forsake all he has known and relied on, and venture into the dark forest ahead? That is the ultimate question the guardian will force him to answer at this point in the journey.

Threshold guardians symbolize the limits of the hero's current life horizon and represent the present state of his limited consciousness —a consciousness rooted in rational self-reliance. Beyond the guardians is a land of greater expanse, an unknown world of infinite power and the mysterious yet liberating way of faith and reliance on this supernatural source, a source that lies deep in the unbounded unconscious. It takes courage, sometimes courage driven by desperation, to face down the threshold guardians and enter this land where the will of reason will be broken down and discarded, and with it the hero's very identity and sense of self.

Examples of threshold guardians fill the stories and memories of man both past and present. The ancient city of Thebes in Greece was guarded by a fearsome creature with the body of a lion, the great wings of a bird, and the animated face of a human. The dreaded Sphinx was renowned as being both treacherous and merciless to all travelers who attempted to enter the city. In order to pass the threshold of the city, weary visitors were confronted by the beast and challenged with a riddle that had to be answered correctly before entrance was granted. The most famous of all riddles was a favorite of the Sphinx: "Which creature has but one voice, but walks on four feet in the morning, two in the afternoon, and three in the evening?"

The answer, which was at once obvious and obscure, was man—who crawls on all fours as a baby, then walks on two feet as an adult, and finally three as a senior using a cane. Only those who could answer correctly were granted entrance into the great city. Other classic stories such as "The Odyssey"[3] and fables such as "The Epic of Gilgamesh"[4] abound with threshold guardians both at the beginning and throughout the adventures.

In recovery, Step Three, "Made a decision to turn our will and our lives over to the care of God as we understood Him," acts as a powerful threshold guardian by challenging the hero to make a firm decision: He must either be willing to surrender his old ideas and self-centered life and commit to living life on a sober and spiritual basis or he can turn back and keep drinking and face an alcoholic decline and death. While this choice might seem an easy and obvious one to the outsider, to the alcoholic it warrants careful consideration as many still harbor hopes of one day being able to control and enjoy their drinking and using again. Then there is the resistance to giving up control to someone or something they don't understand and do not yet trust. As such, Step Three represents a formidable threshold guardian and a turning point for the hero in recovery.

Step Three also challenges the hero's current sphere of consciousness by forcing him to acknowledge and ultimately abandon the selfish and self-centered attitudes and actions that have blocked emotional and spiritual development. Most alcoholics, driven through self-propulsion, power their way through life, oblivious to the effects they have on other people, places, or things. In the rooms they are described as "self-will run riot."[5] The Big Book describes the alcoholic as "driven by a hundred forms of fear, self-delusion, self-seeking, and self-pity,"[6] and, once at Step Three, the first requirement is that he "be convinced that any life run on self-will can hardly be a success."[7] This powerful mix of self-will, egotism, and fear act as formidable threshold guardians that test the hero's willingness and readiness to continue the journey.

It is the sponsor's role at this point to help the initiate break through the limits of their current thinking by helping them examine the consequences of their self-absorbed behavior. The sponsor often directs her to the literature of recovery, both the Big Book and the chapter dealing with Step Three in *The Twelve Steps and Twelve Traditions*. It is here that she finds suggestions on how to cut away the self-will and egotism that has led to a life of spiritual perdition. The first suggestion is to point out that Step Three, like all the remaining Steps, calls for affirmative action, and the first action she is directed to take is to develop a willingness to look beyond herself, her old ideas, and ways of handling her life. To help her do this, the literature offers specific examples of how a life driven by self-will has rarely resulted in happiness, and how the limits of intellect and logic have only served to bolster her ego, cutting her off from the help and guidance of the spirit.

For example, in the *Twelve and Twelve*, as it's commonly known, the hero learns of the falsity of thinking that "we are certain that our intelligence, backed by willpower, can rightly control our inner lives and guarantee us success in the world we live in."[8] At first, many newcomers bristle at the suggestion that their attitudes and motives are responsible for the messes that are their lives, and instead point to their alcoholic drinking and other outside influences. In fact, many become convinced that their newly found sobriety, coupled with even more willpower and discipline, will be enough to turn things around. Unfortunately, their sponsor points out, willpower isn't enough.

Willpower is a highly misunderstood concept where alcoholics and other compulsive behaviors are concerned. For years, people have looked down on alcoholics and wondered why someone who drank too much couldn't muster enough willpower to just lay off the bottle. "What's wrong with that person?" they thought. "If only they had more backbone, more willpower," they often say. Many an alcoholic has also wondered the same thing. "Why am I so weak?" they ask themselves. As it turns out, most alcoholics actually have an excess of willpower. The problem, they learn at this point, is how they have applied it.

While beginning to take a good look inside themselves by examining their use of willpower and other modes of self-seeking, it soon becomes apparent that many of the inner threshold guardians at this point come from their earliest experiences and upbringing. Woven into the fabric of our consciousness are the deeper insecurities and fears passed on to us by the earliest threshold guardians of all: our parents. Our parents were our first protectors, guarding and keeping us safe from the early journeys we were not yet ready to take, such as crossing the street, walking to school alone, or venturing out into the world without their watchful eyes. Unfortunately, while protecting us from danger, parents also transferred many of their own limitations and fears to us, which we innocently internalized. It is these unrecognized and unchallenged fears that also act as powerful threshold guardians blocking us from new journeys that would help us grow and mature.

For Harry Potter, the members of the Dursley family act as his early threshold guardians keeping him trapped in the ordinary Muggle world. Harry is treated more as an outsider than a member of the family, and the Dursleys transfer to Harry their fears of anything magical or out of the ordinary. Harry is further tormented by their bullying son, Dudley, and this early experience makes him both more susceptible to the bullying by Draco Malfoy, as well as distrustful of others. This fear of the unknown and unfamiliar world beyond the confines of the Dursley neighborhood at Number 4, Privet Drive, almost prevents Harry from crossing the threshold to the adventure, and it takes a heroic decision to answer his call and follow Hagrid into the unknown world that awaits him at Hogwarts School of Magic.

On the lonely planet of Tatooine, Uncle Owen is Luke Skywalker's first threshold guardian, and he continually blocks the entrance to any adventure by discouraging Luke from leaving. Uncle Owen is distrustful of the outside galaxy and knows the danger of the dark side, as his stepbrother, Anakin Skywalker, turned to it and became Darth Vader. Uncle Owen transfers his fears and desperation to Luke, and exploits his constant need for help around the farm to keep Luke trapped. Once Luke is freed to begin the journey, new threshold guardians appear in the form of Imperial Stormtroopers who block his entrance to the city of Mos Eisley, the "pirate city" outside the boundaries of the farm he just left. Only by using the Jedi mind trick is Ben able to get Luke past them and into the strange and dangerous world awaiting him in the cantina and soon in the universe beyond.

For Dorothy in *The Wizard of Oz*, her first threshold guardians are Auntie Em and Uncle Henry, who live a quiet and ordinary life on a farm in Kansas. Though Dorothy longs to live a different life "over the rainbow," her aunt and uncle see no reason to leave, and they dismiss her longings as childish whims. Auntie Em and Uncle Henry are decent folks who don't like to stir up trouble, and one of the fears Dorothy internalizes from them is a submissive respect for authority, as evidenced when the sheriff and Miss Gulch come to collect Toto. During this confrontation, they give in and don't stand up for Dorothy, and later, Dorothy won't stand up for herself either during her first visit with the Wizard of Oz.[9]

In the movie *Groundhog Day*, Phil Connors meets a different kind of threshold guardian, one that actually forces him back into the hero's journey. This happens when Phil has refused his call early in the film and is trying to get out of Punxsutawney in the TV van before a threatening winter storm cuts off his retreat. Recklessly fighting his way through the hail and snow, the storm quickly turns into a blizzard, and as he reaches the outskirts of town, Phil is stopped by a state patrolman who is closing the road. When Phil begins arguing with him to let him pass, the patrolman says to Phil, "You can go back to Punxsutawney, or you can go ahead and freeze to death. It's your choice." What this threshold guardian is telling Phil is that his real choice here is to go back to town and answer his call to grow and mature, or he can continue down the road he is on and suffer the sure and lonely death of a frozen soul. The icy blizzard is a fitting symbol that separates both the known from the unknown world for Phil, as well as the fate of choosing poorly. Resentfully, he turns back to town.

The next threshold for Phil occurs the following morning when he wakes up and finds himself trapped in an utterly unknown world: the very same day as the day before. As the new day unfolds, Phil finds that the rational rules and explainable laws that governed his old world are gone. Like all heroes, Phil soon learns that his stubborn reliance on self and his old ideas does nothing to help him navigate this new world, and that only reliance on something outside himself will allow him to grow through this state. Over time, Phil will come to rely on supernatural principles that lie beyond his conscious self, and he will find new direction from a source of power buried deep within his subconscious.

In recovery, it is the sponsor's role at this point to help divest the newcomer from reliance on self and to expose the limits of that self-centered thinking. Through the use of inventories to help her see the consequences of the misuse of willpower, as well as the futility of self-centered thinking, the sponsor slowly reveals the limits of this solitary way of thinking and acting. As the newcomer begins considering, and in some cases accepting, that her old ways of thinking and acting have contributed to and even caused much of the trouble in her life, she cracks the door of willingness open just a bit, and she becomes open to a solution. It is at this point that she begins to move past the threshold guardians of her old ideas and limited consciousness, but what follows next becomes an even bigger threshold guardian: the idea that, once again, surrendering to a Higher Power, or God as she understands Him, is the only way out.

While the alcoholic struggled with the concept of a Power greater than herself in Step Two, now, at the precipice of Step Three, she is asked to go much further and actually make a decision to turn her will and her life over to this Power. This decision acts as an almost impenetrable threshold guardian to many self-serving alcoholics who have been playing God for years. Some, who call themselves atheists, still claim they are unable or unwilling at this point to acknowledge or relinquish control to a Power other than themselves. Others who claim to be agnostics aren't convinced whether there is or isn't a divine source of power or order in the universe, and they, too, claim they are not ready to relinquish control or try living on a spiritual basis. In both of these instances, the known world of self-reliance and logic still seems a better alternative than trusting in something unexplainable and beyond themselves.

And then there are those, too, who come into recovery with a professed belief in God or a divine source of Power, yet many of them still have serious reservations with their current conception of God. Many religious and spiritual people share in recovery meetings that even with their faith in God or in a divine presence, what was baffling and ultimately frustrating was that their faith still wasn't enough to get them sober. "Why has God abandoned me and not answered my prayers to stay sober?" they ask. "If God wasn't willing to help me before, why is He suddenly going to help now?" they wonder. Crossing the threshold into the unknown land of faith and reliance the program of recovery is suggesting can sometimes be harder for those with an existing faith than it can be to the other two groups. Either way, Step Three, and the decision and commitment it asks, poses by far the most challenging part of the journey so far.

The sponsor offers several suggestions based on how others have navigated past these threshold guardians while also sharing his own experience of surrendering to a Higher Power. As the hero struggles with the word *God*, his sponsor quickly points out the last part of Step Three: "God, as we understand Him." The way into the unknown world of faith and protection by a supernatural power, the sponsor suggests, is to first have the choice of defining what that Power means to him and how that Power will manifest itself to him. The sponsor reveals that the real surrender of this part of the journey isn't that the hero comes to believe in God, but rather that she becomes willing to enter the "Great Reality"[10] deep within herself, and, once there, becomes willing to turn her will and her life over to whatever it is she finds there.

While many heroes still struggle with the concept of coming up with their own conception of God, the sponsor reminds them that the only prerequisite is that this Power be something greater than themselves. The sponsor tries to make the path as broad as possible, as it was once made for him, and suggests that the hero can substitute the word *God* with anything she sees fit. She can call it Creative Intelligence or Spirit of the Universe, or it can even be the waves crashing on the beach or the wind that rustles the leaves in the trees. A newcomer once asked his sponsor how the waves could qualify as a Power greater than himself, and he replied, "Can you stand on the beach and stop the waves from crashing down?" "No," the newcomer answered. "Then the waves are a Power greater than you, and for now the Power that moves the waves can be your conception of God." Other newcomers have been directed to think about the Power that aligns and moves the planets, or the silent yet steady energy that keeps their heart beating and their blood flowing. Any conception of a Power that is beyond their immediate control and understanding is enough to open the gateway to surrender and to faith.

As the hero begins his descent into this unknown world of unexplainable mystery and supernatural guardianship, the idea of surrendering control—of turning his will and his life over to the care of God—and the concepts of faith and belief in a Higher Power may still trouble his rational mind. To those who claim they still cannot or will not believe, their sponsor asks them only whether they are at least *willing* to believe. If the newcomer is especially stubborn or fearful and cannot even do that yet, the sponsor suggests that he pray for the willingness to *be* willing. Many times, at just the mention of prayer, the old guardian of resistance rises up again, and the gates of willingness clang shut. Most newcomers equate prayer with religion, and religion with an old concept of a judgmental God, and so become resistant to even trying prayer. This is when the sponsor once again provides guidance. Sponsors often have a simple conversation with newcomers that helps break down this barrier. They ask them whether they ever prayed while drinking or using. "Yes" is the usual reply. "I've prayed many times to just get me home safe while driving drunk, or to get me out of some mess," they say. "And," asks the sponsor, "did you make it home safe or get out of the mess?" "Yes!" they reply. "Well, you see, God *is* listening to you. He is answering your prayers already."

The sponsor recommends that the newcomer spend some time daily to cultivate the practice of prayer. This time, though, he suggests that the newcomer pray to the God of his own understanding to simply keep him sober and to remove the obsession to drink. Given a fair trial, the sponsor says, it works. If the newcomer is angry with God or resentful or feeling abandoned, the sponsor suggests that he tell that to God. "Go ahead and let Him know how angry or hurt you are at Him for letting you down. Tell Him that you don't believe in Him and that you think He is doing a terrible job with the world. Tell Him anything you want, no matter how bad you might think it is. It's been my experience that God is big enough to take it," their sponsor assures him. Ultimately, they know that even if the newcomer is yelling at God, at least he has begun talking to Him. And oftentimes, the sponsor's own experience has shown him that that is enough of a start to begin turning things over.

In the *Twelve and Twelve* it says that when someone becomes willing to reach out to a Power greater than themselves, once they open the door to faith even just a bit, it continues to open as if by itself. The threshold to the zone of magnified power calls to the initiate to cross over and promises her the power to transform her life. As the rational consciousness tugs on the hero to stay in the safety of the known world, she stands at a turning point. The decision to either surrender to a spiritual way of life or turn back and die an alcoholic death once again looms large. At the edge of the precipice of Step Three, the hero has arrived at a jumping off point.

The Jumping Off Point

Once the hero has proved his intention and commitment to the journey and is ready to move past the threshold guardians, he finds himself at a jumping off point. What he quickly realizes is that in crossing the threshold, the challenges he meets will only be overcome by relying on resources he not only doesn't understand but also doesn't yet possess. The hero faces the dilemma of discarding his old ways of thinking and acting while simultaneously trying to discover and trust in a supernatural power and a source of wisdom that is both mysterious and, at times, threatening. Joseph Campbell calls this threshold the nexus "at the entrance to the zone of magnified power,"[11] and it is here that the hero, by surrendering to this deeper pool of power and wisdom, gains access to the unlimited resources needed to complete the journey. The challenge now is to divest himself from a lifetime of self-centered and limited thinking and to rely instead on something greater, to go from the finite self to the infinite possibilities and power of the deeper, more enduring self found in the collective unconsciousness.

This point of the journey represents the time when the hero must act on faith and take action that is contrary to his old established, rational ways of thinking and behaving. In the film *Star Wars: Episode IV—A New Hope,* Luke's jumping off point comes while onboard the Millennium Falcon, which he and his mentor, Ben, have chartered to take them to Aldernaan. It happens while Ben is beginning to teach Luke the ways of the Jedi Knight, by instructing Luke on how to use the lightsaber. At first, Luke tries relying on his own reflexes and skills, but he quickly finds that he is no match for the strange, stinging little balls that evade his attempts to block them. As Luke grows increasingly frustrated, Ben finally suggests that he cover his eyes and trust in the power of the Force to guide him. Luke immediately dismisses the idea as crazy, but after repeatedly failing with his own efforts, he reluctantly agrees to give it a try. At first it doesn't work, and as Luke grows even more frustrated, Ben suggests that Luke let go of his own self-will and try listening for something else. Soon, and to his surprise, Luke finds that he is strangely guided by a Force outside himself, and that by surrendering to this unknown Power, he actually does better than when he relied on himself alone. This first crucial experience is the beginning of reliance on a Power greater than himself, and Luke spends the remainder of his adventure cultivating and deepening his connection to the Force.

Harry Potter reaches a literal jumping off point at King's Cross Station in London as he prepares to take a mysterious train to the unknown world of Hogwarts School of Magic. When he arrives at the station, he is told the Hogwarts Express train leaves from Platform 9¾, and as he studiously searches for this number, he only finds the standard Platforms 9 and 10. Confused, he is told that to get to the special Platform 9¾, he has to do something that goes well beyond any rational thought or logic: he needs to push his luggage cart right into and, theoretically, through the brick wall between the two platforms. Garnering the courage and faith in the unknown laws that might make this possible, Harry is persuaded to put logic aside and jumps into his adventure by charging ahead with his cart through the wall to the mystical platform on the other side. Once through,

Harry finds himself in a magical world filled with owls that deliver mail, chocolate frogs, and talking newspapers. It is a world where the laws he once trusted and understood are of little use to him. Here in this new world, Harry will discover not only a new reality but a new self as well.

By crossing the threshold, the hero enters the "sacred zone of the universal source."[12] Here the supernatural principle of guardianship exists, and the protective power of destiny becomes available to help the hero let go of his old self and begin surrendering his conscious personality to the larger, collective unconscious. The hero will need to rely more and more on the unlimited, intuitive thought and Power available in this magnified zone, for the challenges and trials he is about to face can't be solved or navigated using his old, rational, limited thinking. The mentor's assistance is crucially important in helping the hero adapt to and accept this unknown world, and also what it represents: the sacred world of the cosmic soul. Guidance will now be available to the hero both from the outside, from his mentor and companions and allies, but also from a deeper source: through dreams, intuition, and feelings. This unfamiliar and unexplored zone may seem strange and even threatening at first, but it contains the wisdom of the ages and the very energy of the spirit itself. By tapping into this enduring Power and energy, the hero gains access to the resources needed as he begins the process of disintegration and transformation that takes place on the road of trials ahead.

The Jumping Off Point in Recovery

"Now, there was nothing ahead but death or madness.
This was the finish, the jumping off place."

—*Pass It On*[13]

As the great Sphinx sits at the entrance to the city of Thebes and challenges the traveler with a question before letting him pass, so, too, does the Big Book pose an imposing question to the hero in recovery who has reached this point: "Do I now believe, or am I even willing to believe, that there is a Power greater than myself?"[14] The decision the hero makes at this point determines the success of the rest of his journey. Holding on to old ideas and solutions not only delays the transformation but makes the journey ahead even harder. As the road of trials nears, the sponsor, the literature, and all the heroes who have gone before urge him to be fearless and thorough at this stage and to seek God's care and protection with complete abandon.

Once the hero says he is at least willing to believe or does believe on some level, he has entered the zone of the universal source and a great Power becomes available to him. This is the guiding and protecting Power of destiny itself, and the hero now has access to the eternal and unlimited forces he needs to complete his divine path. Tapping into this Power not only gives the hero the intuitive wisdom he needs to handle the old problems that used to baffle him but also gives him the serenity and ability to handle those new problems that might at first seem unsolvable. The more the hero is able to turn his will and his life over to this Power, the more his conscious personality will be supported by the larger, all-encompassing universal unconscious.

To help encourage the hero's nascent acceptance and reliance on this profound new resource, the sponsor provides still more tools for the hero's spiritual tool kit. The sponsor warns the hero that there are many challenges awaiting him on the road ahead and tells him there will be times when the right path is unclear, when decisions are hard to make. To help the hero deal with these baffling situations, the sponsor directs him back into the *Twelve and Twelve*, and gives him one of the most helpful prayers in all of recovery: the Serenity Prayer. The sponsor leads him to the last part of the chapter on the Third Step, which reads:

> In all times of emotional disturbance or indecision, we can pause, ask for quiet, and in the stillness simply say: "God, grant me the serenity to accept the things I cannot change, courage to change the things I can, and wisdom to know the difference. Thy will, not mine, be done."[15]

The preface to this prayer, "In all times of emotional disturbance… we can pause, ask for quiet," offers the hero the direction he needs when he finds himself at a loss for how to handle the confusing or threatening situations that are to come. This simple beginning teaches the newcomer to open himself up and to rely on his new source of inspiration and Power. It provides him with an alternative way of handling and dealing with the myriad of feelings that come up, and helps him avoid making situations worse by resorting to his old ways of thinking and acting. By reciting the Serenity Prayer, the hero begins reinforcing the shift in his thinking and acting that, when practiced, is the very definition of turning his will and life over to a Power greater than himself. Indeed, each time he uses the Serenity Prayer, he is divesting himself more and more of his old ideas, and relying instead on his new source of Power, which some begin calling a God of their own understanding.

Another amulet the sponsor gives the hero at this stage to help develop reliance on his new source of Power is the idea of the God Box. The God Box is simply a small box that has an opening through which the newcomer can deposit pieces of folded paper. The instructions are straightforward enough and turn out to be uncannily effective: Whenever you have a problem or situation that you keep thinking about, the sponsor advises, or a situation that you are in fear over, simply write that problem or situation down on a piece of paper and put it into your God Box. Once you've made your deposit, you are to stop thinking about the problem and instead shift your focus to whatever you know or feel about God. By doing this, the hero is symbolically giving his problem to God and making an implicit agreement that God will handle it from now on. The best God Boxes are the ones with locks on them so that once a problem has been deposited, it can't be taken back out.

The God Box is particularly suited to the alcoholic personality because of its tendency to obsess and try to control situations and problems. In fact, it is frequently joked in the program that any problem or situation an alcoholic does finally give up has claw marks all over it! But "you can't solve a problem using the same mind that created it," the sponsor warns. "It is best that you turn it over to God, and see what His solution is." The sponsor reassures the hero that his experience has proven, time and again, that with God's unlimited love and resources, the solution He comes up with is always better than what the newcomer's limited, fear-based mind is thinking.

By putting a problem down on paper and depositing it into a God Box, the hero symbolically turns the problem and the solution over to his Higher Power. Once the newcomer has done this, he is next given instruction that if he finds himself worrying or thinking about the problem again (as he inevitably will), he is simply to shift his attention back to God and let go once again. As simple as this solution of turning things over sounds, with sincere and sustained effort, it yields remarkable results. Scary situations often miraculously evaporate, difficult or estranged relationships heal, and seemingly unsolvable problems subside. By learning to "Let go and let God," the newcomer strengthens his budding reliance on a Power greater than himself. And by using the God Box, practicing the Serenity Prayer, and by going to meetings and sharing his experience with others, the hero also begins letting go of his old self and builds the bridge of faith and a working reliance on the God of his own understanding.

The culmination of a supreme surrender, sustained earnest attempts to turn his will and his life over to the care of a Higher Power, or to a God of his own understanding, and the continued practice of relying on this Power give the hero a new footing on which to continue the journey. The ultimate goal of this reliance is summed up beautifully in the Big Book:

> When we sincerely took such a position, all sorts of remarkable things followed. We had a new Employer. Being all powerful, He provided what we needed, if we kept close to Him and performed His work well. Established on such footing we became less and less interested in ourselves, our little plans and designs. More and more we became interested in seeing what we could contribute to life. As we felt new power flow in, as we enjoyed peace of mind, as we discovered we could face life successfully, as we became conscious of His presence, we began to lose our fear of today, tomorrow or the hereafter. We were reborn.[16]

The Third Step Prayer

The prayers in the Twelve Step program are powerful spiritual treatments that, when understood and used consciously, have the amazing power to effect change. The Third Step prayer[17] is a wonderful example of this, and in this compact prayer the whole of the hero's journey is revealed. The prayer contains each phase of the journey: separation and surrender ("God, I offer myself to Thee"), initiation and transformation ("Relieve me of the bondage of self," "Take away my difficulties"), and finally the return with the boon ("to those I would help of Thy Power, Thy Love, and Thy Way of life"). This prayer appears at the end of the description of the Third Step in the Big Book and it is presented to the hero as an acknowledgment of the progress he has made thus far, and also as a road map, as a promise and a preview, of the journey ahead.

THE THIRD STEP PRAYER

God, I offer myself to Thee—
to build with me and to do with me as Thou wilt.
Relieve me of the bondage of self,
that I may better do Thy will.
Take away my difficulties,
that victory over them may bear witness to those I would
help of Thy Power, Thy Love, and Thy Way of life.
May I do Thy will always!

The first line, "God, I offer myself to Thee," represents that the hero has answered his call and has surrendered to the supernatural force he finds there, which he calls God as he understands Him. The second line, "to build with me and to do with me as Thou wilt," acknowledges that the jumping off point between relying on his selfish, self-centered ideas and surrendering his will and life to a Higher Power has been reached and that he has crossed the first threshold. Here a faith has been expressed that his old life will be rebuilt to serve a higher purpose, and there is now a willingness to accept and live this new life.

The next line, "Relieve me of the bondage of self," foreshadows the dismemberment of the old self that is about to take place on the road of trials ahead. The phrase "bondage of self" stands for the self-centered fear, the childish concerns and selfish motives—all the guardians that still keep the hero in bondage to his old self. The term *bondage* is appropriate here and a fitting metaphor for what weighs the hero down, for what keeps his spirit chained, in bondage, to his old self-will. The key here, and in the Steps ahead, is asking and relying on his Higher Power to clear away the ego, which has kept the energy of the spirit imprisoned.

"That I may better do Thy will" speaks of the transformation that lies ahead. This line reinforces the complete surrender and willingness of the hero to be reborn with a new purpose, and on a new footing, seeking only to be of service to others by doing God's will.

"Take away my difficulties" previews the ongoing work of jettisoning the remaining parts of the old self, the character defects, that will be the main work in Steps Six and Seven. When the hero first reads this prayer, he may mistake "difficulties" as meaning the outside circumstances and troubles, that is, the loss of a job, family, health, etc., he has when he first enters recovery. Indeed, many of these difficulties are relieved, but it soon becomes clear that these difficulties are only the outer manifestation of the real difficulties: his self-centered fears, resentments, egotistic, grandiose thinking, and more. These are the shortcomings that keep him from the sunlight of the spirit, and these are the ones only his Higher Power can remove.

"That victory over them may bear witness to those I would help of Thy Power, Thy Love, and Thy Way of life" represents the hero's complete transformation and return to his community with the boon: the lessons and insights from the journey. Reborn, the hero's sole focus is to be of service to others and to share the knowledge and Power he has gained from the journey. In the Twelfth Step, victory over his difficulties has resulted in a spiritual experience, and the hero's purpose now is to carry the message of recovery to other alcoholics and to practice spiritual principles in all of his affairs.

"May I do Thy will always!" hints that the hero has now become master of two worlds. With one foot back in the world of community, he has learned to be a contributing member of society, or as the *Twelve and Twelve* calls it, a "worker among workers."[18] Yet, the journey has also transformed the hero, and he now lives on a spiritual plane with a new purpose. By continuing to pray to do "Thy will always," the hero keeps his connection to God open and continues to be the conduit through which the energy of the spirit flows through him and into his community and to his fellows.

Now that the hero has successfully crossed the threshold and begun the process of abandoning his reliance on old ideas, and as he continues to surrender his will and his life over to a Higher Power, he soon learns that the passage of the threshold marks the beginning of self-annihilation. Once started, this powerful process is one of dismemberment of the ego and destruction of his old life and his old self. To cross this threshold is to pass through the gates of metamorphosis and into the abyss of self. Having found himself here, the hero is now prepared to go within to be reborn, and this begins by making a searching and fearless moral inventory in Step Four.

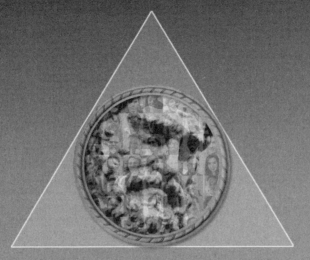

PART TWO
INITIATION

STEP FOUR

Into the Abyss

> "When you look into the abyss,
> the abyss also looks
> into you."
> —Friedrich Nietzche

AS THE STORM GREW more violent, pitching and tossing the near helpless ship, the terrified sailors each cried out to their own gods for relief and salvation. Frantic, they raced around the deck throwing their packages, bags, and cargo into the raging sea, trying desperately to lighten and stabilize the foundering ship. But still the storm raged on, growing more furious by the moment. Finally, the exhausted men huddled together in the captain's quarters and cast lots to find who among them was responsible for the calamity that was about to smash their ship to pieces. As the last lot was cast, they discovered it belonged to the stranger among them, the one who had gone below deck hours before the storm and had not stirred since.

The sailors charged into the bowels of the ship to confront the stranger and to get their answers. "Tell us who your God is and what have you done to anger Him so? What kind of work do you do? What is your country? Who are your people?" they demanded. The man answered, "I am Jonah, a Hebrew, and I worship the Lord, the God of heaven who made everything you see, both the sky above and the land and sea below." Jonah explained that he was running away from the Lord, and the men immediately knew that he was the cause of the terrible storm. "But what should we do with you to settle the sea again?" they asked. "Pick me up, and cast me into the sea," Jonah replied, "the sea will once again become calm, and you will be safe."

The men knew at once this was the only solution, but they were afraid of killing the man for fear their own gods would condemn them. Instead, they lowered a rowboat into the raging sea and tried desperately to ferry Jonah to the safety of the shore. But as they did, the sky darkened, becoming even more threatening, and the storm blew wilder. Finally, the men surrendered to the will of the Lord and begged for His forgiveness for what they were about to do. Together, the men grabbed Jonah and threw him overboard. At once the sea became still, and a great relief overtook the sailors. As they looked for the fate of Jonah, feeling sure they would see a drowning man gasping for his life, they were astonished to see a great whale[1] leap from the depths of the sea and swallow Jonah whole as it disappeared into the sea once again.

While Jonah did not know it when it happened, the great fish had been sent by God to save him from drowning. Jonah remained in the belly of the whale for three days and three nights. During this time, Jonah was forced to go inside himself as well and face his own failings for having avoided the difficult task God had asked him to do.

Jonah had to face his fears and humble his self-will, and he had to become open to accepting the will of God despite his stubborn prejudice. In the depths of his soul, Jonah found the strength and courage to rise above the limitations of self. Eventually the whale came to the shore and expelled the prophet on dry land. Transformed, Jonah went forth to preach repentance to the city of Nineveh.

The passage of the first threshold symbolizes the beginning of the disintegration of the self, where the hero is plunged into the abyss and begins the process of transfiguration culminating in a spiritual rebirth. The image of the belly of the whale represents the worldwide womb and navel of the world where all life began and can be renewed if we have the courage to return to it. While there is great healing here, there is great danger as well, for it is in the belly of the whale that the hero finds the abyss within himself, and while the things he finds here have the power to liberate and transform him, they have the power to destroy him as well. Coming face-to-face with his own demons forces the hero to make yet another decision: to either fan the flames of light he finds inside, however dim and flickering, or to snuff out the embers altogether and remain mired in darkness forevermore. The epic battle that takes place in the belly of the whale determines the course for the rest of the journey, and its successful passage determines the fate of the hero and, ultimately, of society as well.

By descending into the abyss, the hero is immediately forced to navigate the strange and threatening landscape of the primordial zones of his own unconscious. It is here, deep in the depths of self, that he reaches into dark corners and finds the source of his difficulties. The real work of the hero begins here as he confronts the shadows of self and begins the age-old struggle with the parts of himself he needed to discard long ago: the childhood defenses, the selfish ideas, and the destructive beliefs and behaviors that forever keep him chained to self. It is here that the hero will be cast upon the rocks to annihilate completely the ego and the self-will that have kept him alone and helpless. Once the restrictive constructs of his personality—his limiting beliefs and attitudes—have been smashed, the hero becomes open to merging with the sacred power of spirit. And it is only with the help of this transformative Power that the hero can achieve rebirth.

Now that the person in recovery has crossed the threshold of Step Three and has turned his will and his life over to a Power greater than himself, he stands firmly at the edge of the abyss. To continue the journey, the hero must now descend into the spiritual labyrinth of self and do battle with the dragons and monsters he finds there. What seemed like an impossible task just a few weeks or months ago, now becomes possible because of the bond forged, however tenuous at this point, with a God of his own understanding. The hero will rely heavily on this supernatural power, as well as all the resources he's gathered to this point, to emerge from the dark night of the soul that now envelops him, and, in many cases, just to survive it.

Step Four: "Made a searching and fearless moral inventory of ourselves" plunges the hero into the belly of the whale of self. The tools of this Step—writing an inventory list of resentments, perceived harms done, a fears list, etc.—serve to dismantle and expose the old self and its limitations, and this "fearless and thorough moral inventory" is the very definition of ritual dismemberment.[2] The saying in the rooms, "When I was doing my Fourth Step it felt like my life was being turned upside down, but it was really being turned right side up," reveals not only the tumultuousness of this process but also the transformation that is to come.

For the spiritual transformation to take place, the hero uses the Fourth Step as a process to uncover, discover, and discard the disparate parts of the old self, to expose, examine, and dismantle the defects of character that keep the energy of spirit imprisoned in self. The process of listing, looking at, and letting go of these shortcomings and personality traits, the very traits that have defined him, represents the systematic dismemberment of the ego and all its parts. In their place, new characteristics, attitudes, and motives appear: courage replaces fear; responsibility and trustworthiness replace immature dependency and irresponsibility; and a new self is born.

In the story "Our Southern Friend," in the Big Book, the writer describes the purpose of the abyss perfectly by saying, "I am in the bottom of hell. And there, a tremendous hope is born."[3] By "peeling back the layers of the onion"—the saying used in the program to describe the painful process of the Fourth Step—the hero ultimately reaches the core of himself and it is here that he integrates his separated soul and spirit back with the God he finds there. Once this spiritual integration has begun, a miraculous healing, both inside the hero and in the world itself, begins to unfold. But first, the hero must descend into the belly of his own consciousness, into the abyss within, and find a way to survive this part of the adventure. It is the necessary step of cleansing that will ultimately lead to the final absolution.

The universal image of descending into the belly of the whale represents the devouring of the old and the emergence of the new.[4] This symbol of a womb where the hero goes to be reborn has been variously represented in stories as a coffin or a pit (as when the character Indiana Jones, in the movie *Raiders of the Lost Ark*, descends into the pit of snakes and has to confront and overcome his deepest fears), and, most notably, as a cave. Caves were used prominently during the rite of passage ritual, and boys who entered the cave underwent rites of initiation that transformed them, and they emerged as men. The cave is still popular in stories today and is used to symbolize the abyss where the hero goes to confront the darker parts of himself, and, by integrating them, emerges as a more whole, mature, and enlightened person.

In the movie *Ironman*, for example, the character, Tony Stark, goes through the whole hero cycle, starting off first as self-absorbed, then reacting to an external call, and then being thrown into a cave where he undergoes a transformation. The story begins in Afghanistan, where Tony is demonstrating the new Jericho attack missile. Tony is a rich, arrogant, and ultimately heartless defense contractor who is callous and insensitive to how his actions and those of his company, Stark Industries, affect others. Traveling through the desert, his convoy is soon ambushed and he is critically wounded and then captured and imprisoned in a cave.

It is here, in the depths of the cave, that Tony confronts his lack of personal responsibility and accountability. He is now face-to-face with the gruesome effects the weapons he produces have on others, and he is near death as shrapnel from a Stark missile is embedded next to his heart. As Tony lies dying, he looks deeply into the darkness of his own dying heart and compares it with the hatred of the men around him. As he confronts himself in the abyss of the cave, he becomes disgusted and remorseful by his role in it all. It is here that he surrenders to his part in the misery of the world, and recognizes he holds the solution as well. As he begins to transform his attitude and outlook on his life, he also undergoes a physical change as well. A fellow captive named Yinsen has grafted an electromagnet into his chest to keep the shell shards from reaching his heart. Tony figuratively gets a new heart and a new source of power in the form of the powerful electric generator (the arc reactor) that powers the electromagnet that keeps him alive.

When Tony emerges from the cave, he has been reborn. No longer interested in profits at any cost, he is now motivated by a concern for others and sets about changing the course and focus of Stark Industries. His playboy living style also comes to an end when he falls in love with and commits to a long-term relationship with his personal assistant. Ultimately, though, the biggest change with Tony is that he has transformed himself into a superhero called Ironman, and he now spends his life combating the kind of evil injustice and insensitivity in the world that he embodied just a few months before.

In *Star Wars: Episode IV—A New Hope*, Luke Skywalker is swallowed by the belly of the Death Star when he dives into the trash compactor (along with Princess Leia, Chewbacca, and Han Solo) to escape the stormtroopers. Being inside the trash compactor is very much like being in the belly of a whale—it smells of decaying trash, and it's a liquid, swampy mess that begins to devour him when the walls start to close. There is also a terrifying snake-like monster swimming in the soupy ooze that grabs hold of Luke and pulls him down into the depths. In stories and myths, water often symbolizes the subconscious, as it does here, and the serpent represents the monsters and dragons, fears and feelings of inadequacy, that lurk in Luke's subconscious. Here in the abyss, Luke will either be killed or reborn; to survive, he must find a way to confront his deepest fears and to integrate and grow past them.

When Luke is released from the serpent, he emerges from the depth of himself, and his transformation has begun. Even as the walls continue to close, and as those around him struggle in desperation, Luke finds a way to manage his panic and gets the droids to help them escape. Once outside the trash compactor, Luke's actions mirror the change that has taken place as he calls Han foolish for chasing the stormtroopers, and from this moment on, Luke grows both physically and mentally as the road of trials prepares him for the supreme ordeal that lies ahead.

The Third Step required the hero in recovery to make a decision, and in doing so, it prepared her for the rigorous action required to work the Fourth Step. Step Four is a fact-finding and fact-facing process during which the hero searches for the causes and conditions in her life that have led to the state of spiritual bankruptcy, and to her physical, emotional, and often material bottom. By examining each area of her life and making a fearless and thorough inventory, literally listing on paper the exact causes, conditions, and consequences of her thoughts and actions, she is finally able to discover the attitudes, thoughts, beliefs, fears, actions, behaviors, and patterns that have blocked her from a life of usefulness and purpose.

Step Four represents a search and an accounting of the true costs of the old self. The Big Book likens it to a shopkeeper who must take stock of his inventory to know which items are rotten and in need of replacement. No establishment can remain a going concern, it says, unless a thorough and strenuous inventory is regularly conducted. So, too, is such a sweeping inventory needed with the old self. The search in this case is for the distortions and twisted influence of the self-centered ego. By use of the Fourth Step inventory, the hero lists where her defects of character have manifested themselves and interfered in her relationships with her fellows and with God.

In helping the hero uncover and understand her defects of character, the *Twelve and Twelve* compares these defects to instincts and natural desires that have gone well beyond their intended purpose of allowing her to survive and grow to this point. While instincts to be secure, to reproduce, to socially interact with others are natural and normal, for the alcoholic—self-centered, immature, and self-serving in the extreme—these instincts turn into physical and mental liabilities and maladjustments. Through the process of taking an inventory of these "serious violations of moral principles,"[5] and by examining our part in their manifestations, the hero moves toward correcting and, eventually, incorporating these disparate parts into a new and integrated self. While at first a daunting process to consider and complete, the hero once again relies on the help, guidance, and experience of her sponsor.

The sponsor, having traveled into the abyss of her own Fourth Step, knows the perils and promises ahead, and provides the hero with specific suggestions on how to navigate each part of the inventory process. To start with, the sponsor reinforces the need to be "fearless and thorough," reminding her that fearless means being rigorously honest with herself, and that only through a thorough moral inventory, including facing up to even the gravest of behaviors and thoughts, will she be able to emerge from the abyss a free and new person. Despite these suggestions, many newcomers struggle with honest self-inspection, and in many cases self-centered pride blinds them to their own part in their troubles. The sponsor works tirelessly to help them find a crack in their armor of ego, even the merest of openings through which recovery and truth can shine through.

The first resource the sponsor uses is the three-column formula for listing resentments found on page sixty-five of the Big Book. This simple list—"I'm resentful at," "The Cause," "Affects my"—captures the perceived wrongs and hurts that are the source of the spiritual disease of resentment that destroys many alcoholics and addicts. The sponsor has the newcomer list all the people, institutions, and principles that rub the alcoholic the wrong way or make them angry and resentful. Next, the sponsor has her list the cause. Was she snubbed at work for being late or irresponsible? Did the police boot her car for unpaid traffic tickets? And what about her parents or siblings, and so on? Finally, the sponsee is directed to list what effects or injuries she suffered as the results of these actions by others. Was her pride hurt? Or was her financial, emotional, or physical security threatened? How about her sexual relations, pursuits, or needs?

At first, most initiates are resistant to face how angry, hurt, or resentful they really are. Once they get started, however, many are relieved to finally get everything out, to finally make a list of how the world and its people have done them wrong. Suddenly, their anger and drinking seem justified. "You'd drink too if all this had been done to you!" they indignantly claim. It is at this point, however, that the sponsor shows them the road into the deeper and darker parts of themselves and into the real causes and conditions.

The road into the unexamined and unwanted parts of the self is through a new fourth column the sponsor introduces and calls "my part." She instructs the hero to begin listing her own defects in each part of her resentments. While clearly others may have been at fault, what part has her own selfish self-centeredness played in each situation, the sponsor asks? Where has she defended her frightened or hurt ego? How has her own dishonest attempt to get her exaggerated needs met interfered with or provoked others to retaliate? While the suggestion of this column often meets fierce resistance at first, the sponsor explains the purpose of this column and the key to freedom it holds.

The sponsor explains that while much may be wrong with other people and with the world in general, in the end we are powerless to change people, places, and things. While this at first may seem disheartening, the sponsor reminds the newcomer that the fourth column offers the way out. By listing her own part in the perceived wrongs and resentments, she is given the key to freedom because, by identifying where she has contributed to or caused the wrong to begin with, she is immediately given the means to change it. You see, the sponsor says, while she may not be able to change others, she can always work at changing herself. With the help of her Higher Power and a true willingness to change her attitudes and actions, she will finally escape the resentment and hurt pride that has kept her in bondage to her old self. This is the beginning of the transformation and rebirth that provides the great freedom that is the gift of the Fourth Step.

In order for this great change to take place, the sponsor provides the hero with the second suggestion for the Fourth Step inventory: that she be willing to examine and expose the shadow parts of herself and where her ego has tried to exert itself in virtually every area of her life. To do this, the sponsor suggests that five inventories make up a comprehensive Fourth Step: a resentment list, a harms list, a fears list, a sexual inventory, and a seven deadly sins list. Each of these inventories represents a separate path down the corridors of self, and as the light of the spirit is shined on each area, the underlying character defects are systematically dismantled, smashed, and scattered. In this ritualistic way, the ego, with its myriads of manifestations, is broken down by the Fourth Step dismemberment process, clearing the way for spiritual rebirth and regeneration.

The first inventory is a list of resentments against people, places, and things (the construction of this list is made by using the four columns described earlier). The Big Book calls resentment, in all its forms, the "number one offender"[6] and explains that it destroys more alcoholics than anything else. As such, resentments represent a spiritual sickness that triggers powerful character defects of the ego including self-pity, unwarranted pride, anger, self-righteousness, dishonesty, denial, retaliation, and a host of other shortcomings. The ego conceals itself in resentments as the problem is always perceived to be "out there," and so the fault of someone or something else. The fourth column of the inventory list, "my part" is the key to freedom from resentments, and it is the sponsor's job to help the hero honestly identify where these defects of character contributed to or even caused these situations to begin with.

Nothing is as important here as the willingness to be rigorously honest. The sponsor likens the uncovering and discarding of character defects during this Step to pulling out weeds in a garden—if you don't pull them out from the root, if you don't dig deep enough, then the weeds come back. Only by digging deeply into the garden of the old self, identifying the root causes and conditions of the resentments and character defects, can the hero clear a space for the new self to be planted and to grow. As each defect of character is exposed and cast away, a little piece of the old self dies. The ego loses its grip bit by bit. And with each little death, each defeat, the spirit of God grows stronger and takes hold a little more each time.

The results of this spiritual process begin manifesting themselves almost immediately, starting with a change of attitude and outlook. As the initiate begins to shift his focus from where others have been wrong to instead asking where he has been selfish, dishonest, self-seeking, or frightened, a new set of personality traits takes their place. Tolerance replaces judgment, patience replaces self-righteousness, and self-pity is replaced by a sincere desire to see where the initiate has been at fault. The initiate begins seeing that when others have acted unreasonably, they were, in many instances, simply reacting to his own selfish and unreasonable behavior. He realizes that instead of people being out to get him, in many cases others have also been spiritually sick and acted out of their old selves and old ideas as well. With his new focus on his part and his own faults, the newcomer begins to shift his focus from blame to a more helpful and open approach. The sponsor encourages the hero to follow the guidance in the Big Book by asking, "This is a sick man. How can I be helpful to him? God, save me from being angry. Thy will be done."[7] By changing his reaction in this way, the newcomer opens himself up to a new way of seeing and living and, thus, begins the spiritual rebirth of the Fourth Step.

But opening oneself up to a new way of seeing and living isn't always easy, as Phil Connors finds in *Groundhog Day*. When Phil wakes up to the Sonny and Cher song "I've Got You, Babe" in the cold motel room in Punxsutawney, he is trapped in the abyss of self. Instead of letting go, he stubbornly holds on to his immature ego, and each new day he awakens to the same abyss as before. Phil is experiencing what Saint John of the Cross called the "dark night of the soul," and it is the phase in the journey when the hero is left alone to battle the deeper demons of self. Spiritual development is possible here only if the hero is willing to develop his character by honestly facing his shadow. Phil is not yet ready; his arrogance won't allow it. For Phil, and many other would-be heroes, his ego has to be smashed completely before he can be reborn.

Ritual Dismemberment Continues

Now that the hero has entered the depths of self and has begun to navigate the spiritual maze he finds there, the process of dissolving the old personality structure in preparation for the emergence of his new self has begun. For the hero to achieve the radical transformation needed for this new self to be assembled in a whole and integrated way, his old self must be torn apart and scattered completely, in the same way as parts of an atom are smashed apart before they can recombine to from a new entity entirely. Here in the caldron of self, the hero continues the greatest and most dangerous part of the journey: the complete ritual dismemberment of the ego and all its tentacles of self.

To continue this dismemberment, the sponsor suggests the next inventory, a harm's list, which is used to uncover another strategy the ego uses to justify its resentments and retaliations. The alcoholic feels deserving of just about everything, and he often thinks, *Don't you know who I am?* (a fabricated self-image, of course) along with perceived disrespect, harm, or unreasonable denial. The outsized instincts of "His Majesty the Baby" often come in collision with those of others, and in his mind, justify a defensive response when his demands aren't met. By making a harms inventory, the hero lists what his part was, where he has been at fault, which once again gives him the keys to freedom. The harms inventory helps uncover another shortcoming the newcomer has: his skewed perception. It has often been said that alcoholism is a disease of perception, and once the hero clearly puts things down on paper they finally begin to see how their unbridled ego has not so much been harmed as has, in many cases, caused the harm itself.

One example of this occurs in the workplace. Alcoholics are a bewildering mix. They can be willful, creative, hardworking, lazy, prideful, and ambitious people. Their erratic behavior at the office often leaves them being passed over for promotions, raises in salary or prestige, and a variety of other perks they see others enjoying. This perceived harm done has caused many a resentful alcoholic to blame others and has fueled even more selfish and irresponsible behavior. Only when the complete picture has plainly been laid out in a harms inventory does the alcoholic begin to see his part in the situation. The sponsor helps the newcomer clearly list what behavior may have contributed to him feeling passed over or disrespected. Have they ever trampled on their work associates to get ahead? Have they always been honest in their dealings? Have they gone beyond what was asked of them? Have they always sought to be of service to others and their company, or have they only thought about what was in it for them? On and on these questions go, until the alcoholic finally begins to see their part.

The power of the harms list comes once again from the freedom from the old self it provides. Before examining the fourth category of "my part" in the perceived harms done list, it is easy for the newcomer to feel victimized. This feeds the immature ego, causing it to be defensive, on guard, and always quick to act in its own interest in an attempt to prevent others from taking supposed advantage of him. Once his own character defects have been revealed, however, true recovery begins as the initiate starts to recognize and take responsibility for "their side of the street." As the shackles of victimhood come off, the initiate emerges from the prison of self and sees the road to freedom that forming a true partnership with others and with God offers.

Before attempting this partnership, however, he must be willing to clean up his side of the street. This is achieved by continuing to search for his part in the discord between himself and others. As the sponsor helps him search out the defects of character that have played a role in the resentments he feels, and as he continues to sincerely accept responsibility for his part, his awareness begins to grow and he becomes, however slowly, willing to acknowledge and become open to making things right. This huge shift in perception is necessary for the personality change needed for the humbling work of amends later in the journey. The gift of the Fourth Step inventory process is the awareness of and willingness to change, but as his list of character defects begins piling up, the task of doing away with them all seems overwhelming. As the newcomer turns to his sponsor for help, the answer he receives seems like a riddle from the Sphinx, giving him hope but then dashing it away: "There is too much to change," the newcomer says to his sponsor. "It is hopeless!" The sponsor replies, "Don't worry; there is only one thing you need to change." "Thank God! What is it?" demands the newcomer. "Everything," the sponsor says.

Seeing the desperate look this answer evokes, the sponsor quickly reassures the initiate that this is easier than it at first appears, and tells him the answer and the solution is to be found even deeper in the abyss. "When you're going through hell, keep going," the sponsor suggests. As the inventories keep exposing and breaking down the old self, the hero becomes more and more willing to make that all-encompassing one change. And, as he will soon discover, this change becomes possible as the ego's stranglehold has been demolished and enough willingness to let the light of spirit in has been achieved. But first there is more work to be done, and the dark night of the soul continues with an inventory of fears.

At the first mention of a fears inventory, the impenetrable ego feels no chinks in its armor. "Afraid?" it balks. "Not me! Others need to be afraid of me," it booms. So goes the bravado of the fragile ego.

Yet, as a thorough fears inventory soon reveals, the old personality structure is shot through with it, and barely any aspect of the hero's life has remained untouched by its corrosive thread. With this inventory, the hero begins to construct a fears list with the same four columns, and here, too, he looks at people, places, and things in an attempt to get the whole picture of this destructive emotion.

Cataloging the full impact of how fear is affecting the newcomer and, strangely, at the same time fueling his ego, he starts by making a list of the specific people, situations, and things he is afraid of. Once again, when stuck in this area, the sponsor is quick to lend a hand. Authority is a good place to start, he suggests. Many alcoholics owe money to a variety of sources, including unpaid fees or fines to governmental agencies, including the IRS. "Do you owe any money on back taxes?" is a common question the sponsor asks. "How about unpaid parking tickets? How about a student loan or any other delinquent payments on loans from the past?" he persists. Once a thorough list of his fears of institutions has been made, the newcomer moves on to other areas such as his fears surrounding his job or finances, his fears surrounding his relationships, and even existential fears such as the fear of death and even of living. Once a thorough inventory has been rendered, the extent of the real problem with fear emerges: self-righteous denial.

With each fear added to the list, the ego grows increasingly defensive and indignant. With self-righteous pride, the ego balks at each attempt to list its part. "The government doesn't need my money!" it screams when faced with IRS debts. "Parking should be free on my street, that's what my tax money is for!" it reasons unreasonably. On and on such arguments go as the ego retreats and tries to defend itself. But as the newcomer lists his fears honestly, they expose the underlying problem that a life run on false confidence and self-reliance has ultimately failed him. The fears inventory finally reveals that the sum of all his fears is wreckage everywhere, and now the fear of retribution surrounds and threatens to destroy him.

At this point, the sponsor offers the hero the amulets of surrender and humility to help him deal with the feelings of shame and hopelessness he feels. Reminding the hero that recovery comes by focusing on the part he can control and change, namely, his part in what is causing the fear, he encourages the newcomer to focus on what he is truly afraid of. Isn't it the fear that he will lose what he has or that he won't get what he demands, his sponsor asks him? Isn't it truly self-centered fear that has kept him in bondage to his ego all these years? With an honest appraisal of these shortcomings, coupled with a true willingness to own his part in the creation and perpetuation of his fears, the hero takes the first steps in overcoming them. As the hero continues to uncover, discover, and discard the real causes and conditions surrounding his fears, the ego's hold becomes weaker, and as it does, the dismemberment of his old self continues.

The next inventory the hero makes takes him even further into the most intimate reaches of himself: the fearless and thorough sexual inventory. Few things can dismantle the ego as effectively as an in-depth inventory of the pursuit, avoidance, or excesses of sexual relations. When it comes to sex, the spectrum of emotion and opinion vary widely, and attitudes can range from self-righteous justification of the excesses of sex to concealed guilt or shame over other kinds of thoughts, desires, and behaviors. Helping the initiate make sense of the often-bewildering range of feelings in this area, the sponsor sets the bar for self-examination on a straightforward and easy level.

He simply asks the newcomer to be honest about when, where, and with whom he has been selfish, dishonest, or inconsiderate. How has jealousy, for example, made his and others' lives unmanageable? Where has he been the cause of bitterness and suspicion in his intimate relationships? Honestly and thoroughly making a list of these shortcomings, as well as what the appropriate behavior should have been instead, is the purpose of the sexual inventory.

While the process of making a detailed sexual inventory sounds simple enough, it is rarely easy to do. The needs for love, physical affection, and procreation are some of the most basic and beguiling of all instincts, and much of the identity of the immature ego is locked into pursuing and satisfying them. Because so much energy and validation are tied to the pursuit and attainment of sexual relations, the threat to the fragile ego and sense of self this inventory poses causes stiff resistance, and even rebellion. At times, the sponsor has to take a step back to reassure the initiate that the purpose of this inventory isn't to punish or prohibit sexual behavior but rather to have God restore him to sanity in this area, and to have Him mold his ideas and help him live responsibly and with dignity. By carefully helping the newcomer see where and how his obsessive urges have contributed to his difficulties and unhappiness, the sponsor helps him begin his first attempt at an honest self-appraisal in this area.

Focusing on his own behavior is the most direct path to the root causes and manifestations of the ego in sexual situations. By writing down the situations, attitudes, and desires that have led to his compulsive behavior, the initiate begins to recognize recurrent character defects that are at the source of his troubles. Examining these shortcomings and becoming willing to own them help dismantle their compulsive influence and prepare the newcomer to reach out to his

Higher Power for a solution. By allowing the light of God to shine into what at first seems to be the darkest recesses of the self, the hero begins to transform both his attitudes and outlook. As the ego lets go of its selfish designs and desires, the sponsor helps him replace his attitudes with a focus on thinking about, praying for, and helping others. Adopting this new perspective represents yet another fundamental change in the structure of the self and serves as an important building block in the creation and rebirth of the new self.

By now, with the completion of these four fearless and thorough moral inventories—resentments, harms, fears, and sex—a recurrent pattern of character defects of the old self has been thoroughly exposed. The hero has traveled far into the abyss of self, past the river of denial and self-justification, and has swallowed some big truths. In many cases, the recurrent theme is that self-centered fear has been the corrosive and consistent driver of a whole range of self-seeking motives and shortcomings. The ego at this stage in the journey is usually reeling, grasping to justify itself and reassert its control. In struggling to reestablish itself, it argues that the very existence of the initiate is dependent on it for the fulfillment of his most basic instincts for survival. At this point, the final inventory, a seven deadly sins inventory, is conducted, which at last reveals the ego's vain attempts at domination rather than survival, and shows why, by locking the energy of spirit in the prison of self, a life run by self-will always ends in pain, misery, and suffering.

The seven deadly sins of pride, greed, lust, anger, gluttony, envy, and sloth serve as the final paths into the spiritual center of self. The chief offender of the alcoholic is pride fueled by a host of conscious and unconscious fears that results in wanton self-justified actions and reactions. It is this pride that has effectively blocked true growth and progress and, most importantly, the healing light of God. And it is this pride that takes the final fall as the edifice of the old self is exposed and smashed by this last, comprehensive inventory.

The writing of the seven deadly sins inventory is unlike the previous lists in that it consists of four different questions:
1. What is the definition of each sin?
2. Has the hero ever practiced it?
3. What did he hope to gain from practicing it?
4. And finally, what *did* he get from practicing it?

While again a seemingly simple and straightforward process, the results are powerful in the way they reveal the wreckage of the ego's demands by matching the distorted desire with the often-tragic outcome. Once clearly set on paper, the ego, confronted with its own carnage, often dissolves away as does the Wicked Witch of the West in *The Wizard of Oz*.

The first thing the sponsor suggests to the hero is that he consult a dictionary to arrive at an accurate and objective definition of each sin. To use greed as an example, one standard definition is: "Excessive or rapacious desire, especially for wealth or possessions." If words such as *rapacious* are not thoroughly understood, those are then looked up as well. In this case, *rapacious* means: "Given to seizing for plunder or the satisfaction of greed; predatory; extortionate." Each new definition peels back yet another layer of the ego's hidden, self-serving, and even devious attempts to get its demands met. Once its full motivations are uncovered and understood, the sponsor moves on to the next question: "Has the initiate ever practiced it?"

Newcomers usually have no trouble citing examples of when they have indulged in greed, and if they hesitate, the sponsor gently directs them to look for evidence of it in any of the inventories they just completed. If the initiate is honest, examples abound. The greed for money, property, and prestige easily arises, and a careful examination reveals many attempts to acquire more than his share of these things, and by any means necessary, despite the consequences. It is truly humbling to look at the ego's ravenous attempts to dominate and exploit, but the true impact and consequences are yet to come.

By answering the next question, "What did I hope to gain?" the initiate finally feels brief relief by being able to justify what at first seems like natural and harmless reasons for his behavior. Isn't everyone out to make as much money as they can? Aren't we supposed to try to acquire as much as we can so we can be secure and provide our families with the best of everything? Isn't a strong drive for success to be celebrated and encouraged in this dog-eat-dog world? These questions fuel the ego, and it usually has no trouble coming up with justifications for almost every kind of behavior.

Just as the ego is flying high and looks to escape any kind of condemnation, down comes the club. In the next question, "What *did* I get?" a stark realization is thrust upon the whole scene, and once again the ego is forced to retreat. When the newcomer answers this last question honestly, all kinds of havoc are soon revealed. When, for example, greed is the motivating force in business, the greed to make money, acquire status, advance in careers, etc., the result seldom matches the intention. Hoping that the excesses of money, property, and prestige will bring him the concurrent excess of security, comfort, and accomplishment, he often finds they bring just the opposite. In their place instead is an excess of trouble. Careful examination reveals that others who have been used or neglected often retaliate, and the money that has been accumulated is never enough. The initiate finds that the security he was after has been replaced by a deeper insecurity; freedom from money troubles is replaced by overspending, debt, and worry, and the acquisition of possessions hasn't filled the hole he feels but instead spurs the desire and demand for even more.

As he continues to review what he *did* get, the initiate finds that greed, driven by the ego's insatiable demands, has twisted his natural instincts for safety, security, position, and status. All the things he had tried to acquire to feel accomplished, secure, or successful have only led him to feel less than, unsuccessful, and, worse, on the defensive from the attacks from others. As he examines the consequences of greed in other areas, he finds a similar result: the greed for sex, food, possessions, attention, etc., have also led to unmanageable results. By honestly facing the ravages of his rapacious ego, the hero sees, often for the first time, just how insidious and extensive—and how damaging—its influence has been.

As the seven deadly sins inventory continues, even more is revealed. As the hero winds his way down into the very bottom of himself, he discovers that pride has led to self-righteous justification, lust has brought the opposite of pleasure, gluttony has caused problems unforeseen, and anger has been turned inward and transformed into rage and self-loathing. Each Fourth Step inventory acts as a spotlight shining awareness into the unseen depths of the old self, and as each dark corner is illuminated, the ego dissolves. And it is only through the dissolution of the ego that the power of spirit can enter.

Sister Ignatia, the Angel of Alcoholics Anonymous

Sometimes the internal dismemberment process is preceded by a physical event, as can be the case when extreme emotional upset manifests as a nervous breakdown. The effect of such a traumatic event can often be enough to cause a complete rearrangement of consciousness, bringing about a transformation that forces the hero further into the journey. This is what happened to Mary Ignatia Gavin, more widely known as Sister Ignatia, a nun with the Sisters of Charity of St. Augustine, whose work with Dr. Bob in the early 1930s was crucial to the growth and success of Alcoholics Anonymous. Sister Ignatia is called the Angel of Alcoholics Anonymous because of her tireless work to get treatment and hospitalization for alcoholics at a time when alcoholism was seen more as a moral failing than as a disease. Because of her position in the admissions office of St. Thomas Hospital in Akron, Ohio, and her friendship with Dr. Bob, Sister Ignatia was instrumental in hospitalizing the first alcoholics that Dr. Bob helped get sober. Her assignment to the admissions office turned out to be an act of fate brought on by the nervous breakdown that changed both the course of her and Alcoholics Anonymous's journeys.

For years, Sister Ignatia struggled with balancing the demanding life in a convent, where she practiced a strict and austere religious routine, which included harsh fasting and other forms of self-denial, with her artistic expression and love of music. A gifted musician, she was assigned to teach music to orphans, and she maintained a rigorous training schedule in addition to being responsible for organizing several intensive musical events. Sister Ignatia's grueling physical demands, exacerbated by the self-mortification required of convent life, coupled with her internal conflict of maintaining and fulfilling her musical responsibilities, finally resulted in a physical breakdown. In February 1927, Sister Ignatia collapsed and was rushed to St. John's Hospital.

When she arrived at the hospital, Sister Ignatia's arms were paralyzed and her stomach riddled with bleeding ulcers. Exhausted both mentally and emotionally, Ignatia had reached the abyss. Believing that she was terminally ill, the nuns at Saint Augustine began to scatter the remains of her life at the convent, much like Set scattered Osiris's[8] body in the Egyptian myth. They disposed of her possessions, including her veil and habit, and even burned a satchel of personal letters and other mementos in her music studio. Nothing was left of her old life, and after six months, when Sister Ignatia recovered and finally returned to the convent, it was as a new and wholly integrated person.

In her book, *Sister Ignatia, Angel of Alcoholics Anonymous*, author Mary C. Darrah answers the question of why God would allow a debilitating breakdown to take away the musical talent that seemed central to the Sister's sense of self and purpose:

> The answers seem precisely why Providence suddenly struck Ignatia: to redirect her course of action; to re-channel her creative drive and energy; to refine and purify her spiritual path; to reintegrate her physical, mental, and spiritual natures; to teach her the power gained by letting go of self; and to open her heart in preparation for a new direction. Thus a total breakdown for Ignatia might be better likened to an illuminating *breakthrough* that finally allowed truth and a living vision of the will of God to reawaken and quicken her spirit.[9]

Through complete dismemberment of her old self, Sister Ignatia had been reborn to a new purpose. By surrendering to a singleness of focus (her days as a musician died with her old, conflicted self), she was able to develop her gifts of perseverance, organization, caring, and creative problem-solving, and return to her community as a channel of love and healing. Sister Ignatia emerged from the abyss transformed and spent the rest of her life as a healing instrument of God, turning the boon of her experience into a living legacy that impacts the program of Alcoholics Anonymous even today. "Total surrender freed Ignatia and transformed her life. The healing graces of a second birth strengthened her spirit and opened her wide to be used for God's divine purpose."[10]

In the movie *Groundhog Day*, Phil Connors takes the process of ritual dismemberment literally as he repeatedly attempts suicide as a way to annihilate his old self. After living in the purgatory of a repeated day for months, if not longer, Phil's ego has exhausted itself by manipulating nearly everyone and every situation he encounters, day after endless day, until he finally realizes that his vain and childish self-will no longer make him happy by getting what it thinks it wants. Each selfish path he takes only leads him deeper into the belly of his old self, and it is here that he finally surrenders and decides that no matter what happens next, even if it's death, it will be better than living in the nightmare of the abyss.

Phil tries a variety of ways to die and so to disintegrate completely: He steals a truck with Punxsutawney Phil in it and drives it off a cliff and into a chasm at the local dump; he tries electrocuting himself with a toaster in the bathtub; he jumps off the town's highest building; and he even stands in front of a moving truck. Each new morning, however, he wakes up to the same song, and each new day he tries to find a new way to destroy his old self in what becomes an ongoing ritual of dismemberment. Finally one morning, Phil wakes up with a new awareness and purpose, and he realizes that a new self has appeared and that he has emerged from the abyss. In the most fundamental way, Phil's psyche has been reassembled, and he has been reborn. Phil spends the rest of his days building, strengthening, and improving his new self until, one day, he is ready to return.

The result of the dismemberment process is that, in the end, the ego is finally forced to surrender its control because there is nothing left to hold on to; the parts of the old personality structure, its attitudes, beliefs, and concerns, have been annihilated and cast aside. And it is here, in the darkness of the ruins of the old self, that a new light begins to shine; a new awareness and purpose and connection to others is reassembled to give birth to the new self. In addition, an even more momentous event has occurred: A deeper connection and union with a supernatural power have been forged. The experience in the belly of the whale establishes a new starting point for the journey, and the hero, now spiritually reborn and mentally rearranged, is ready for the initiation of the new self that comes in the road of trials ahead.

Death and Rebirth

> "And where we had thought to find an abomination, we shall find a god; where we had thought to slay another, we shall slay ourselves; where we had thought to travel outward, we shall come to the center of our own existence; where we had thought to be alone, we shall be with all the world."
> —*Joseph Campbell*, The Hero with a Thousand Faces[11]

As the hero in recovery sits torn and exposed in the belly of the whale, a great transformation is at hand. With the ego crushed and the wreckage of its incessant demands laid bare, it is finally forced to relinquish control. As the hero confronts the ego's wreckage, he also confronts the limitations of self and realizes that by the self alone, he can accomplish nothing. To go on relying on egotistical self-will and the finite resources of a separate self will always lead to a life shot through with fear, worry, and unrest. It is here that the hero finally lets go completely and, in doing so, dies to the old self. It is also here that he is reborn.

With the walls of ego swept away, the healing power of spirit rushes in to rebuild the broken personality structure, to reassemble and meld the disparate parts of the self into an alloy stronger than before. Gone is the limited, fragmented personality, constantly on guard of attack, and in its place a new entity entirely, a new person with a new purpose. It is this person that continues the journey from here, and only the new man would be able to withstand the road ahead. Each challenge will test this new self, as well as the hero's reliance on his new source of Power. With each victory comes experience, strength, and a rekindled hope for himself and others.

This new, integrated self achieves the vital spiritual experience Jung described to Roland H. all those years ago, as the emotional displacements and rearrangements brought about in the Fourth Step result in the hero being driven by a completely new set of conceptions and motives. Indeed, the "Ideas, emotions, and attitudes which were once the guiding forces of the lives of these men"[12] have been cast aside, and the hero is now on a new footing. Being finally convinced that a life driven by self-will can only bring ruin and unhappiness, the new self that goes forth from here seeks to give rather than to get, to be of service rather than to take.

At the center of this new self is a complete reliance and dependence on the infinite power of God. The hero has been rocketed into the fourth dimension of existence, one where the answers to any problem are the same: Let go and let God. Situations that used to baffle him will now resolve almost of their own accord, so long as the hero continues to be willing to turn them over to a Power greater than himself. Fueled by this new Power and armed with a new set of motives, a new man begins the rest of the journey—a journey back to the wholeness made possible by establishing a true connection with his Higher Power. His task is to remain humbled enough to allow the energy of spirit to help him repair the damage he's done, to build bridges back to the many relationships he's burned, and finally to channel the energy of spirit to help heal society.

Examples of this rebirth are mentioned throughout the A.A. literature, including this passage in the Big Book that describes the person who has just completed the Fourth Step:

> For we are now on a different basis; the basis of trusting and relying upon God. We trust infinite God rather than our finite selves. We are in the world to play the role He assigns. Just to the extent that we do as we think He would have us, and humbly rely on Him, does He enable us to match calamity with serenity.[13]

And there will be calamity on the road ahead. The old self roared its way through the lives of others, and not everyone the hero approaches will be willing to forgive or forget. People have been hurt. Institutions and others will want their recompense. Situations will test and push and challenge the hero's new faith and way of life. One of the biggest and most persistent challenges will come from his old self. The damaged ego will mend and want to return. It will constantly try to justify itself when the going gets tough, and it will look for every opportunity to reassert itself. If he is to survive the initiation process in the upcoming Steps, the new man will need all the tools in his spiritual tool kit. These include the continued help and guidance from his sponsor and from his companions, as well as the need to stay close to the program and his new source of Power. To grow the new self, he will need continued willingness, constant vigilance, and an ever-deepening humility. These new, untested personality traits will receive their first real trial in the next Step of the journey as the hero lays the shattered pieces of his ego and his very soul before another person and God Himself in Step Five.

STEP FIVE

Initiation
The Road of Trials

"Only birth can conquer death—the birth, not of the old thing again, but of something new."[1]
—*Joseph Campbell,* The Hero with a Thousand Faces

UPON EMERGING from the abyss, the hero enters a new landscape, an uncharted world where he must meet and survive a succession of trials that further require him to release old ideas and attitudes and that force him to rely on the new tools and skills he has acquired on the journey thus far. Only the reborn self, with its new reliance on a Power greater than himself, would attempt the rest of the journey, and the hero's dedication to the path will be repeatedly tested and tried. As each trial is met and overcome, the hero's connection to this Power grows, and with this comes a deepening faith that his passage is indeed protected and supported by a supernatural power.

The initiation phase of the journey represents a transition stage between two states: the first being where the hero has come from and, more importantly, who he was, and the state not yet entered, where the hero has yet to fully embrace, trust, and act intuitively from his new self. The series of initiations[2] that lie ahead serve to strengthen the untested skills of this new self and expand the hero's awareness, allowing him to grow more in tune with who he is becoming. With each test passed, and with each victory won, the hero grows in confidence, becoming more and more capable of surviving and accomplishing the ever-increasing tasks that lie ahead.[3]

In *Harry Potter and the Sorcerer's Stone*, Harry's classic initiation phase begins (and yet spans the entire series of books) and is characterized by a string of tests and trials that help him grow by developing his problem-solving skills and confidence, by expanding his knowledge and use of magic, and by helping him develop into the new person he is becoming—a wizard. Since he is in school, some of the tests are regular exams given by his teachers, but through other, more dangerous tests and trials, Harry grows by accumulating new skills, amulets, and talismans. By developing the knowledge and use of magical spells, such as the levitation spell he uses to defeat the Halloween troll in defense of Hermione, or by growing his physical skills, such as those he develops by playing Quidditch, Harry becomes more capable, confident, and able to handle the increasingly dangerous challenges and opponents to come.[4]

Step Four challenged the hero to uncover and discover the old personality structure, to seek out the root causes of his troubles, and to dismantle the ego that has kept him chained to his old self. Now, as the initiation of the new self begins, the hero undergoes a series of escalating challenges and obstacles that force him to discard those parts of his old self he is still hanging on to and that require him to have increasing faith in the journey and in his reborn self. In Step Five, the hero is faced with his first great test: Has he deflated his ego enough so that he is now willing to reveal all his faults to himself, another person, and to God?

Step Five: "Admitted to God, to ourselves, and to another human being the exact nature of our wrongs" is the first obstacle on the recovery road of trials. Facing and overcoming this obstacle means facing and overcoming one of the inner demons many alcoholics suffer from: the tremendous sense of shame, loneliness, and isolation they feel. For years, drinking and using has isolated the alcoholic, and the walls his ego has constructed to defend its behavior have effectively cut him off from other people. The emotional, spiritual, or physical isolation this creates leaves him with a lasting sense that he has never quite belonged in the world of other people. It is often said in the program that alcoholics feel as if everyone else was given the owner's manual to life, but on the day it was passed out in school, he was absent. Overcoming this perception is a daunting first test of this part of the journey. Subsequently, the idea of intimately approaching another person and of revealing his innermost, shameful parts is truly terrifying; at its core is the very real fear that once someone else knows his ugly secrets, the vague hope of ever being a part of society will evaporate.

But facing and overcoming this trial is crucial to being able to successfully continue and complete the journey of recovery. In fact, the success of the rest of the Steps is determined by how sincerely and honestly the hero has worked Step Five, and in how thoroughly he has been able to reveal himself to another, to himself, and to God. In order for his new self to blossom and achieve a spiritual experience, his past regrets, shame, and secrets, and even his selfish desire to hold on to his remaining character defects must all be abandoned. It is a common experience in recovery that one of the persistent causes of irritability, anxiety, remorse, and even depression results from holding on to undisclosed or unacknowledged secrets of the old self and ego. The obstacles of pride and selfishness must be swept away for the hero to succeed for they can lead to the very real danger of avoiding this Step, or of not working it completely, of falsely believing that just listing and examining his character defects has been enough. The alcoholic ego wants to turn to what it believes is an easier way of dealing with these defects, which doesn't include self-disclosure. These easier, softer ways didn't work before, and they will certainly not work now. The hero is reminded of the ego's cunning nature by the saying "Your ego is not your amigo," and he is instructed instead to trust in the Steps and take the next indicated action.

To gather the courage to proceed with Step Five, the hero must rely on the tools in his spiritual tool kit, and, in particular, he will need to further develop the attributes of humility, fearlessness, and rigorous honesty. Of these, humility is often the toughest challenge at first, not only because of how misunderstood a concept it is but because of how much the ego rails against it. By the old way of thinking, to be humble always meant to be weak or vulnerable, two things the ego would never stand for. To arrive at a new perspective and proper understanding of true humility, however, the sponsor suggests the hero read the definition offered in the *Twelve and Twelve*. Here, humility is described as "it amounts to a clear recognition of what and who we really are, followed by a sincere attempt to become what we could be."[5] This new understanding of humility helps the hero accept who he had become as the result of his alcoholism, and makes him more willing to approach and disclose to others the exact nature of his wrongs. Viewing humility in this light also allows the hero to reframe the purpose of Step Five and see it for what it is: a path to freedom from his shame and secrets, and the beginning of true fellowship with others and with God.

Honesty is the next tool the hero cultivates to thoroughly work Step Five. Because the hero is now in transition, having one foot in the old self and one in the new, he is still driven by the old fears and persistent self-pity, and many hurt feelings still grip and try to drive him. All these feelings, along with the ever-present ego demands, make an accurate self-disclosure seem a nearly impossible labor. Besides, the solitary ego still tries to trick the hero into thinking that making an admission of its grosser handicaps and defects is unnecessary. After all, it reasons, I've just listed them down and been honest. Now that I know better, I won't indulge in those character defects again, and this time I'll be good. While gaining a clear understanding of his grosser handicaps is important, it is only the first step in learning how to be free of them.

Experience in the program proves that self-knowledge avails the alcoholic nothing if it is not followed by rigorous honesty and constant action. Being honest with the self on paper is something altogether different than being honest with another person. Because of this, it is clear that the next indicated action is for the hero to find someone he can disclose his innermost self to, someone who can help him develop the honesty needed to evaluate and appraise not only where he was wrong but also to point out the good in himself.

There is a saying in the program that to achieve sobriety and work the Steps, you must "find someone you can tell the truth to. We don't do this alone." The person in the best position to do this with is usually the hero's sponsor, as he often knows the hero the best and because he also has experience with both working his own Fifth Step and of hearing those from others. The sponsor, well aware of the hero's shortcomings, as well as his level of willingness and readiness, can carefully guide the hero past the early obstacles of his own bravado and any attempts to hide his secrets and shame. The sponsor also helps the hero avoid the pitfalls of wallowing in his shortcomings, or from exaggerating his defects, both common ways for him to hide his guilt and remorse. Thus, there is danger here, and even with the path clearly laid out, and with sponsors and others standing by and willing to help, some heroes still balk at the need for a Fifth Step and threaten to refuse this crucial Step.

The literature of the program warns, over and over, that refusing the call of this Step, and thus denying the freedom from self it offers, is not only dangerous but it becomes one of the main reasons people fail to achieve long-term sobriety or happiness. Carrying the burden of shame over acts he feels he either can't or, worse, won't reveal to anyone becomes a heavy rock to carry. It often leads to continued isolation, and many heroes suffer as they remain stuck in the transition: anchored to the old self and sinking under the constant weight of the remorse, resentment, and anxiety over acts committed and not yet purged. Instead of achieving a spiritual experience and release, these heroes labor on, haunted by secrets and the feelings of shame and self-loathing they bring. The *Twelve and Twelve* warns, "It seems plain that the grace of God will not enter to expel our destructive obsessions until we are willing to try this (Step Five)."[6] It is clear, then, that for the hero to gain a new freedom from his character defects, and for him to forge a deeper relationship with his Higher Power, one that will continue to protect and assist him throughout the tests and trials ahead, a sincere attempt at Step Five must be courageously made.

Obstacles on the Path

While the challenges on the road of trials are most dramatically represented in myth and tales as dragons and monsters, as well as other dangerous situations encountered, it is often the demons that still reside within—the deep emotional weaknesses and fears, and the resilient ego with its resurgent demands—that present some of the most formidable obstacles to overcome. Each hero faces trials that reflect his most glaring weaknesses, forcing him to recognize and resolve the shortcomings that keep him tethered to the old self. By meeting and overcoming these specific weaknesses and needs, the hero grows in maturity, skill, and confidence, thereby turning weaknesses into strengths. As he does, the process of transformation deepens.

We see this process unfold many times with Luke Skywalker as he continues his trials in *The Empire Strikes Back*. The adventure begins when Luke continues his training with his new mentor, Yoda, on the planet Dagobah, and it's clear in the beginning that he doesn't fully believe in or understand the power of the Force. Deep down, Luke is still struggling with the internal obstacles of ego, youth, and inexperience, and like a child, he is easily discouraged. While training with Yoda, for example, his spaceship begins sinking in the marshy bog. Yoda urges Luke to use the power of the Force to save it, and though he tries briefly, he quickly gives up and whines, "I can't. It's too big." Yoda wisely replies, "Size makes not," and explains that the Force is an energy that exists in everything, including the trees and the land and even in one as small as himself. Luke listens and then falls back to his limiting beliefs, grabs his jacket, and says, "You want the impossible" and then goes off to sulk. Yoda decides to teach Luke by doing the seemingly impossible by himself, and concentrates and channels the Force to lift the ship out of the quagmire and onto dry land. Luke watches in stunned silence as it lands right in front of him, reaches up and touches it as if to verify it's really there, and then rushes over to Yoda and breathlessly exclaims, "I don't believe it." Yoda slowly nods his head and knowingly closes his eyes and replies, "That is why you fail."[7]

In the spring of 1927, Sister Ignatia was a patient in the recovery ward of St. John's Hospital, and it was here that she began the long road out of the abyss of her complete breakdown. There were many obstacles ahead, for in addition to the challenging physical rehabilitation she had yet to undergo—healing her painful, bleeding ulcers, regaining the use of her paralyzed arms due to hysteria, and recovering from the debilitating symptoms of exhaustion—she also had to face the trials and challenges that matched the inner obstacles that had blocked her growth for years. The first of these challenges was her compulsive overworking and need for perfection, both of which drove her relentlessly and contributed to her breakdown. For years Ignatia hid behind these character defects to hide her deep fear of failure, and it is this unresolved fear that is tested over and over again as her new self takes on demands and responsibilities again. In order to survive these trials, Ignatia's first challenge was to accept her own limitations and learn ways of balancing and integrating both her personal needs with those of her community and to come to terms with the steep conflict she felt over continuing her musical career.

In helping Sister Ignatia to convalescence, her physician, Dr. Doran, kept her in the hospital for over six months and began her recovery by addressing her immediate physical needs. To assist in her recovery, Ignatia's parents rented an apartment nearby to also help support her, and the other sisters at the convent attended to her constantly. Sister Ignatia's fragile new self was constantly in danger of the recurring and overwhelming stress that led to her breakdown, namely, her conflicted feelings over balancing her musical career and the physical demands of convent life, so Dr. Doran posed a question to her that would finally overcome this internal obstacle once and for all. He simply said, "You can either be a live nun or a dead musician. Which is it to be?"

The choice Sister Ignatia had to make represented an early trial that had the power to free her and give life to her reborn self. Once she became willing to surrender her musical career, the obstacle of conflict disappeared and she was finally able to completely turn her will and her life over to divine providence. The passing of this trial transformed her life and set her on a course that would help transform countless other lives as well.

The continuing series of inner trials Sister Ignatia went through tested her fears of authority and challenged her strict upbringing as a nun that taught obedience beyond all else. While she was working in the admissions department at St. Thomas Hospital in 1939 in Akron, Ohio, she met Dr. Bob Smith, the cofounder of Alcoholics Anonymous. Dr. Bob approached her with the request to admit alcoholics for a few days so they could "dry out" and receive the A.A. message. At the time, hospitals did not consider alcoholism a disease and regularly refused beds to drunks. Sister Ignatia was in an uncomfortable position because of her vows to be of service and her inclination to help those in need, but she didn't want to go against the authority or rules of the hospital administration. The challenge Dr. Bob's request presented led to a jumping off point for Sister Ignatia and forced her to confront another internal obstacle and make a choice: she could either go against what she felt was the right thing to do, or she could take a leap of faith and push past this limit, and thereby past the limits of her old self, and continue to grow.

Leap of Faith

At this stage of the journey, the hero is acting in a new way, a way that is out of character with the old self, but not quite in consistent alignment with the reborn self. At times he chooses to rely on his new resources, and when he does he grows, but at other times he falls back on old ideas and gets mired in old results. To help integrate more fully with the new self, the hero often meets key situations that require him to commit or make a decision to fully trust in his new source of Power, and act on the intuitive wisdom of the new self. Once the hero makes the decision to believe and act on faith, he is then required to take an action that requires a leap of faith to confirm this belief.

Taking this leap of faith is a defining experience during the road of trials, and there are numerous such extraordinary moments when this commitment to the transformation is called for. With each successful passage of these timeless moments, the hero accumulates rich experience that builds his courage for when the journey requires another difficult decision to be made or action to be taken. Taken together, these actions turn a tenuous faith into a reliable and working part of the intuition, and as these moments are accumulated, the hero begins sourcing even more from his new self, and moving closer to the center of a spiritual awakening. Each leap of faith requires more and more from the hero, but the growing pool of experience expands his consciousness and becomes a reservoir for right action for many adventures yet to come.

As Sister Ignatia deliberated over Dr. Bob's request to help, she prayed continuously for guidance and the strength to do God's will. Finally, she made a decision and took one of the most dramatic leaps of faith a nun in her position could take: She chose to go against the authority and hierarchy of both the hospital and the convent by deciding to secretly admit and treat drunks in a makeshift ward she put together at St. Thomas Hospital. At great personal risk, she at first hid them in closets just large enough to hold a bed, and sometimes even parked the alcoholics in corridors for a few days. This wasn't ideal, though, because of their unpredictable and unruly behavior, and Sister Ignatia knew she would soon have to find them a more private place. After much continued prayer, she remembered how a fellow nun, Sister Isabel at Cleveland's Charity Hospital, had secretly admitted alcoholic priests to private rooms while they, too, dried out. Taking another leap of faith, Ignatia came up with an ambitious plan to house alcoholics in the same way, and so set about planning the details of another ambitious idea.

The first obstacle she faced was finding a suitable room away from the none-too-sympathetic nursing staff. Complicating this problem, the room also had to be big enough for two beds, as she found that two drunks drying out together had the ability to relate to each other and so helped calm themselves. This not only helped prevent many chaotic episodes, but it also directed and confined to one area of the hospital the constant flow of traffic from other sober A.A. members who came to support them, including frequent visits by Dr. Bob. After she secured the right room, she next had to overcome the challenges of admitting these kinds of patients by coming up with an acceptable medical diagnosis that would not draw undue attention. She creatively alternated between things such as "medical observation" or "nervous breakdown." Sometimes, if they had a black eye, for example, she would list their diagnosis as a possible head injury. Once she had these basic logistics worked out, she next turned to the more complicated and ongoing obstacles that would need to be overcome if the fledgling program was to survive.

As Sister Ignatia continued to work with Dr. Bob to get alcoholics the help they needed, the clandestine recovery operation began to show dramatic results. Not only did most of the alcoholics recover, but, once released, they spread the word to others in need of help, and soon more alcoholics showed up looking for beds. Sister Ignatia saw that she would soon need to establish a legitimate program at the hospital if her work was to continue, and this required yet another leap of faith. The only way to expand the program meant that Sister Ignatia would have to come clean about the work she had been doing, and this meant meeting with the hospital administrator, Sister Clementine, and not only disclosing what she had been doing, but also, even harder perhaps, laying out a case that not only met all the hospital's standards but also proved beyond a doubt that the unprecedented program was worthwhile. She knew this meant overcoming several more difficult challenges, starting with two very practical and basic issues: religion and money.

The first of these obstacles had to do with A.A.'s affiliation with the Christian organization the Oxford Group. Because St. Thomas Hospital was a Catholic hospital, she knew A.A.'s affiliation with any organized religion would be challenged. Coincidentally, this very issue was causing some conflict within Alcoholics Anonymous as well, and as a result, Bill W., Dr. Bob, and the majority of the early members of A.A. decided to sever ties with the Oxford Group and declare A.A. a lone entity that was dedicated to spiritual development rather than to any religious doctrine. In November 1939, A.A. took its own leap of faith and ended its affiliation with the Oxford Group, and began holding its own meetings at King's School in Akron, Ohio, starting in January 1940. This momentous split established A.A. as a separate movement apart from all religions, and in doing so, it removed an important obstacle in Sister Ignatia's way.

Next came the challenge of the alcoholics' inability to pay for the hospital services they were about to receive. By the time most drunks arrived at the hospital, they were at or near a complete bottom, and this often meant they didn't have the resources to pay for their hospital stay. In what would become a hallmark of the spirit of A.A., Dr. Bob and other sober members of the fellowship decided to contribute whatever they could to help another alcoholic cover his hospital bills. It was expected that once the treatment "took hold," that they, too, would be willing to pass this help along to another. With these and other challenges overcome, Sister Ignatia was now ready for the final leap of faith: facing and admitting to Sister Clementine that she had not only been secretly admitting drunks against the hospital's established policies but that she now wanted to change that policy altogether.

While Sister Ignatia seemed to have all the evidence needed to plead her case, she wavered one last time. Wanting to be certain that A.A.'s spiritual purpose was not allied with any religion, she enlisted the help of a local priest, Father Haas, and dispensed him to an A.A. meeting just to be sure. Father Haas was extremely impressed with A.A.'s independence and reliance on a nonsectarian "Higher Power" and reported back to Ignatia that all members were free to pursue whatever religious practice or leaning they had. Sister Ignatia now felt certain that she had overcome all potential obstacles, so she arranged a meeting with the hospital's administrator, Sister Clementine, along with Dr. Bob and a few selected A.A. members to offer direct testimony. With great fear and trepidation, Ignatia confessed to Sister Clementine that she had been secretly treating alcoholics at the hospital, and then she laid out a compelling case for a full-time treatment program to be established at the hospital. Dr. Bob and the other A.A. members then gave sincere evidence of the success of the program, and by the end of the meeting all were relieved and gratified by Sister Clementine's complete support. The final hurdle was next crossed after Ignatia applied for and received official approval from both the hospital trustees and the local diocesan authorities for a comprehensive program of alcoholism treatment policies.

The great courage Sister Ignatia demonstrated in overcoming all these initial obstacles resulted in St. Thomas Hospital becoming the first religious institution in history to officially recognize and establish a permanent policy acknowledging the rights of alcoholics to receive hospital treatment. Moreover, the established five-day "treatment" plan Sister Ignatia and Dr. Bob developed became essential in establishing that alcoholism could be treated, though never fully cured. Through constantly reinforcing this distinction, the word *treatment* became the recognized term that defines the role an institution plays during the early, managed phase of recovery. Today *treatment* and *treatment programs* are commonplace terms and a living legacy to Sister Ignatia's enduring triumphs.

In the film *Star Wars: Episode IV—A New Hope*, Luke Skywalker also reaches a point where he must take a leap of faith and test his new self shortly after he and his companions emerge from the abyss of the trash compactor. Once they are freed by C-3PO and R2-D2, Han, Chewbacca, Luke, and Princess Leia are under immediate attack by the Imperial stormtroopers, and Han decides to charge them, giving Luke and the Princess time to get away. As Luke and Princess Leia escape down another corridor, they soon reach a dead end and are trapped at the edge of the Death Star's core. With the stormtroopers closing in, the only way out is to take a leap of faith by swinging over the seemingly bottomless pit of the Death Star's core to the other side. Luke, in a courageous display of new action, doesn't hesitate: He throws a rope over the top of a railing, sweeps Princess Leia into his arms, and literally leaps off the ledge and swings to the other side. In this swashbuckling moment, Luke's transition to his new self is underway as he makes a decision and takes an action that his old self, the self in the cantina, for example, was unable and unprepared to take.

The kind of leap of faith a hero takes doesn't always involve a dramatic action but instead is more often driven by the kind of growth the hero has to make at the moment. Because of the emotional growth needed for the new self to develop, many times the leap of faith involves reaching out and connecting with someone else in a deep way, as Step Five indicates, and letting another person see them for who they really are. This can be a significant moment in the journey, which signals the end of isolation of the separate ego and reveals the transition to joining with and beginning to trust others. This happens to Phil Connors in *Groundhog Day* after repeated suicide attempts succeed in dismantling his ego enough that he surrenders and so gives birth to his new self, signaling a new willingness to let others in. Emerging from his dark night of the soul, Phil is now ready to take a leap of faith and reveal his vulnerable new self by telling someone else what's been happening to him.

He does this by taking a risk to disclose his truth to Rita, the woman he's in love with and whom he fears rejection from the most.

As they settle into a booth in Punxsutawney's downtown diner and he begins talking with her, it's clear he has changed; his old selfish ego is gone and in its place is the calm resignation and serenity of his reborn self. Without his old bravado, he struggles at first to find the right words, but he finally just tells Rita what he thinks is happening to him. "I'm a god," he says in a matter-of-fact way. Rita smiles thinking Phil is kidding with her, and says skeptically, "You're God?" Phil replies, "I'm *a* god. I'm not THE God, I don't think." Rita remains suspicious, so Phil explains, "I have been stabbed, shot, poisoned, frozen, hung, electrocuted, and burned; every morning I wake up without a scratch on me, not a dent in the fender . . . I am an immortal." Rita is still unconvinced, so Phil sets out to prove to her that he has powers and knowledge only a god would have. He starts by introducing Doris, the waitress, to Rita, revealing her lifelong dream of visiting Paris. He then takes her around the diner introducing her to other patrons and service staff, also revealing intimate details about them that he says only a god would know. Rita is overwhelmed by Phil's familiarity with everyone, and agrees to stay up all night with him to see whether what he's saying is really true. By taking a leap of faith and being honest with her, Phil's new self has begun to pave the way back to connecting with others, and this will soon lead him to rejoin the real world as well.

Navigating the early part of the initiation phase of the journey requires the courage to repeatedly take contrary actions, the willingness to remain open to change, and the increasing awareness of and dependency on a newfound source of Power. Each new obstacle challenges not only the remnants of the hero's old self but also forces him to continue expanding his emotional, spiritual, and physical skills. But as his proficiency grows, so do the challenges grow in strength and complexity, and each new adventure tests the hero in ways he couldn't possibly anticipate. As the road of trials deepens, so does the danger. Constant vigilance is required of the hero lest he fall back on old solutions that not only won't work in this new world but can actually sabotage or even eliminate progress thus gained. As he is hurtled toward his destiny, the hero continues to encounter ever more threatening obstacles until he finally comes face-to-face with the supreme ordeal that will challenge the very core of who he is becoming.

Leap of Faith in Recovery

Once the hero makes the decision to work Step Five, it takes a courageous leap of faith to actually go through with it. In addition to pride and ego, which still scream their resistance to any revelation of their base defects, the hero is driven by an intense fear of what the results will really be. Many of the secrets and shame the ego has hidden for years still haunt the hero, and the biggest anxiety the hero faces is whether he will be accepted or rejected by the process. What will his sponsor's reaction really be when he hears all the horrible things he has done or thought? How can God truly forgive him for the darkness and selfishness he has harbored in his heart? What will others think of him when the truth finally comes out? These very real worries act as fearsome threshold guardians that block the way to freedom from isolation the Fifth Step offers. Surrendering to this process requires the leap of faith that, once all has been disclosed, he will not only be accepted for who is but still be offered the support for who he is trying to become.

When he is ready, the basis of working the Fifth Step is for the hero to read his entire Fourth Step—with emphasis on the fourth column—to his sponsor. Like all rites of passage, the actual process of working this Step is carried out as an intimate ritual. First a time and location are agreed upon. Picking a place that is relatively quiet and free from distractions is important, and allowing enough time, usually beginning early in the day or afternoon, is also key as Fourth Step inventories tend to be rather long. Some inventories can fill whole notebooks. Once the sponsor and sponsee are ready to begin, the ceremony commonly opens with a prayer, either the Third Step prayer or the Serenity Prayer, after which the Fifth Step begins. The hero is then directed to read each line and each column of what he has written, and then encouraged to explain or elaborate where necessary. The work often continues for hours and alternates between daunting and intense, to light and humorous, as the sponsor shares parts of his own experience to help normalize some of the more shameful or embarrassing situations. As each hour passes, and as each secret is revealed, the bond between them grows stronger, and the weight the hero has carried for years begins to lighten.

Through the sponsor's careful guidance, when indignant feelings arise, or when the hero focuses on other people or the hurts they have inflicted, the sponsor gently guides his attention back onto the fourth column: his part. Whenever the hero blames or points fingers at other people's misgivings, the sponsor patiently reminds him that he is working on *his* inventory, not taking someone else's. By steering the hero back to his part, the sponsor keeps the process in the realm of recovery because, as he constantly reminds the hero, it is only the fourth column, his part, that offers the opportunity to recover. He reminds the hero that he has no power to change other people, places, or things, but he does have the ability to change himself. This is the truth of recovery, and this message is revealed and reinforced over and over again during the Fifth Step.

As the hero nears the end of this exhaustive process, the sponsor poses a question that surprises the hero and catches him off guard. "Have you been thorough and disclosed everything?" he asks. "Yes...," the sponsee responds hesitantly. Then the sponsor asks a question the sponsee doesn't expect, "What secret are you keeping in your back pocket?" Feigning innocence, the sponsee usually shrugs his shoulders and throws back a puzzled look, mumbling, "Ah, nothing." "You know," the sponsor prompts, "what is the one thing you swore you wouldn't share with me today, the one thing you are determined to take to your grave?" Indignant, the sponsee replies, "Why do you want to know?" "Because, that's the thing you'll end up drinking or using over. That one secret or shame will remain the barrier to forming an intimate relationship with yourself, with God, and with another human being. That one thing will keep you in bondage and isolation, and will keep you from the light of the spirit," the sponsor answers.

And so, with a little coaxing, the hero is nudged to reveal all. Sponsors have heard many answers to this question, and while sometimes surprised, it remains the sponsors' experience that whatever it is, the newcomer can recover from it—if he is willing to surrender it, too. At this point, he usually relates some of his own dark secrets and things that he also swore he would take to the grave. As the process of open and honest sharing continues, a bridge is built out of the loneliness of self, and for the first time the hero can fully and openly connect with another and, in doing so, with God. It is at this moment that the embers of forgiveness are stoked, and hope enters into what was before a dark pit of shame.

Once the ritual is complete, the hero is directed to go home and find a peaceful place where he can be quiet for an hour or so. During this sacred time, he is asked to review each of the previous Five Steps he has taken and evaluate how thorough and honest he has been. Has he omitted anything? Has he been as diligent and forthright as he can? This is a crucial step in the journey as he is reviewing the foundation on which his newborn self is built. The roots of a new life depend on the soil he has just tilled. If he can answer with assurance that his work is solid, then he can reenter the stream of life a free man, unburdened by the past.

End of Isolation

By completing the Fifth Step, the hero in recovery ends the isolation of the separate ego and walks over the bridge she has built back to freedom through an honest relationship with herself, another person, and her Higher Power. The tortured loneliness of isolation dissolves, and the hero begins to see that she does belong and that her old way of living and past mistakes can receive redemption. While revealing the darkest parts of herself, the hero has felt the hand of humanity extend to her by her sponsor, and she has made peace with herself and her Higher Power. She can now walk down a new and broader highway to a spiritual way of life that leads to healing.

And this healing begins with forgiveness. Buried in shame and regret, the hero used to feel hopeless. But once she has shared her deepest secrets with another and not been cast out, a revelation occurs. She realizes now that her secrets could only keep her in the prison of self if she held them in, but once brought out into the sunlight of the spirit, they also have the transformative power to free her. Once released from their grip, she intuitively knows that she will be able to receive forgiveness, and she will have the courage to extend it, too. This is the beginning of a true connection with God and with others.

As this revelation sets in, tranquility begins to replace the restlessness she has lived with for so long. Calm replaces the pain, and hope tempers the fear—though it will still take time to fully heal. The hero can, however, and often for the first time, begin to feel at ease with the world and experience the peace that seems to come so easily to others. In a moving and powerful way, she has rejoined and starts to feel a part of society for she no longer feels the need to hide. But most of all, this revelation brings her a deeper understanding and relationship with her Creator.

Throughout the journey, a supernatural power is guiding, protecting, and supporting the hero. In the beginning, this Power is often just a vague idea heard discussed at length in meetings and often in private with a sponsor. Though many new to recovery have various spiritual or even religious beliefs, now the sense of actually having a spiritual experience begins to take hold. It is often at this phase of Step Five that release from the driving need to drink begins, and as that obsession begins to fade, the awareness of a Higher Power becomes palpable. Suddenly, the presence of God becomes a working part of the hero's everyday reality. By completing the Fifth Step, the hero has achieved the disintegration of ego and annihilated her separate sense of self and acknowledged her oneness with God. The power of spirit, which was trapped in the labyrinth of self, has finally been released. Freed from the bondage of self, the energy of spirit now flows to others where it completes its unification with society and fulfills its quest for wholeness.

The road of trials is a chronicle of this ongoing spiritual journey where the new self continues to be tested and tried as it forges and strengthens its connection back to the larger self. Although newly reborn, remnants of the old self remain and pose serious hurdles in the ongoing journey of redemption and ultimate transformation. As the hero is still new, all things are also new to her, and the perils on the road of initiation mirror the inner obstacles that still need to be resolved. Continued willingness, humility, and faith are required as each new task is encountered, and courage, honesty, and reliance on her Higher Power are needed to successfully complete them. Each continuing Step in the adventure will add confidence, skills, and experience to the hero thus preparing her for the supreme ordeal ahead.

STEPS SIX AND SEVEN
Revelation
The Curiously Fluid Stage

> "Destruction of the world that we have built and in which we live, and of ourselves within it; but then a wonderful reconstruction, of the bolder, cleaner, more spacious, and fully human life—that is the lure, the promise and terror, of these disturbing night visitants from the mythological realm that we carry within."[1]
>
> —*Joseph Campbell,* The Hero with a Thousand Faces

AS THE HERO VENTURES DEEPER, the increasing challenges and tests he encounters result in a series of revelations that fuel the transformation taking place. A growing realization for the hero is that to survive and succeed, he must continue to jettison old ways of thinking and acting that continually come up and threaten to derail him. As he makes his way through this new landscape and begins incorporating the lessons he learns, he undergoes a "curiously fluid"[2] part of the journey where he struggles to overcome both the temptations of his battered ego and other new obstacles. Each revelation uncovers something about his old self and something about the new self he is becoming. Integrating these two essential parts of himself is the goal of this phase of the journey.

To help him during this process, the hero meets additional helpers and spiritual guides, many of them offering support and guidance, yet some who might try to trick or confuse him as well. All these guides serve to strengthen the hero by reminding him who he really is and of what his real purpose is. They also serve the crucial function of keeping the hero humbled and therefore open to receiving the gifts and learning the lessons from the challenges he undergoes. As the hero grows through this phase of the journey, he grows even closer to his new source of Power, relying on it more and more to make it through each increasingly difficult obstacle. Every successful passage through these challenges forges a deeper level of faith, thus transforming fear into courage, and limited awareness into an unfolding enlightenment.

As the hero travels deeper down the road of trials, he also travels deeper into the spiritual labyrinth of his consciousness. Enlightenment is a journey into the self and out of the catacombs of a neglected and dark psyche. The essential spiritual energies he finds there must be transmuted and focused on spiritual ideals. Transcending the infantile ego's limited sphere, and seeing beyond his personal past to glimpse what he might become, is the ongoing challenge of this stage of the journey. The trials are a ritual for purifying[3] the hero, cleansing him of both his sins and his fears and preparing and humbling him for the spiritual experience to come.

This purification phase of the journey washes away the contamination and restrictions of the existing consciousness, clearing the way for the growth and maturation of a more expansive and encompassing new self. As the hero goes through the tests and trials of this stage, his soul is renewed, and a new outlook and attitude are developed; with this new awareness there also comes a threatening and nearly impossible task as well. For deep within his psyche, where all the real battles for the soul are fought, the hero is suddenly confronted by a profound revelation that exposes the terror and challenge of this phase: that the disparate parts of the psyche, the darker parts that cause him the most shame and regret, are an integral part of who he is and of what makes him human, and, moreover, they will not go away. Once the hero comes face-to-face with these immovable parts of his own consciousness, he faces the real work of this stage of the journey: to embrace and make peace with the energy of his own dark side, his shadow, for only through acceptance and integration with it can he achieve the transformation that will make him whole.

In Jungian psychology, the shadow is an archetype that represents the powerful, darker parts of the personality: a chaotic mixture of repressed desires, demands, defects, and instincts that the ego has disavowed and refuses to identify with. The shadow includes all the material and impulses hidden from the light of consciousness, and the more the hero refuses to recognize or examine these aspects of his personality, the darker they grow and the more unconscious power they exert. Instinctive and irrational, the shadow is also considered the seat of creativity, and thus acknowledging and integrating this vital energy are key to the successful rebirth of the unified new self. The only way to incorporate this essential energy, though, is for the hero to once again brave the depths of his own psyche, to descend back down into the abyss of self, to search out and face the opposite and disowned parts of himself.[4] If the hero is successful at meeting this darkness without being swallowed by it, then he has the chance of assimilating and transforming this power for the greater good. But the very real dangers of this descent act once again as mighty threshold guardians, and any failure or resistance to complete this phase of the journey can derail or unravel the journey altogether.

When the hero in recovery arrives at Step Six, "Were entirely ready to have God remove all these defects of character," and Step Seven, "Humbly asked him to remove our shortcomings," he enters the curiously fluid phase of recovery. The tests and trials he encounters in trying to live a sober life result in a series of revelations about the lingering defects of character of his old self and about the work required to grow his new self. As the hero makes his way through this part of the recovery landscape, he struggles with overcoming the remaining shortcomings of his ego, with overcoming his still dominant old ways of thinking and acting, and with attempting to live more in alignment with the new spiritual principles of the program. During this phase of the journey, the hero learns the importance of continued surrender, honesty, and willingness as he continues to jettison the defects of character he identified in his Fourth and Fifth Steps. He learns to rely even more on his Higher Power to make the transition to his new sober and spiritual way of life. The goal of this phase of recovery is finding a way to reconcile the multitude of emotions he has—the incessant needs, wants, hopes, fears, rage, and shame of his old self—with the spiritual ideals of faith, humility, and service he is striving toward.

In trudging through this stage of the adventure, a large part of the hero's challenges is self-made and comes from refusing to fully live life on life's terms rather than his own. Overcoming a lifetime of self-serving actions and thinking is not easy, and, as the *Twelve and Twelve* says, "Rebellion dogs our every step at first."[5] Because the overriding way of thinking for the alcoholic is still selfish and self-seeking, each new situation often triggers a character defect and so an old way of reacting. If the hero chooses to act on these old ideas, the resulting spiritual development is nil, and many heroes in recovery have become lost in the rationale of old thinking and acting, and so have become trapped in the purgatory of being a "dry drunk": physically sober but mentally, emotionally, and spiritually the same as before. Remaining in this unrecovered state often becomes unbearable, and this path often leads to the hero abandoning the journey altogether, called in the program "going back out." It usually starts with the hero reducing the number of meetings he is attending, then refusing to reach out to his sponsor and others, and soon, once there is no spiritual or mental defense against the first drink, the disease of alcoholism takes over, triggering the old self to pick up a drink or other substance. If a hero is not vigilant during this stage of the journey, this heartbreaking ending becomes a very real possibility.

However, each new situation also offers an opportunity for growth through right decisions and right actions, and so making the right choices during this part of recovery becomes the ongoing challenge of Steps Six and Seven. During this fluid phase of the journey, the hero alternately makes both good and bad decisions, each resulting in a series of victories and defeats that continue to test, reward, and move the hero through the growth and development of initiation. In practicing these Steps, the hero is repeatedly directed to rely on and use the tools in his spiritual tool kit until they become an integrated part of his automatic and intuitive responses. To help him integrate these new ways of thinking and acting, the hero is encouraged to keep checking in with others, to run his thoughts, feelings, and potential actions by his sponsor, and to repeatedly turn to his Higher Power for support and guidance. This is how the hero grows ready to have God remove his shortcomings during this phase of recovery.

The sponsor's primary role during the tests and trials of these Steps is to keep the hero on the recovery path by helping him meet the situations and trials in his life by acting from his new self and by reminding him who he really is, a channel of God, and what his ultimate spiritual purpose is: to be of maximum service to others by doing God's will. This new way of thinking is difficult to practice, though, for oftentimes the newly recovered hero is facing challenging situations sober for the first time in years—dealing with difficult family members or relationships, getting a new job or starting a new career, confronting the wreckage of his past, and even attending social gatherings, or dating and being intimate—and his first reaction is to act from the character defects of his old self. The test of this phase, then, is to source from his deeper spiritual self, to reach and maintain a level of humility that enables him to continue to deflate and transcend the ego while at the same time grow and develop his new self. Humility, a key to remaining open to change, is taught through action, and the sponsor encourages selfless actions such as helping others, becoming more active in the program, and inspiring the hero to think and act more from the perspective of what he can contribute to a person or situation rather than what he can take. The goal of these actions is to help the hero overcome the shortcomings that continually threaten to retard his growth or keep him stuck in his old self.

As the hero moves further into this part of the journey, a key to making the transition into this new way of thinking and acting is to develop a deeper relationship with his Higher Power. As each sober experience triggers an old reaction, the hero can easily feel overwhelmed by all the work he must do to change and stay on the spiritual path. It soon becomes clear that, by himself, he has neither the strength nor the interest in changing some behaviors, and a growing revelation during this stage is that only by relying on God to remove these defects of character will he finally be able to be free of them. Becoming and remaining willing to turn these shortcomings over to God then becomes the real work of these Steps. To help the hero develop this willingness, the sponsor reminds him that although he may not be ready to give up some of his character defects at the moment, as long as he remains *willing* to have them removed, or in some cases, willing to *be* willing, then God will do the work when the time is right. As with alcohol, the hero soon learns that by himself he is powerless to overcome many of his shortcomings, but now, through increasing faith and willingness, his growing realization is also that when he is ready to surrender these defects, God can and will remove them, too. As such, the ongoing work of this stage of the journey is to achieve the level of surrender needed to become entirely ready.

This part of recovery represents the purification of the self during which the hero's ongoing thoughts and motivations are examined, cleansed, and transformed to align with the rebirth that is taking place. In a continuation of the work that began during the Fourth Step, the hero continues to observe his thoughts and actions in other areas besides alcohol, and the process of uncovering, discovering, and discarding his remaining shortcomings becomes his primary focus. In attempting to live a more sober and spiritual life, the hero is earnestly trying to do the right thing, but this isn't as easy as it sounds. At almost every turn, he comes face-to-face with automatic and unsuspected old ways of doing things and finds, to his dismay, that his character defects are very active in other areas of his life. Moreover, like the Lernaean Hydra, when one character defect is dealt with, it seems as if two more spring up in other areas. As an obsessive alcoholic, the disease that was once manifested as alcohol abuse soon mutates into a myriad of forms, such as an abuse of smoking or eating or sex or spending, etc. Other defects soon emerge as well, such as the greed to accumulate money or property, or the opposite defects of procrastination or sloth can set in. In helping the hero understand and deal with these emerging defects, the sponsor points back to the Fourth Step inventory in an attempt to once again understand their root cause.

By reexamining his inventories, especially the seven deadly sins, what the hero soon discovers is that his character defects are tied to the expression of his old self and ego in many other areas of his life, and most of them center on getting, taking, or demanding more than he either needs, has, or deserves. Most of his defects spring from an abuse of natural instincts: the instincts for security, comfort, love, or sex, and while these instincts are natural and necessary to survive and flourish, the alcoholic finds they are distorted and drive him in ways that still pit him against others and, when indulged, make his life unmanageable. The obsessive, self-centered ego is always ready in the background, like a computer program icon on a desktop, to spring into action once activated. As soon as the alcoholic opens up a program by engaging in a seemingly natural activity such as getting into a relationship, or wanting to get ahead in a career or job, or even getting something to eat, the program for selfish, self-serving accumulation and the demand for more than his fair share automatically take over. Reconciling these natural instincts with his ego's incessant demands for more soon becomes too much for the hero to resolve alone, and this leads to a realization that he must rely, once again, on a source of Power greater than himself to restore him to sanity in these areas.

As the hero makes his way through this initiation period and struggles with the countless character defects that still drive him, he comes to the vital realization that while he may have turned the drink or drug problem over to his Higher Power, he has, in a very real sense, still hung on to control in almost every other area. Because his old self is still in charge in these areas, the unremitting emptiness he feels in his core remains unquenchable. Regardless of how much money or shopping or sex, etc., he pursues, he soon realizes that there will never be enough of anything to fill the spiritual void he now feels. In the program they say that ego stands for "edging God out," and as long as it is still in control in these other areas of his life, the presence and healing energy of God cannot enter.

Some people in recovery spend a long time fighting to control their behavior and their instincts, and they pay dearly for this struggle. Like Phil Connors in *Groundhog Day*, who indulges his ego daily by acting out in every area, including stuffing himself at the diner, having sex indiscriminately, repeatedly punching Ned Ryerson, or robbing an armored car, some alcoholics can spend years trying to control and enjoy their excesses. Still chained to their old selves, they remain convinced that material things—money, property, or prestige—are the keys to happiness. Although sober, many still suffer from the anxiety and discomfort that comes from pursuing these outer things that can never satiate their inner spiritual longing. The saying "it's an inside job" in the program takes on real meaning at this stage in the journey, and as the hero in recovery reaches a bottom in these other areas, he moves closer to a surrender and to a spiritual solution.

God Shots

The *Twelve and Twelve* describes Step Six as the Step that "separates the men from the boys."[6] Indeed, the rite of passage of this Step symbolizes the surrender of the childish ego *in all* its manifestations, and in Step Seven, the hero is further directed to let go of ego's selfish demands and desires and to focus instead on character-building and the development of spiritual values. An unfolding revelation for the hero here is that character-building and spiritual growth, rather than the satisfaction of instincts and desires, is the true path to happiness, and convincing the alcoholic of this, and keeping him on the path of pursuing it, is the true work of these Steps and this part of the journey. The sponsor continues to direct the hero to focus on seeking his Higher Power's will in all situations, and to praying for the willingness and humility to do what's right, rather than on what feels right.

As the hero continues to make progress by taking contrary action and surrendering his will and his life over to his Higher Power, he encounters a series of unexpected results known in the program as "God shots." God shots appear as unforeseen outcomes to events and situations the hero has truly surrendered to, and once he puts the results in the hands of his Higher Power, he finds that things start working out far beyond his limited expectations. Outcomes begin exceeding his selfish demands and designs, and situations unexpectedly resolve themselves and turn out far better than anything he could have thought up on his own. Results of these situations turn out for the benefit and welfare of all involved, not just himself, and the hero begins recognizing God shots for what they are: the true gifts of surrender and faith in his Higher Power's will. There is a saying in the program that if you are truly willing to pray for God's will instead of your own, then you'll find that

"God has only three answers to your prayers,
1. Yes.
2. Yes, but not now.
3. No, because I have something better for you."

Learning to believe in, surrender to, and trust the wisdom of this saying represents the spiritual development the hero is seeking during these Steps.

The more the hero practices turning his thoughts and actions over to God, the more these series of God shots lead to the realization that God can do for the hero, in all areas of his life, that which he cannot do by himself. As God's peace and serenity begin to fill the emptiness of self-centered interest, the hero moves away from his limited objectives and more toward what God's will is for himself and others. As the hero's consciousness grows and changes in this way, his spiritual development accelerates. His tolerance for dishonest or self-seeking actions goes down, and he is quicker to choose the right thoughts and actions. The "emotional displacements and re-arrangements" that Jung described in the Big Book start to become a working part of the hero's new personality, and the "ideas, emotions, and attitudes which were once the guiding forces"[7] of his life are, one by one, cast aside as God consciousness slowly yet steadily takes their place. As the hero develops genuine humility and surrenders even more of himself and his ego, his reborn self is strengthened and his spiritual experience deepens.

Moving through this transformative phase of the journey, the changes the hero is undergoing can be subtle and sometimes hard for him to see. It's easy to get frustrated during these Steps, and sometimes the transformation taking place is clearer to others than to himself, and it occasionally takes a little help for the hero to recognize the progress he is making. To evidence the internal changes taking place, the sponsor occasionally has the hero go through an exercise of bringing out any lists he made at the beginning of the journey of all the things he wanted and thought he would get from being in recovery. The list often reveals the sharp contrast and development of the new man. Most items on the list, which were driven by the old self and ego, consist of outer things such as money, career advancement, material possessions, and prestige. In reviewing this list with his sponsor, the new self realizes that none of these outside things will ever bring him the peace and serenity needed to make him truly happy. The new priorities of being of service, practicing honesty in all his affairs, improving his conscious contact with his Higher Power, and such reflect the transformation he is undergoing. The new set of priorities is firmly in place, and the hero now seeks actions and ways of thinking and being that will fulfill him spiritually and that, as a result, will enable him to achieve the one goal he never even thought of in the beginning: feeling comfortable in his own skin.

As the hero continues to receive God shots and revelations that lead to preliminary victories over her character defects, she often experiences moments of ecstatic hope and breakthroughs called "pink cloud" experiences. These are euphoric moments where she glimpses the ultimate peace that is available once she is truly aligned with God's will, but these moments don't always last and can be followed by a descent once again into the pit of self-pity and despair. This curiously fluid stage of recovery is known in the program as the roller-coaster ride of early sobriety, because emotions rise and fall seemingly indiscriminately. Once at bottom again, the hero can quickly become overwhelmed with the self-pity and shame that seem incurable, and with character defects so ingrained and automatic they seem necessary for her basic survival.

To work through these temporary emotional bottoms, the sponsor urges her to keep "peeling back the onion" layers of self. As she continues this work, she once again descends into the abyss of her own consciousness, searching for the shortcomings and character defects that still need to be purged, and it is here that she confronts her shadow. Deep in the recesses of her psyche, she discovers that the urges and needs of her basic instincts have been twisted into defects and fueled by a psychological power that even she is afraid of. These serious character flaws—her extreme self-centeredness, her demands to get more at the expense of others, her mistrust and resentment of people, places, and things—are the shadow parts of herself that caused her retreat into addiction, and that she has tried to hide from for years. So dark are they, and so mixed with shame and remorse, that she has not dared to try to integrate them into her life, or even admit she has them. The task of facing these demons and finding a way to either banish them for good or to integrate them into the new self becomes the final trial of this part of the adventure.

At last, the hero is confronted with one of the deepest mysteries and paradoxes of being human: that within each of us we carry both the energy of the dark as well as the light, and that both are necessary to achieve wholeness. As the hero journeys once more through the depths of his psyche, he comes to see that the many unacceptable parts of his shadow—the selfishness, hostility, fear, and greed—are the lingering aspects of the dark and unacknowledged side of his residual ego. To achieve integration of the reborn self, he realizes that the task he began in the abyss, the dismemberment of the ego, continues during this phase, and that assimilating the remaining dark energy is the key to his return to the oneness of life. As he gains more awareness, he begins to see that the unique tests and trials facing him in the initiation phase are mirrors reflecting back to him the different manifestations of his shadow, and that as each test brings a new part of the darkness to light, the real challenge is in owning, integrating, and growing from it. Yet, once one defect of character has been cut away, many more seemingly spring up, as the ego constantly morphs into different areas and expressions. This phase of the journey is thus populated by an endless series of initial victories and defeats, and of revelations that motivate the hero to transmute the dark energy once and for all, and so complete the transformation.

After Luke Skywalker completes his ego deflation in *Star Wars: Episode IV—A New Hope*—which culminates during the rebel attack on the Death Star when he voluntarily turns off the missile guidance system (effectively his ego) and surrenders to the Force—the real work of facing and assimilating the dark side of his shadow takes place on the road of trials during the next two films, *The Empire Strikes Back* and *Return of the Jedi*. For Luke, the lingering qualities of anger, resentment, hostility, pride, and ambition are mixed in the darkness of his psyche and exemplified by his father, Darth Vader. Darth has given in to the power of his shadow, and Luke's greatest trial is to resist being swallowed by these very qualities within himself. In a triumphant final scene with Darth in *Return of the Jedi*, Luke makes a decision that not only allows him to accept the darkness in his father, and so in himself, but that also offers redemption to his father by allowing Darth to assimilate his remaining light with the darkness and so transmute it for a force for good that saves Luke.

The scene takes place on the new Death Star, which is now fully operational and poised to destroy the rebel resistance once and for all. In a classic showdown between the light and dark, Luke faces Darth with the evil Emperor Palpatine looking down from an elevated place, as if in judgment, as the eternal battle between the two opposite forces takes place. Luke feels the good that is left in Darth and tells him that he feels his conflict over doing the right thing, and yet Darth tells Luke that his hatred makes him strong and encourages Luke to give in to the dark side and join him. As they both struggle with the opposites in themselves, Luke uses the energy of his own darkness to defeat Darth but then surrenders to the power of the Force and to his destiny by refusing to kill him. In this moment, Luke has faced and assimilated his own shadow and has finally completed his journey of becoming a Jedi Knight. Luke's decision to spare his father's life allows Darth the chance at his own redemption and atonement as he then saves Luke by destroying the evil Palpatine. Mortally wounded during the battle, though, Darth refuses Luke's pleas to save him, saying, "You already have, Luke." As the father dies in the arms of his son, both are transformed, and Luke is now capable of returning to the world as an eternal force for good.

While struggling to accept the shadow elements within herself, the hero quickly discovers that in addition to the darkness, there is valuable light contained there as well. Not everything hidden in the psyche is negative. There are powerful creative forces contained in this deep pool of the self, but they, too, must be brought to the surface, integrated, and channeled, lest their power be turned inward, where they can destroy. For Sister Ignatia, it was this part of her conflicted psyche, her musical talent and endless need for perfection, which drove her relentlessly, that contributed to her breakdown and physical collapse. On her road of trials, the challenge of acknowledging these essential parts of herself and finding a way to assimilate them into who she was becoming became one of her greatest trials.

Sister Ignatia did this by channeling this energy and pouring it into her greater calling in serving as a nun. While she no longer played, taught, or coordinated musical events, she didn't give up the tremendous creative energy inside her. Instead, she infused it into the work she did with Dr. Bob, and in doing so she found creative ways to overcome the myriads of challenges she faced in establishing the alcoholism ward in St. Thomas Hospital. Sister Ignatia realized, for example, that in order for the alcoholism program to succeed, she would need to build and shape it into a respectable and valuable part of generalized hospital care, and so she directed her artistic energy into A.A.'s growth and activities in her spare time. For thirteen years, Sister Ignatia tended to the procedural and practical development of the alcoholism ward, all in addition to her full-time duties in the admitting office. The successful integration of the creative part of her shadow gave Sister Ignatia the inner resources and wisdom to develop and grow the alcoholism treatment ward in the late 1930s and early 1940s. The thought, energy, and time she invested in this recovery program went on to become the model of modern alcoholism treatment today.

Just as the opposites of light and dark are contained in the shadow, so, too, are energies of the male and female present deep within the psyche as well. The hero, in struggling to integrate his consciousness, must also come to terms with these powerful yet opposite forces. Jung called the female aspect in the man the anima and the male energy in the woman the animus. The universal energy of the anima is often represented in stories and myths as a young girl or fairy princess, and also as a witch or earth mother. The energy is pure, spontaneous, and intuitive; it is deeply emotional and tied to the spirit energy itself. The male energy, the animus, is found in the figures of the wise old man, sorcerer, or shaman. This male energy completes the anima by adding the qualities of logic and order; it represents rationality and can even be argumentative or aggressive. When combined together, the yin and the yang, they temper and complement each other. At this stage on the road of trials, the hero's task is to find and merge with this opposite energy, to incorporate its power and wisdom, and so pass through the final gateway to the wholeness and completeness he seeks.

Meeting with the Goddess

In many cultures, the earth mother is the living embodiment of the planet, giving life, nourishment, and protection. The hero, who has now passed many tests and merged his fragmented psyche, longs for a relationship with a figure who exemplifies these qualities of the mother, the unconditional love and support, and the capacity to accept the good and the bad, the pain and the bliss of life. The hero searches for this union in the opposite sex or in another who exemplifies the energy and qualities he or she lacks. By joining with this other half, the hero completes a sacred marriage by merging the essence of two souls and so gains greater power and wisdom. For the hero, the meeting with the goddess represents this mystical opportunity.

The goddess figure is most often portrayed as a woman who represents the totality of creation, the beauty and the ugliness, the noble and the banal. Her embrace includes all life on Earth and extends throughout space, encompassing the known galaxies and the unknown solar systems reaching to the edge of time. She gives joy at the beginning of life; hope, growth, and maturity in the middle; and finally wisdom and satisfaction at the end. But she also gives the pain of birth, disappointment and struggle in the middle, and regret and suffering at the end. She represents the wholeness of life, and in her the opposites of good and bad are merged and blurred, forcing the hero to accept them both as flickering aspects of the essence of life. Through the goddess, the hero finally sees past his limited ego, judgments, and resentments, and he is awakened, through transcendence, to the true nature and meaning of life.

The goddess is also a mirror for the hero, reflecting back to him his perception of the world and, his understanding of his place in it, and her reflected image soon becomes the measurement for his internal development. In childhood she represents and defines the difference between the two sexes, but in the transition from youth to adulthood, she becomes the image of sexual attraction and lust. Through this lens of separateness and erotic compulsion, she is often reduced to an object of fulfillment, something inferior yet necessary, something to covet and use. The goddess can never transcend the image projected onto her but rather waits and evolves with the consciousness she is engaged with. She beckons the hero toward the light of knowledge, intriguing him with the promise to fulfill more than he currently comprehends, luring him with the promise of completeness and enlightenment. Both the hero and the universal energy of the goddess are redeemed and set free by the right understanding, respect, and acceptance. Once the proper submission is attained, the evolution of consciousness is complete, and the hero assumes his proper place in her world.

The goddess also symbolizes the attainment of every goal the hero sets along the way of his journey, eventually teaching him that the elusive happiness for which he reaches is possible beyond his mundane life and dangerous struggles. She is the reason the hero ventures forth; she represents the goal of a better, more fulfilling life. Surrendering to her energy means returning to the unconditional love she bestowed all those years ago, the love and acceptance for which his enduring thirst has never been quenched. Once the hero finds his soulmate, his muse, and his reason for life—to give life and love and to create life through this union—that is when he has achieved a destiny beyond self, beyond thought, beyond time.

While the goddess, by its very name, has most often been represented as a woman figure, in its true transcendental meaning, the symbol of the goddess stands for the true understanding and acceptance of the two sides of the human experience: bliss and suffering. By submitting to and merging with the energy of the goddess, the hero surrenders completely to the duality of life, accepting the good with the bad with equanimity. Gentle acceptance of both sides of life leads to seeing with reverence the preciousness of experience in a birth as well as a death, and once so achieved, the hero has finally transcended his attachment to ego and moved into the realm of the spiritual.

Because the goddess represents the total life experience, she can appear to the hero in a myriad of forms throughout his journey. At times, she embodies the motherly aspect, serving to protect or guide the hero, or she can surface as a sisterly figure contributing to the journey as a companion by teaching or aiding the hero through his trials. Sometimes she appears as a temptress, exemplifying the shadow aspects not yet integrated, threatening to distract or even derail the hero, and often she appears as the romantic figure the hero eventually merges with. These different manifestations are prevalent in many hero's adventures, and during Harry Potter's journey, for example, he meets all these forms of the goddess on his way to becoming a wizard. Each expression enriches and completes his experience, culminating in a sacred marriage that results in the unconditional love he has searched for his entire journey.

Several women play the role of mother for Harry and display varying attributes of the nurturing aspects of the goddess. Lily Potter, Harry's birth mother, gives her life in the beginning to protect Harry from Voldemort, and continues to provide a nurturing and protective love for him throughout the adventure. Molly Weasley becomes Harry's surrogate mother at the beginning of his journey and provides him with the stability, warmth, and caring he never had in a family unit. In a sense she is a cosmic mother for Harry, offering him the unconditional love and sense of belonging he has been searching for. Her acceptance and comfort are so inviting for Harry, they almost become a threshold guardian as they offer an early temptation to resist the dangers of the journey and instead retreat into the safety of her motherly protection.

Once Harry enters Hogwarts, he falls under the protection of Minerva McConagall, who assumes an active and motherly role with him. Although a bit strict and standoffish, Minerva has nonetheless been protective of Harry from the beginning and was even against placing him with the Dursleys as a baby. Minerva takes on the surrogate role of mother for Harry and assumes a direct personal guardianship for him, including, on several occasions, preventing him from being expelled from school. She guides, encourages, and supports Harry as when she recognizes his talent and places him on the Quidditch team in his first year. Minerva also has aspects of the goddess of wisdom, living up to her being named after the Roman goddess, Minerva, representing wisdom, defense, and magic. She is a loyal and fierce supporter of Dumbledore, and fights, as any mother would, to protect her home, Hogwarts, and those under her care.

As Harry's faithful companion, helper, and protector, Hermione Granger represents many aspects of the goddess as well. Throughout his journey, Hermione provides the amulets and guidance Harry needs to survive the obstacles he meets, and she also challenges him to become his best self as a student, wizard, and person. Hermione also has many of the traditional qualities of the goddess including knowledge of both the ordinary Muggle world and that of the magical world, representing the totality of what can be known. Lower-consciousness characters such as Draco Malfoy and Pansy Parkinson project their own ugliness onto Hermione, making fun of her frizzy hair and buck teeth, but others, such as Viktor Krum at the Yule Ball, see her for the complete woman she is becoming and find her beautiful and alluring. Like the Greek god Hermes, the god of transitions who became the messenger of the gods moving freely between the worlds of the mortal and the divine, Hermione also becomes a master of both worlds as she moves through time itself with the use of the time-turner. Ultimately, Hermione evolves the skill of transfiguration, symbolizing the spiritual experience of rebirth, and throughout Harry's journey she provides the unconditional acceptance and support he needs for his own growth and transition.

Harry eventually merges with the romantic figure of the goddess at the end of his adventure after he survives his supreme ordeal by defeating Voldemort. Ginny Weasley serves the role of the traditional goddess, and her own development reflects Harry's growing maturity and ultimate transformation. In the beginning of his journey, Ginny's crush on Harry makes him embarrassed, and he sees her more as a figure to be protected rather than as a peer or potential love interest. As she matures, however, she begins attracting more attention from boys and is comfortable in the realm of the opposite sex, coming into her own and freely expressing herself. Ultimately, as Harry changes by the end of his journey, he is able to see the enduring capacity for love and acceptance Ginny has for him, and they marry and have a family together. In this union with the goddess, Harry has finally fulfilled his quest for unconditional love, acceptance, and completeness.

In *Groundhog Day*, Rita serves as the goddess figure for Phil, constantly reflecting back to him his level of immaturity and eventual growth. In the beginning of his journey, Phil considers Rita childlike and hopelessly naive, and he is interested in her on a purely physical level. He reduces the purity of the goddess in her to something banal, something to be used and discarded. As Phil moves through his adventure, he struggles to integrate this ugliness of his shadow, but after his road of trials is complete, he is able to grow past it. Once he has changed, he sees Rita as a representation of the pure form of life that he now longs for, and her version of "good clean fun" becomes his own. By assimilating his own darkness, he is finally transformed and able to merge with the goddess and find the love and acceptance even he didn't know he longed for.

As the goddess represents all aspects of life for the hero, both what he is striving to become and trying to avoid, she can sometimes appear to him in her shadow form as a temptress, seeking to divert him from his path. When appearing as a woman, she offers temptations of a physical or pleasurable kind, luring him to abandon or stray from his quest by appealing to the base side of his consciousness not yet integrated. As such, women in this role become a metaphor for the physical or material temptations of life, and their siren call has diverted many would-be heroes from their journey.

But the temptress isn't always represented by a woman, for any worldly distraction that pulls the hero's energy and focus from the spiritual back to the material world can serve as temptation enough to suspend or abandon the journey altogether. This nearly happens for Harry Potter when Sirius Black is killed and Harry is distraught enough to quit. He is tempted again to abandon his quest when he learns at King's Cross that he can choose to die and so avoid the supreme ordeal of destroying Voldemort. Luke Skywalker is repeatedly tempted by the power of the dark side of the Force and by the temptation to join with his father, Darth Vader. For years, Sister Ignatia was tempted by her musical career and talent, both of which diverted her energy from a higher spiritual purpose. For people in recovery, other addictions and obsessions abound, diverting or delaying the true spiritual work that will offer ultimate redemption and freedom.

In dealing with the dual nature of the goddess, the enchantress and the temptress, the hero is forced to reconcile and assimilate the light and the darkness of both his consciousness and the world itself. Wanting to avoid death and struggle, as Harry did, and wanting to join with the father, as Luke did, are natural emotions and desires, both of which would have led the hero astray. Ultimately, though, there is a higher calling for the universal hero, and becoming worthy of the magical union with the goddess means accepting these temptations as part of the experience of life but also choosing to transcend them to reach the bliss of the spiritual experience. Truly understanding and accepting this essential dichotomy of the goddess and of life, and finding a way to merge and assimilate them both, characterizes the hero's choice at this stage of the initiation process, and the proper decision leads, finally, to transfiguration and eternal life.

By finally merging with the goddess, the hero's assimilation of all that life is, what it can become, and what it has always been is complete. This mystical union represents a permanent rearrangement of consciousness within the hero and elevates his awareness to an enlightened state. With this final revelation of the essence and truth of life, the hero has transcended the limitations of right and wrong and good and evil, and through the sacred marriage with the goddess, he has achieved a total mastery of this world.

An enduring consequence of this transcended state is that the measurement of pain and suffering, or of any problem or failure of any kind, is no longer linked to the things of this world, but rather to a constraint of consciousness, indicating that there is something wrong *with us*.[8] Anger and frustrations, once blamed on outside influences, are now seen as reflections of an inner lack of faith and understanding—resentments as forgiveness never rendered. The hero's work from this point on is entirely internal, in the proper realm where reality is conceived and manifested. Now that illusions have been shattered and all the ghosts banished, the hero is at last free to live and give to life. His rebirth is now complete.

Integration

As the hero in recovery works through Steps Six and Seven, he moves toward the final integration of self and the union with God. By accepting and integrating his shadow, and assimilating his past mistakes, the hero completes the integration of opposites and fully accepts both the good and bad as necessary and valuable elements of his own humanity. Having reached this state of self-acceptance, the hero is now ready to attempt a true union with another person. To find the same love and acceptance from another that he has been able to find for himself is the equivalent of meeting with the goddess at this point in the journey, for this represents the road back to the beginning, to that idealized state where the helpless child and ego were accepted completely, when there were no stains, no mistakes, only forgiveness and love. Finding this in another person, and, more importantly, being able to accept the opposites of their nature as well, brings a whole new set of tests and challenges in the stage ahead. Consummating this union requires even deeper humility, understanding, and surrender. Once achieved, however, the hero in recovery will have evolved the capacity to accept the light and the dark in others, to truly forgive, to live and let live without self-righteous judgment. The result will be a new level of humility, one that prepares and sets the hero off on the road of amends, culminating in the supreme ordeal.

But achieving this union is especially difficult for the hero in recovery. Having entered the journey emotionally stunted at the age he first started drinking or using, many of the relational skills—such as the tolerance for disappointment and the ability to give and receive freely, which are necessary for a healthy relationship—are either absent or severely underdeveloped. Oftentimes, too, having been raised in a chaotic or abusive environment, the mother figure was less than perfect, and the lessons they learned, coupled with the treatment they endured, instilled a whole range of defense mechanisms designed to keep people out. Many of these defense mechanisms evolved into the character defects they have used to survive and now have been struggling to overcome. Despite these shortcomings, the instinct for connection is deep, and this causes a challenge in early sobriety: overcoming the urge to enter into an intimate relationship too early, before the work of integration and recovery of the self has been achieved first.

As such there is a strong suggestion in recovery that a person beginning the program should not get involved in a new relationship during the first twelve months. Many people, newly sober and awake to life again, are hungry to taste the joys of love, and they disregard this suggestion, often to their dismay. Unrecovered and still ego driven, they find that getting into a relationship before they are ready acts like pouring Miracle Grow on their character defects. All the longing, lust, and demands of the insatiable ego come roaring to the surface. Hearts are broken, emotions torn apart, and behaviors requiring steep amends are the usual result. Sponsors try to warn of these consequences by explaining that relationships usually don't work out in the beginning because in the newcomer's self-centered and unrecovered state, he has little to offer another person. This is often unwelcome advice, and the newcomer frequently puts up resistance and challenges this suggestion. At this point, many a sponsor has leveled with him and told him the truth: that at this stage in recovery, "nobody wants what you have."

For heroes that disregard this advice, the goddess figure, and the multitude of emotions she contains and elicits, often acts more as a temptress, luring the hero from his spiritual path with the promise of physical comfort or pleasurable distractions. There is an acronym that in the first twelve months of recovery relationship stands for: Real Exciting Love Affair Turns into Overwhelming Nightmare; Sobriety Hangs in Peril. The very real danger for the hero is that the emotions he encounters not only drive him beyond his limits to accept but drive him back out of the program altogether. Temptations at this stage of the journey aren't only represented by a woman though. Anything that feeds the old ego—the drive for material possessions and prestige, physical pleasures or sensations, including other drugs or distractions, or anything that leads him from his spiritual path—becomes a temptress for the hero. The long road back to dealing with and accepting the complex nature of relationships with others, and with the other diversions, requires both the work of recovery done in the Steps to this point, as well as the additional work coming in Steps Eight and Nine.

The way past all these temptations is by repeatedly working Steps Six and Seven on the character defects they activate. By humbly surrendering the desires and demands of the old self and ego to God, the hero is cleansed of these temptations over time, and he experiences, often for the first time, true peace of mind. The growing awareness he gains is that the humility he is trying so hard to develop and maintain is indeed the key to this freedom and serenity. In each situation, the hero comes to see that humility heals pain and transforms weakness and fear into courage and strength. This evolving attitude about humility reflects the profound change of consciousness taking place: his awareness and true acceptance of a God of his understanding working in his life. As the miracles of transformation manifest themselves in and around his life—feeling comfortable in his own skin for the first time, accepting and understanding others, relief from not only the alcohol or drug problem but many other types of obsessions that made his life unmanageable—the hero sees that God is doing for him what he could not do for himself. His reliance on a Higher Power has gone from a theory to an everyday practice that has led to freedom from the bondage of self. The final surrender and revelation of this stage are summed up by the Seventh

Step Prayer:

> My Creator, I am now willing that you should have all of me, good and bad. I pray that you now remove from me every single defect of character which stands in the way of my usefulness to you and my fellows. Grant me strength, as I go out from here, to do your bidding. Amen.[9]

By becoming entirely ready to have God remove her defects of character, the hero finally overcomes the resistance of forgiving, accepting, and integrating her shortcomings. As she asks God to remove them, one by one, she begins to assimilate the disparate parts of herself and comes to realize that what she at first thought of as opposites turns out to be two essential elements of the same thing. She learns that she is neither all good nor all bad, but instead, she contains the multitude of contradictions that make her human. In God's hands, however, she can become whole once again, and as she lets go of her shame and secrets, she receives the ultimate gift and knowledge that her "dark past is the greatest possession you have— the key to life and happiness for others. With it you can avert death and misery for them."[10] The boon of this part of the process is not only total freedom from the remnants of the old self but the new power and purpose to do God's will by helping others.

By developing and maintaining enough humility, honesty, acceptance, and courage throughout the curiously fluid stage of Steps Six and Seven, the unification with the self, along with the awareness, peace, and forgiveness it brings, the hero has finally developed enough willingness to begin repairing the damage done to his relationships. Armed with the spiritual tools of the program and with a new purpose and employer, the hero is at last ready to enter the last phase of the initiation journey: the daunting and difficult road of atonement and amends. During this part of the adventure, the hero will come face-to-face with the people and situations he has caused damage in, culminating in the supreme ordeal during which the hero will face his ultimate fears. By meeting and surviving this ordeal, the hero paves the way back to others, and to life, and so completes his journey of wholeness.

STEPS EIGHT AND NINE

Atonement

> "Luke, I am your father."
> —*Darth Vader*, Star Wars: The Empire Strikes Back

THE ROAD OF TRIALS has led the hero through the labyrinth of life, requiring him to grow beyond his childish, immature self and to finally arrive as an adult. He has met and assimilated the opposites, not only within himself, but in the world as well. By rising above the limits of his consciousness, the hero has reached a great revelation: that the goal of the journey to this point has been to unite dual concepts and so transcend the ordinary world of delusions and restrictions, and pass into a more complete understanding of the true state of being. By accepting and becoming one with the totality of himself, and with the duality of all things and others, the hero becomes whole. And now, with a new personality and perspective, the final challenge of the journey begins: to assume the mantle of the father figure—the figure of responsibility and power. The child who answered the call in the beginning wouldn't have the strength or the interest in meeting the ultimate test ahead, the supreme ordeal, and it is a testament to how far the development of the new man has come that he is now ready to meet this ultimate trial and put his newly formed self, his reborn self, to the true test of adulthood: meeting and overcoming the things that still control him—be it a parent, another person, or situations and past actions that still cause him shame or keep him afraid. The hero is now ready to face, to merge with and thus transcend the father figure, and by meeting and conquering the ultimate obstacles still blocking his passage into a new life, he will assume the power of an adult and a new position in his community. This final challenge becomes the bridge back to the world of other people through the healing of relationships, which in turn leads to the wholeness and integrity of the world.

Both Steps Eight and Nine focus on personal relationships, and as such, they represent the symbolic return of the transformed child back into his community to assume his proper role as an adult, and therefore take his place as the father figure within the society of his fellows. Paving the road back to his community and rejoining the fellowship of humanity began when he answered his call and started connecting with other people in the rooms of recovery, and it was accelerated in Step Five when he formed a true bond of trust with another by admitting the resentments he felt, and his part in the wrongs he had suffered. This path of union with others and himself was honed in Steps Six and Seven when the hero came to terms with and accepted the imperfections and opposites in himself and came to recognize them in others as well. Now, in Steps Eight and Nine, the hero takes the final step in his spiritual development as he begins to repair the broken relationships by atoning with others for the damage he has done.

Many tools will be needed to face this ultimate test of the journey, including continued willingness, reliance on his Higher Power, and the support and guidance of his sponsor. The precious quality of humility that was the goal of Steps Six and Seven become the cornerstone for success in Steps Eight and Nine. While Step Eight asks only for the action of preparing a list of people the hero has harmed, much willingness is needed to do even this and to overcome the fear, shame, and resentment he still feels as the result of his previous actions. When the hero becomes resistant and even self-righteously indignant at compiling such a list, his sponsor reminds him of the decision he made during the Third Step to continue on with this journey and to go to any lengths for victory over his problems with alcohol and other obsessions. But there are many hurdles yet to be overcome.

The first obstacle the hero faces is the resurgence of his broken ego. Like the serpent Medusa, the ego raises its ugly head yet again and taunts the entire process of making amends. Its first act of rebellion is to look at the list of possible candidates and point out the harms done to himself and to focus on the faults of others first. By concentrating on the wrongs committed by other people, the ego easily justifies its resistance to making amends, and once again the walls of isolation come up. Much prayer and meditation are suggested during this stage to stay humbled and to develop continued willingness to stay focused on his part alone in the hurts he has both suffered and inflicted. Though real harms may have been committed, the sponsor reminds the hero that true recovery and freedom can only come by cleaning his side of the street. Thus, the ultimate act of atonement during these Steps is as much about facing himself as it is about facing others.

When Luke Skywalker, in *The Empire Strikes Back*, faces Darth Vader, he sees not only his father but a reflection of himself as well. As his father calls Luke to come with him and join the dark side, Luke pauses for a moment and sees himself as he could be, and might become if he makes the same decisions his father did. In facing his father's darkness, he at once faces the same temptation of darkness inside himself. Luke's encounter with his father suddenly becomes an encounter with himself, and at this moment Luke faces the duality of the choice he must make: to pass Vader, he must defeat him, but he also must accept his father, and therefore part of himself, to complete his transformation. As the final lightsaber duel comes to an end, Luke has made his decision. He refuses to turn to the dark side, and he refuses to kill his father. As Luke stands surrendered to the truth of his new position as a Jedi Knight, his courage ignites a vestige of hope that once burned in his father as well. In the last moment of his life, Darth asks Luke to remove his mask so he can at last see his son with his own eyes. As Luke does, he beholds the face of his father and sees himself. For the first time he understands, and in this moment, both are atoned.

By forgiving his father, Luke finally lets go of the one thing that had the most power over him: his resentment over his abandonment of his father to the dark side. His father's betrayal was the one thing that held the ultimate power over Luke's life, and the supreme ordeal of the journey for every hero is to confront these things and either be initiated or destroyed by their power. As such, this power, though classically represented by the father figure, is frequently represented by other people or things that wield incredible power or influence over the hero. The great courage of the hero at this stage, indeed, the culmination of all the trials and tests so far, led to this meeting with that which seems impassable. In meeting this ordeal, the hero faces his deepest fears, which act as the guardians of the ultimate threshold into his new life and position. This supreme trial is at the center of the journey; all previous steps have been moving into this place of redemption, and all that follow move out from it. It is the apex of the spiritual transformation, the beginning and the end, the alpha and the omega.

Arriving at this ultimate place of redemption, Step Eight offers the hero the first step in this process of unification. Looking back over the damage he has done, the hero is encouraged to not only look at the wrongs he has committed but to look further into what the dysfunctional relationships reveal about his twisted motives and self-serving ego. For here is where the real problems lie, and only when the deeper character flaws are uncovered, and a true willingness to surrender them comes, will the hero finally be ready for the supreme ordeal of making direct amends—a task that would only be attempted by one who has accepted his or her responsibilities, in other words, a grown-up. The defects the hero discovers in his Eighth Step list are often responsible for the whole pattern of his life, but in admitting and facing them, they also hold the transformative key to full recovery as well. The sponsor urges thoroughness and courage as the hero uncovers and prepares to discard the final barriers that stand between him and his relationship with others.

But still, the pugnacious ego tries to defend itself: *What if by exposing and listing my wrongs I get fired from my job, or my wife divorces me, or worse?* Very real dangers do exist at this point, as some behaviors can seriously jeopardize careers, relationships, standings in communities, and, in some cases, even their very freedom. Many alcoholics or drug addicts have done things that were illegal including burglary, embezzlement, and worse. *What would happen if you went to jail?* the ego demands. *And what about those people who have been harmed but are unaware of it? Why bring those things up and unnecessarily disturb them? What about a business partner or relationship that is still good as they are unaware of the harm done? Must these situations be uncovered as well? What about a spouse who may be aware of some irresponsible behavior but not of more glaring defects such as affairs? And what about all the harms and wrongs done by other people who deserved the retaliation?*

As the ego builds its case for not making amends, the sponsor reminds the hero of the task at hand and the point of Step Eight: to simply make a list of all people he has harmed and then just become willing to make amends. Relying on the talismans from earlier in the journey, sayings such as "One day at a time" and "Just take the next indicated action," helps restore the hero to the sanity of the moment and focuses him on his only job right now, which is to be fearless and thorough in just making a list. If he has trouble coming up with any amends he needs to make, the sponsor directs him to look at his Fourth Step inventory, paying special attention to the fourth column of his part. Here is a premade list of amends he must attend to if he is to be free from the bondage of both self and his past. While the resistance and fear of making amends may still be fierce at this point, his sponsor constantly reminds him that the focus of this Step is not to make the amends but, rather, to simply become willing.

To help achieve this willingness, the sponsor reminds the hero of the whole point of the journey and what all the Steps he has taken have led him to: to heal himself in such a way so that he can be of maximum service to God and to others. With this proper perspective of his life and purpose in mind, the hero is encouraged to actively examine how the newfound knowledge of himself and his character flaws can be used to repair the damage he has done and so build back up the relationships he has torn down. Once again, honesty and humility are the keys that will help transform these relationships, leading to the most powerful healing force of all: forgiveness.

As the hero works through his Step Eight list, grappling with his own faults and still hurting from both the real and imagined wrongs done to him by others, indignant pride can still block the willingness to forgive certain people for their actions, motives, or misdeeds. Once again, the sponsor lends the benefit of his experience, teaching the hero to leverage the forgiveness he found for himself when he integrated his own shadow and to extend this same forgiveness to others. Accepting both the light and the dark in ourselves enables us to see and accept it in others as well, the sponsor teaches. If the hero still has trouble developing the willingness to forgive others, he is reminded that in the process of making amends, he is going to seek forgiveness as well. Remembering this, true humility becomes not only a needed quality but one that is sincerely sought.

Once the hero has made his list and has become willing to begin the process of making amends, he has left his childish ways behind, has accepted his new role as an adult (merged with the father figure), and stands at the doorway to a new life. The completion of Step Eight represents the culmination of the revelations that have led up to this point of the transformation and reveal a new man: one that is ready to leave the isolated darkness of self and join with the light of others. Being ready to admit his faults, and ask for and offer forgiveness for wrongs done, is what frees the spirit and allows the energy of God to flow back into society. This integration finally ends the isolation from God and from his fellows, and his new life can truly begin.

As Harry Potter moves through his journey toward his supreme ordeal with Lord Voldemort, he, too, has to grow and become an adult, and he does this by reconciling with the many father figures in his life. There is James Potter, his actual father; Vernon Dursley, his father figure of memory; Albus Dumbledore, his protector; Sirius Black, who becomes a surrogate father; and, ultimately, Lord Voldemort, the demon who created Harry's destiny by killing his parents. While Voldemort holds the ultimate power to destroy or redeem him, it is James with whom Harry first struggles to understand and integrate with.

At first, Harry idolizes his father, even though he knows little about him. The more he learns about him, the more he discovers that James was good at just about everything, and Harry tries to live up to this image by becoming a Seeker on the Quidditch team, like his father, and by joining the same cause his father had in defeating Voldemort. But as Harry learns more about his father, he also discovers the ogre aspect as well. James was a bully, especially to Snape, and more arrogant that Harry would like to admit. Accepting these opposites in his father, and reconciling the image he has of him with the contradictions he is uncovering, forces Harry to grow past the delusions of opposites and ultimately allows him to atone with the image he has of his father. Once Harry evolves beyond the limited understanding of all good or all bad, he comes to accept the totality of his father, and the totality of others, including even Lord Voldemort. Once Harry reaches this level of understanding and consciousness, he has taken the place of his father and is ready to fulfill his destiny.[1]

In addition to the symbolic father figure, other obstacles that hold the most power over the hero can include other people, situations, or other ideas that still tether him to the world of opposites, to the illusion of good and bad, right and wrong. Attachment to the ego, along with its corresponding limited and self-obsessed perspective, prevent the hero from accepting his new role as an adult and from accepting the realities, the verities of life itself. Still driven by his demands for how life should be, atonement in these situations becomes about learning to accept life on life's terms by transcending the delusion of having control and coming to terms with the limits of being human. One of the biggest challenges, then, is to accept that life isn't fair when viewed through the lens of self and ego, but rather, when taken on its own terms, life *is* whole, perfect, and just as it is supposed to be. Thus the final threshold to the enlightened experience is to fully surrender, to accept and revere all the manifestations and outcomes of the life experience.

In *Groundhog Day*, Phil Connors's transformation isn't complete until he atones with the homeless man he meets on the street each repeated day. For much of Phil's journey, the man he passes is nothing more than a bum—sick and destitute—so he tries to avoid him. Viewed through the limited perspective of his infantile ego, with its exaggerated and distorted perspective of right and wrong, good and bad, the man is easily dismissed as something repulsive, the very opposite of how Phil sees himself and how he thinks life should be. Reconciling and accepting what the man truly represents—the duality of life with its realities and consequences of differing paths—becomes Phil's supreme challenge and the ultimate test of his awakening.

Phil's spiritual experience comes in stages. The first is when he is reborn and starts acting differently by saving people, instead of taking advantage of them, becoming interested in art, and in relating to Rita in a more respectful and mature way. At this point his perspective toward the old man begins to change as well. With the new eyes of one reborn, Phil now sees the humanity in him and sees that this ending could have been his fate as well had he not changed. With this new perspective, Phil realizes how near the opposites of life really are. The alternative, or what he thought of as the "bad" path or outcome, is always possible. One side is as real and as near as the next. This realization bridges the gap between himself and others, and he now sees the shared humanity in the old man and even begins calling him *Father*. But Phil's ego still prevents him from fully accepting the man's end-of-life experience, and his own powerlessness to alter it, and it takes a final surrender before true atonement can come.

While the old man's declining health offers Phil the opportunity to see death as it truly is, a part of the cycle of life, he is still too attached to his ego to accept it. Thinking he is now a demigod, Phil believes he can fix anything, including controlling life itself by saving the old man. After numerous failed attempts to keep the homeless man alive, Phil realizes that he must not only let go of the old man but he must give up the illusion of control as well. This deep surrender finally leads Phil to let go of the last remnant of his ego, which had crept back into the new, better self he had become.

His complete transformation occurs in the wonderful scene at the hospital where he has brought the homeless man, demanding that they do something to save him. When the old man passes, a hospital nurse tries to console Phil, but he fixates on trying to find out why he died. The nurse's simple response sums up everything Phil has been struggling to reconcile: the mystery, the madness, and the wonder of life itself. She simply says, "It was just his time." In this moment, Phil understands life and his place in it. He finally accepts his limitations and more importantly understands his new role— that to just be kind and do the right thing is enough. Phil's failure to save the old man, to cheat both death and life, finally open him up to the suffering and the joy of those around him. This realization leads to Phil's atonement, and it is only after this scene that he is truly humble and able to return to his community.

As the hero finally detaches and integrates the remnants of her ego, and learns to accept the complexities of life and her true role within it, she comes to embrace her real purpose, which is to act as a channel for her Higher Power. The final test of atonement represents the passage into this new world of cooperation and service. Guided by this new understanding, the hero intuitively knows how to handle situations that used to cause frustration, doubt, or fear, and by meeting them with the new tools of faith, patience, and humility, the hero is now able to transcend them. By becoming "at-one" with others and with life itself, the hero's rebirth is complete, and her ability to fully contribute to the flow of life is effortless—and sometimes even miraculous.

In the summer of 1952, Sister Ignatia faced the supreme test in her journey as the Angel of Alcoholics Anonymous when she was reassigned to a new hospital in Cleveland, St. Vincent's Charity Hospital. With an unclear job description and without the power of the administrative position she had held at St. Thomas Hospital, Ignatia feared that this transfer was the first step into a forced retirement. Anxious to continue her work with A.A., but with no alcoholic ward in the hospital, and with the hospital's administrator, Sister Francetta Morrison, indifferent and perhaps even opposed to it, Ignatia faced a situation that seemed to have ultimate control over her life and destiny.

Sister Ignatia's challenge in her new position was to find a way to integrate the two opposites in her life at this point: her great desire and need to establish an alcoholic treatment ward at St. Vincent's and the current administration's antipathy to the idea. Lacking the influence of her previous position to bulldoze her initiative through, her will and her ego were neutralized. Atoning with the power of this situation meant that she would have to source deeper; she would have to trust God completely and surrender her plans and ideas, and listen for the direction she felt would surely come if only she could remain in faith long enough. That direction did come, but following it required sustained patience, prayer, contrary action, and faith—all attributes of the transformed self she had become.

Sister Ignatia began this last phase of her journey by humbly going about her duties as the second-floor surgical wing's spiritual advisor, offering comfort and support to the patients and their families. She next acquainted herself with the local A.A. chapter in Cleveland and further developed relationships with those members she had known and even treated when she was in Akron. This fellowship with whom Ignatia had for so long dedicated herself welcomed her to Cleveland, and she became at one with her new community, her journey having come full circle. In addition, the A.A. groups were keen to offer her help, and Ignatia was guided by members such as Eddie G. and Lou C., whose suggestions and ideas buoyed her spirit by keeping her focused on planning and preparing for the day she would be tasked with opening a new wing. In the spirit of reliance on her Higher Power, and with the support of the very community she was committed to helping, Sister Ignatia was finally ready to transcend the world of seeming opposites and integrate the needs of both for the benefit of all.

The convergence of these differing needs came on October 7, 1952, when Sister Ignatia was unexpectedly summoned to Sister

Francetta's office. Sister Francetta was an intensely practical woman and had been the perfect selection to take over as Charity Hospital's administrator earlier that year. Crisp mannered and formal to a fault, Francetta's sole focus was to the hospital, and, as she would admit later, she was not particularly interested in an alcoholic ward. But Sister Francetta had a problem: Charity Hospital had a shortage of nursing personnel and an overabundance of empty hospital beds. As a professional nurse, Francetta had shrewdly developed special-care units, such as the intensive care and surgical recovery room units, which effectively pooled nursing resources while also offering more effective patient care. With an eye to solving the empty-bed problem while at the same time not stretching the already limited pool of nursing resources, Sister Francetta considered the opening of an A.A. ward as a viable option.

As Francetta saw it, after the initial intake into the hospital, which she would leave up to Sister Ignacia, an alcoholism ward was nearly a self-running unit as A.A. members were constantly present and committed to helping one another recover. Therefore, opening an A.A. ward would essentially accomplish her twofold goal of both filling beds and, because the patients were often self-monitoring, not taxing the skilled nursing care of her limited staff. To this end, Sister Francetta finally reconciled her indifferent attitude toward an alcoholic wing with the need and desire of Sister Ignatia, and together these seemingly opposite outlooks were atoned. Success had come at last for Sister Ignatia, and it had come through the merging of patience and perseverance, surrender to her Higher Power, and the active support from the A.A. community. In a transcendent moment of understanding and "at-one-ment" with one of the fathers of Alcoholics Anonymous, Sister Ignatia named the new alcoholic ward

"Rosary Hall Solarium." She later explained that the initials, "R.H.S.," stood for Dr. Bob's full name: Robert Holbrook Smith.

At the end of Dorothy's journey in *The Wizard of Oz*, the person who holds the most power over her is the Wizard in Emerald City. After Dorothy defeats the Wicked Witch of the West—who acts as the temptress aspect of the goddess figure—her supreme ordeal is to confront the final person who seemingly has the power to grant her return home, allowing her to complete her journey. When she returns to the Wizard's castle, she is no longer the child she was in the beginning, and as an adult she now has the courage to look behind the curtain of illusion he hides behind, and what she finds is that the Wizard is just an ordinary middle-aged man. Discovering the truth, Dorothy is finally liberated from the prison of delusion, and this breakthrough leads to her final realization, with Glinda the Good Witch's encouragement, that she has always held the key to her return deep inside her.

By atoning with the father figure, or with that which holds the ultimate power to ignite the ego and keep him chained to the worldly illusion of opposites, the supreme ordeal represents the final expansion of consciousness for the hero. By transcending the limited awareness of his own humanity, the hero passes into a cosmic realm where the revelation of being is bestowed. Divested of ego at last, the hero is now a representative of the power of the universe; the energy of the cosmic spirit is released and flows through the hero, initiating, healing, and enlightening others. By becoming the father, the hero is twice-born, and the resulting transformation leads to acceptance of all form, experience, and consequence.[2]

Step Nine: Making Amends

In the *Twelve and Twelve*, the chapter on Step Nine, "Made direct amends to such people wherever possible, except when to do so would injure them or others," begins with a description of the attributes of the new person who is about to face the supreme ordeal of atonement: "Good judgment, a careful sense of timing, courage, and prudence—these are the qualities we shall need when we take Step Nine."[3] These qualities are a far cry from the childish old self that answered the call, and they evidence the spiritual rebirth that has now taken place. The new man who goes forth to restore his relationships with others and assume responsibility for the wrongs he has caused is now ready to live and act as the new self, to find peace and harmony with it and, through it, with his fellows and the world.

For the hero in recovery, taking Step Nine is about atoning with the society of his fellows as an adult, someone finally capable of assuming this role by not only making amends for harms done, but also by taking responsibility for the ongoing welfare of others and his community. This Step completes the process of ego deflation the other Steps have been working toward, and evidence that the qualities of humility, willingness, and reliance on the will of a Higher Power are the hero's new guiding forces. With all the elements in place—the personality changes sufficient to attempt this task, the ongoing support and guidance of his mentor and others in the program, and a completed Eighth Step list of amends—the hero is now ready to build the bridge back to humanity by atoning with the father figure, or with those people, situations, or institutions that hold the most power over his life. That power, in many situations, is often the shame, regret, and remorse the hero still feels for his past actions. The fear he now feels and the remaining obstacle of this Step is often,

"Will I be accepted?" The supreme ordeal is facing this ultimate fear of rejection and retribution while finding a way of making amends for the damage wrought by his ego and his past actions. Only though a sustained and sincere sense of humility and complete surrender to this process will the hero succeed in overcoming this ultimate challenge.

Through transcending the illusion of good and evil during Steps Six and Seven, and learning to reconcile his shadow and accept these qualities in himself and others, the hero was given the keys needed to survive this Step. By accepting and integrating the darkness and contradictions in himself, the hero is now aware of what it will take to do the same with other contradictions. But here in Step Nine, the hero must further transcend the remaining attachments to his own will represented by the expectations of selfish demands for outcomes still tied to the remnants of his ego. The hero must be on guard for wanting to control the results of the amends, and for becoming resentful if amends don't go the way he wants them to. Redemption will only come through complete surrender of the results to God and His will. Only through this total submission to God's outcome can the hero's remaining ego completely annihilate, thus allowing him to achieve the peace and understanding offered by these amends Steps. This is the true path to acceptance and integration back into the community.

Once the hero is set to begin the amends process, a careful strategy of whom to approach first and what that approach should entail is discussed with her sponsor. General categories are drawn up such as family members, work associates, friends, or previous relationships, and those categories including institutions, such as the IRS, the DMV or street parking authority, or shopping stores that she has been less than honest with, etc., make up the list as well. There will be those, too, who are not readily available to make direct amends—people who have either moved or whose whereabouts are unknown—and the course of action here is to be ready and willing to make the amends should and when the opportunity presents itself. Sometimes a carefully worded letter may be indicated, a phone call or other method as decided upon after careful deliberation with her sponsor.

In addition to knowing to whom to make amends, there are also situations where knowing whom not to approach, or what not to disclose, is just as important as well. Step Nine reads: "Made direct amends to such people wherever possible, *except when to do so would injure them or others*," and the wisdom of this process is knowing when making full disclosure will cause more harm than it will heal. In the cases of a marital indiscretion, for example, while it may feel liberating to admit the harm of an affair to a spouse, it is often best to leave the names of the other party out of it. Doing further harm to others is not the point of making amends. It may be that an amends needs to be made to that other person, but that is a separate matter. If other people are involved in these and other matters, then a direct conversation must be had first so as to avoid creating even more wreckage. In all these matters, the hero turns to her sponsor and relies on the guidance of her Higher Power through much prayer and meditation. The answers always come if she is sincere in her desire to atone.

Another difficult category of amends is to those who may have caused more damage to the hero than she has to them. This is often further complicated if she is still resentful over the harms she has suffered, or if the other person is still acting out. Here again, the hero is reminded that the point of making amends is to come clean about *her* part, the recovery coming from the freedom she experiences by taking responsibility for her part and then taking the next indicated action to break the cycle of abuse or mistreatment. Another area that requires careful consideration is in those situations where the other person who might be injured is the hero herself. Sometimes the amends indicated in these situations is a living amends, one where the hero disengages in harmful behavior on a daily basis, making an amends by contrary action and new behavior. Other situations require the utmost willingness to set things right, however, by making direct amends to the person or institution when warranted, and each situation must be thoroughly discussed with her sponsor to be sure she is not avoiding an amends simply because she is afraid or reluctant for other reasons.

Once the hero is ready, the actual process of making amends follows a straightforward formula designed to keep the focus on her part of the relationship and wrongs done, and to offer the maximum opportunity for the proper amends to be identified and carried out. Amends are most effective when conducted face-to-face, and after a meeting or get-together has been arranged with the other party, they often proceed along the following course: The hero begins by explaining that she is a member of a Twelve Step program, what that program is, and what she is trying to accomplish by working it. She can either emphasize the spiritual side of the program or emphasize that she is trying to get over her addiction to drinking or other compulsive behaviors, but that in order to recover, it is crucial that she admit and own up to her previous misbehavior, thoughts, or deeds. In some cases, it comes as a surprise to the hero that the person receiving the amends already knows that she has struggled with alcohol or other substances, and that such an admission is barely news at all. Regardless, the hero next pushes on to explain the reason for the amends.

This next part is the most important. The hero then explains, with sincerity and humility, all the harms she is aware of, and the character defects in herself that caused them. She then apologizes for the hurt she has caused and asks two things of the person. The first is if there are other harms or hurts she has caused that she is not aware of, and the second is what she can do to atone for these harms. It is important at this point to hear the other person out—regardless of their level of upset or opinion—remaining open to taking in the other person's experience and to making the amends the other person feels are needed. Remaining willing to accept responsibility for herself and for another is the essence of Step Nine and the cornerstone to the transformation of becoming an adult.

The result of this earnest attempt to make things right is often liberating for both people. Years of resentments, misunderstandings, or petty feuds can often be cleared up in a matter of hours as the power of love and understanding infuses the relationship and the energy of spirit sets them both free. Making amends represents the final initiation for the hero, and as she passes this last test, she merges with the father figure, or with that ultimate power that still chained her to the realm of this world (and to the secrets and shame that kept her in the prison of her old self). Divested of the consequences of her past, she emerges twice-born with the power now to guide, heal, and free others.

A story is related in the program of the freedom offered by this Step about a thief who had broken into nine homes in a local neighborhood. This newly sober person was not willing to face up to this because he feared he would go to jail, and when he told his sponsor about his fear and unwillingness to make these amends, he was certain his sponsor would force him to make them regardless. To his surprise, the sponsor said he didn't have to do it if he didn't want to. The sponsor suggested instead to see how long he could live with himself, and what level of peace and serenity he could attain with this hanging over his head. "When you are ready," he told him, "you will either become willing to do it or you will likely drink."

Several months passed and the hero, still resistant, grew more irritable, restless, and discontent. One day, however, he finally became too uncomfortable to keep this secret in. The man he had become no longer had the tolerance for pain he used to have, and he soon realized that any consequence that might come from making amends for his actions wouldn't be worse than going back out and drinking. The sure consequences of that, especially how he would suffer inside himself, weren't worth it. So he met with his sponsor again, and together they laid out a plan to make the amends.

Trembling but willing, he began knocking on doors and introducing himself to the homeowners as the person who had broken into their home months before and stolen their property. He was met with mixed reactions as he explained that he was now sober and trying to do the right thing by cleaning up his past and making amends. He told the people he met that he was now willing to make any amends they felt were right, including even going to jail should they decide to call the police. To his great relief, none did.

Many expressed their anger and feelings of violation at having been robbed. Others expressed their resentment and their ongoing fear caused by his behavior. Some demanded to be paid back the value of the property he had stolen and the repairs they were forced to make. Others were so surprised by his forthrightness that they said just knowing who it was and that he was committed to doing the right thing was enough. With those who demanded repayment, he agreed to terms he could afford and set up a monthly repayment that he could honor.

At the last house, though, he got a reaction he could not have expected. When he knocked on the door, it was a while before it was opened. Just as he was about to leave, an elderly woman answered and looked up at him with tired eyes through thick glasses. As he explained why he had come, he saw a startled look come over her face. And then to his amazement, the woman asked if he would come in for a moment.

She led him into the kitchen and told him to sit at the table. She offered him a cup of tea, which he accepted. After she brewed the pot and poured two cups of tea, she sat down and told him what a wonderful gift he had just given her and how happy he had just made her. Surprised, he listened quietly as she then related the following story.

At the same time as the robbery, her grandson, who also suffered from the disease of alcohol and drug addiction, had been staying with her as he had been kicked out of his parents' house because of his lying and untrustworthiness. When her house was robbed, she was sure it was he who had done it, for what she thought was money to buy more drugs and alcohol. The grandson denied it vehemently but she, and his parents, thought they knew better. Their relationship deteriorated over this matter to the point that she asked him to leave her home and they stopped talking altogether. This lack of relationship with her grandson caused her heart great pain, and each night she went to sleep with deep regret.

With this man's visit, though, she now realized that her grandson had been telling the truth all along. The amends he made brought a powerful sense of relief and freedom for her and her grandson. When the man asked what he could do to make amends for his actions, she just took his hand and cried, saying that he had already made more than enough amends simply by coming and telling the truth. This brought tears of redemption from the man as well, and together they wept over their tea and felt the power of forgiveness wash them both clean. When the man left, he left as a free man, forever changed by the experience of atonement. He wondered why he had waited so long and was now ready to make the other amends that he had resisted before.

The absolute freedom and universal redemption resulting from the amends of the Ninth Step catapult the hero into a new dimension. Looking into the face of his fellow man, the hero glimpses the cosmic reality uniting them. Merging with his fellows leads the hero back to the source, back to the beginning where there was only one. Realizing his connection to the whole of humanity, the universe, and God Himself, the hero emerges from this Step at one with himself and with the world.

It is at this point in the journey that the boon begins to appear. The gifts of this stage of the journey reveal themselves in the day-to-day reality of the hero and are commensurate with the thoroughness of the surrender to the amends process. The Big Book lists these as promises of the Ninth Step, and says they always materialize so long as the person works for them:

> If we are painstaking about this phase of our development, we will be amazed before we are half way through. We are going to know a new freedom and a new happiness. We will not regret the past nor wish to shut the door on it. We will comprehend the word serenity and we will know peace. No matter how far down the scale we have gone, we will see how our experience can benefit others. That feeling of uselessness and self-pity will disappear. We will lose interest in selfish things and gain interest in our fellows. Self-seeking will slip away. Our whole attitude and outlook upon life will change. Fear of people and of economic insecurity will leave us. We will intuitively know how to handle situations which used to baffle us. We will suddenly realize that God is doing for us what we could not do for ourselves.[4]

Living in and from this new God consciousness, the adventure of a new life lies ahead. The next Steps of the journey strengthen the new self and deepen the connection to this unlimited source of Power, and through a series of continuous submissions and surrenders, the hero is made ready to return to the center of life, where his contribution and presence as a channel of God will be complete.

STEPS TEN AND ELEVEN

Attunement

> "Those who know, not only that the
> Everlasting lives in them, but that what they, and all things,
> really are is the Everlasting, dwell in the groves of the wish
> fulfilling trees, drink the brew of immortality, and listen
> everywhere to the unheard music of eternal concord.
> These are the immortals."[1]
>
> —*Joseph Campbell*, The Hero with a Thousand Faces

BY INTEGRATING the seemingly disparate parts of himself, and learning to accept these opposites in others and in the world, the hero crosses the last threshold and evolves beyond the illusion of separateness from humanity and from God, beyond the boundaries of his limited consciousness, beyond the land of fear and hope. In meeting with the goddess, the hero learns to revere both the joy and suffering of life, and in atoning with the father, he comes to accept both the power of creativity and destruction as equal parts within himself and others. Accepting what has been, what is, and what will be, the hero has moved into the realm of the divine, knowing and accepting all of life, outside of consequence and even choice. In dying to the self, the hero now lives in the kingdom of the spirit, and by moving beyond the pairs of opposites, he returns to the one divine state of love, compassion, and bliss. This is the apotheosis of the hero.

Shedding the delusion of duality liberates the hero from the collective dream of humanity, and finally allows him to complete his quest for wholeness. Driven by a longing to merge back with the source, the hero has been on a journey from ignorance to knowledge of his own divinity. What he finds in his breakthrough of consciousness is that even this concept of separateness from God has been a delusion. At this point, he realizes that he doesn't as much merge with the divine as come to the knowing that he already *is* the divine. Once the veil of separation and division has been lifted, he sees that all there ever was, and is, is the divine reality of which he has always been a part.

With this great awakening, the hero enters a state of enlightenment as he returns to the paradise of the original concept of Oneness, the state of non-duality from which everything springs, remains, and returns. The primordial concept of androgyny underlies this and is found in early myths such as that of Hermaphroditus, in spiritualties and religious figures such as Dyava-Prithvi, or "Sky-Earth," who subdivides into masculine, feminine, and neuter parts in Hinduism, as well as in early interpretations of the Old Testament when Adam is seen created by God as androgynous. Duality began when Eve was created from the One, Adam, symbolizing the fall from perfection and the introduction of the opposites into the world of good and evil, fear and hope, and, more importantly, beginning the illusion of separateness from the source itself. The apotheosis represents the completed journey back to paradise by dissolving back into the One. This final dissolution of the self leads the hero past the last construct of duality—time itself. Just as Eve was taken from Adam, time emerged from eternity and is thus eternity in another form. Dying to the illusion of time, the hero is born back into eternity, transcending once and for all the limits of the material world.

With his idea of reality forever altered, the hero at last sees a larger, interconnected, world and comes to recognize his proper place within it. In a land now without ego, without boundaries, the hero sees his connection and responsibility to others and the world, and this awareness brings to the hero the willingness of the final surrender: the ability to sacrifice himself for the greater good of the world. This becomes not only the hero's new driving force, but it is the only concept that still holds meaning. This final surrender and death is the beginning of life eternal, not only for himself, but for all others as well. This is the truly heroic act and the one he has been preparing himself for during the whole journey.

This ability and readiness to sacrifice himself defines the hero, and in a very real way, he cannot be a hero without sacrifice. This willingness to sacrifice himself for others grows out of the overwhelming compassion he now feels for others as he sees them struggle with the delusion and terror that he has fought to overcome. Sacrifice can come in many forms, from deciding to leave the blissful state of Nirvana to return to the delusion of the world of time and pain, as the Buddha did, to sacrificing his own wants and desires by putting the needs of others first. The ultimate sacrifice, of course, is the willingness to even die a physical death if the circumstances warrant it.

Obi-Wan Kenobi does this in *Star Wars: Episode IV—A New Hope* when he duels with Darth Vader. Taken by itself, the scene and the sacrifice don't seem to make sense. But when viewed through the lens of the hero's journey, the meaning becomes clear:

Darth Vader: "I've been waiting for you, Obi-Wan. We meet again, at last. The circle is now complete. When I left you, I was but the learner; now I am the master."

Obi-Wan: "Only a master of evil, Darth."

As they fight, Darth seems to grow in strength as Obi-Wan's lightsaber begins to flicker.

Darth Vader: "Your powers are weak, old man."

Obi-Wan: "You can't win, Darth. If you strike me down, I shall become more powerful than you could possibly imagine."

As the fight moves into an open passageway, Obi-Wan sees that Luke, Leia, Han, and Chewbacca are safely escaping and making their way to the Millennium Falcon. As he feels his power waning, he knows that only by sacrificing himself will he be able to distract Darth long enough for the others to get away. With great faith and wisdom, Obi-Wan decides to sacrifice his physical self for the greater good. He surrenders by holding his lightsaber up, and Darth seizes the opportunity by cutting him down. Once Darth's saber slices through him, however, Obi-Wan's robe simply crumples into a pile on the floor. Darth suspiciously pokes through the empty robe, not understanding what has happened.

What we find out later is that Obi-Wan didn't die. Instead, he just passed away in a physical sense to become one with the Force again. We know that the essential part of Obi-Wan is still alive in the Force and present in Luke's life because he speaks to Luke when he is losing faith or needs to be reminded of the truth. "Use the Force, Luke," he encourages him when, for example, he is fighting the battle of the Death Star. In this seminal moment, Luke does indeed surrender to the higher power of the Force by using it to guide him in firing the missile into the belly of the Death Star.

Luke also makes the decision to sacrifice himself physically in *The Empire Strikes Back*, when he duels with Darth Vader. Darth's power and experience are too much for Luke, and toward the end of the fight he slices a part of Luke's hand off, rendering him defenseless. As Darth pleads with Luke to come over to the dark side with him, Luke retreats further over the Death Star's core. Just when Luke's only option for survival seems to be to surrender himself to Darth, he, too, makes the decision to sacrifice himself physically by surrendering to his death. Luke is miraculously saved, but his willingness to sacrifice himself transforms him. From this point forward, Luke's worldview expands beyond just himself, and he is now more interested in the greater good and in contributing by being part of the larger rebel cause.

The apotheosis represents the hero's death, either literally or figuratively, and his resurrection or restoration to a more complete and enlightened self. Once transformed in this way, the hero is prepared to perform the final task, as Luke did in defeating the Death Star. Sacrificing oneself results in the final cleansing of any remaining doubts or reservations, and as impurities in the soul are purged, the hero becomes a vessel of spiritual energy and so becomes sacred. The apotheosis can also be a time of rest and fulfillment for the hero, allowing him to consolidate his new energy and to integrate the revelations and lessons of his journey. Harry Potter does all this during his apotheosis in the final part of his adventure in *Harry Potter and the Deathly Hallows*.

Before his final battle with Voldemort, Harry learns, by viewing Snape's memories, that Voldemort made him into the seventh Horcrux when he attacked him as a baby (this is the true meaning of Harry's scar) and that in order to destroy Voldemort, Harry must die. During the duel with Voldemort that follows, Harry makes the decision to sacrifice himself for the greater good of the wizarding and Muggle world. When Harry enters the Forbidden Forest and presents himself to Voldemort, Voldemort casts the Killing Curse at him, which causes Harry's physical death and destroys the fragment of himself, which he placed in Harry's soul. With this impurity now expelled, Harry enters a kind of stasis where he meets with the spirit of Dumbledore.

It is during this period of rest that Harry is able to make sense of all that he has been through, and he grows in understanding and knowledge as his questions are answered by Dumbledore. Harry experiences a time of fulfillment here in this King's Cross dreamlike state, and the new awareness he gains prepares him to achieve his final goal. As Harry's understanding grows, though, he is faced with the hero's final dilemma of either staying in this state and then moving on to the afterlife, or of returning to his physical form and to the world of ignorance and duality. When Harry decides to return, he is resurrected and restored to wholeness as he no longer has the parasitic darkness attached to him. Now on the plane of an enlightened being, Harry is ready to complete the final task of facing Voldemort for the last time.

The hero's final great sacrifice is to return to the world of duality to help those who are still suffering from their own delusion of separateness. The hero's journey has brought great change to the hero, and the suffering he has endured during his transformation has opened his heart to the experience of others. By becoming more vulnerable at each phase of the journey, the hero learns about the vulnerability of others, and by seeing past the illusion of opposites, he has gained new insight into the terror and ignorance others are still tormented by. This final realization leads to the universal principle of compassion for his fellows, and with the veil now lifted, he is able to glimpse the divinity in others as well. In this enlightened state, the hero longs to return to them and is at last fully ready to merge with all of humanity.

Those who return to the world are vastly different from their old selves and from the community into which they return. They see things others can't see and do things others can't do. With their expanded consciousness, they are now open to the true nature of existence, and life on Earth becomes nirvana. In nirvana, the hero gives up desire, hostility, death, and delusion. They now see the eternal in the world of time and live within the eternal moment, not within time itself. The One who achieves this state, who is able to identify with universal consciousness and yet return to the world, is known in myth and religions as the savior of the world.

Heroes may be recognized by those in the world, or they may become an unseen force for the good and benefit of the world. Their apotheosis results in a new level of awareness and is a permanent transfiguration. The final stage of the journey is now at hand, and that is to return and bestow the boon, the gifts he has acquired on the quest. This return will complete his journey, and he will annihilate back into the world transformed and fully willing to give and to serve, and by doing so he will live forever in and through others.

Step Ten: Attunement

As the hero emerges from the Ninth Step, he finds that the journey of recovery has corrected the imbalance that caused him to answer the call to begin with. The contradictory feelings of fear and false courage, shame and entitlement, and the secrets and demands of his ego that kept him separated from others have finally been resolved by a sincere amends process. Seeing past the illusion of duality in himself and others, and finally humbling his ego enough to let the power of God heal him and his relationships, the hero is at last reborn to the dimension of the spirit and reinstated to his place in the society of his fellows. To strengthen his new self and his connection to spirit, and to move him closer to the state of apotheosis, the hero works Step Ten: "Continued to take personal inventory and when we were wrong promptly admitted it." This daily inventory and amends process represents the ongoing process of attunement with the spiritually reborn self and allows the hero to maintain emotional sobriety while keeping his ego in check.

In addition, Step Ten serves an even more important task: to keep the channel to his Higher Power open. Having just established a working reliance on God that helped him through his Ninth Step amends, the hero must now be vigilant for situations and feelings that trigger the old self and his old reactions to life. The main threat to this channel is, as always, the recurrence of ego. As life continues to happen, with its multitude of demands, stresses, and desires, along with the impingement of the wants, needs, and wrongs of others still suffering from the illusion of separateness, it is easy for the old, childish ego to react and justify selfish, dishonest, or resentful behavior. These qualities of the old self often take over without warning and block the energy of the spirit. It is only later, upon calm reflection and the use of a daily inventory, that these reactions can be examined, and a new willingness can be achieved to correct them. In this way, a Step Ten inventory allows the healing light of God to continually cleanse the new self, and by identifying the proper amends, it reinforces the new behaviors and new ways of thinking that maintain attunement with the spiritually reborn self.

The daily personal inventory also prepares the hero for the next stage of his spiritual development: to continue to grow in compassion, empathy, and effectiveness. In order to achieve this higher spiritual state, it is crucial to examine his motives and reactions to others and to the situations in his daily life. Through honest self-appraisal, the hero can confidently acknowledge his continued shortcomings and strengthen his connection to his Higher Power by asking for the continued willingness to set things right. With each inventory and humble request for help, the channel to spirit is expanded, and his working relationship and reliance on God is fortified.

There are a variety of inventories that are useful in correcting emotional imbalances throughout the day, and the hero is encouraged to use the tools in his spiritual tool kit to correct them. The first is called the *spot check inventory*, and this is suggested for whenever the hero is feeling fearful, anxious, or discontent—all signs that his connection to God has been temporarily lost or is threatened. When the hero finds himself feeling this way, it is useful for him to H.A.L.T., and ask himself if he is Hungry, Angry, Lonely, or Tired. Any of these states are easy triggers for old behaviors, and the solution is for the hero to attend to that state, then to search for which character defect is activated by them, and then to immediately ask God to restore him to sanity by reconnecting him to spirit. During the peace that follows, the hero is directed to make an immediate amends if possible, or to make one as soon as he can. The spot check inventory, like the others that follow, are designed to reestablish connection with his Higher Power so the hero can once again focus on others and on doing God's will. As the Big Book suggests, it is helpful to constantly turn our thoughts over to our new spiritual purpose and repeat: "Thy will be done."[2]

Another tool the hero relies on to facilitate a spot check inventory is to pause when agitated or doubtful. When hurt or in fear, it is often a sign that he has taken his will back and assumed control. In this state, the self-righteous ego is quick to defend itself and retaliate. When one reacts harshly or impetuously, the connection to spirit evaporates on the spot, and the resulting willful reaction can seriously hurt relationships with others. There is a saying in the program that you don't have a rewind button, only a pause button, and that if you use the pause button more often, you won't wish you had a rewind button later. Practicing pausing before reacting allows time for the hero to consider why they are hurt, what their part is, and pausing can often prevent the need for an amends later on.

Another form of pausing before reacting is to practice restraint of pen and tongue. Again, when hurt, fearful, or indignant, it is easy to react unwisely or to fire off an ill-tempered email or text. When the hero is boiling with hurt pride or a threatened ego, the calmer, more spiritual approach is to pause before responding. In the program it is suggested that many amends and misunderstandings can be avoided if the hero adopts a "ten second" rule between any event and reaction. So, for example, rather than honking a horn or gesturing at someone when cut off in traffic, or responding with some choice words to someone who has offended them (and that would then necessitate an amends), by waiting ten seconds and asking for God's will and wisdom to flow in, much ill will can be avoided. A spot check inventory is still useful in this situation as it gives the hero a chance to calmly examine the shortcomings these situations have triggered, plus it allows even more time to examine his part.

The spot check inventory is a useful, necessary tool for helping the hero attune with his new spiritual self. As he pauses throughout the day to examine his motives and reactions, he keeps the channel to God open and realigns himself with God's will. Continually checking in with God also helps to keep the reemerging ego in check. As the hero spends more time in the world of the spirit, it becomes easier to discern what God's will is and to understand His true purpose. A saying in the program about the difference between God's will and the hero's will is: "The difference between God's will and my will is that my will starts out easy and then gets hard, whereas God's will starts out hard, then gets easy." While the Tenth Step seems hard at first to practice, eventually it becomes a working part of the new self and leads to an easier, calmer, and more joyful life.

The next inventory, the *nightly inventory*, is more comprehensive. In this inventory, usually conducted before retiring for the evening, the hero reviews her day asking herself where she has been selfish, resentful, or disrespectful, or where she acted out of fear or from the old self. By humbly and honestly reviewing these instances, the hero looks for the character defects that led to them. By carefully identifying where she acted from the old self, she then looks for opportunities to set things right as soon as possible. Often, a simple apology suffices, but in some cases a more complete amends is called for. In these instances, the hero is encouraged to consult with others.

The first person the hero consults with is her sponsor. The sponsor has the benefit of knowing the hero well and is familiar with her more egregious character defects. In helping her discern the fears, shortcomings, and motives that led to the old behavior, the sponsor helps the hero see past her ego and envision what a more spiritual approach might be. By keeping the hero out of resentment and focused more on her part, a willingness can develop to set things right and make a more complete amends if necessary, which might include both an apology coupled with an explanation of the character defect or fear that led to the behavior. While the Tenth Step inventory is at its core a simple process, it is not always easy to work, as the ego often balks at the need for continued introspection and amends and is quick to justify its behavior by pointing out the wrongs of other people. This is dangerous as the ego can quietly build itself back up by pointing to injustices done as justification for any retaliation taken. It is here again that the careful guidance of a sponsor is invaluable.

The ego—quick to defend, protect, and justify itself—remains a formidable foe even at this point in the journey. To overcome its cunning and sometimes baffling influence, the sponsor relies on one of the fundamental teachings in the recovery program for this phase of the hero's spiritual development. In the *Twelve and Twelve*, it states that "it is a spiritual axiom that every time we are disturbed, no matter what the cause, there is something wrong *with us*."[3] While real harms may continue to be done to the hero, the way to spiritual freedom can only come by examining, admitting, and making amends for "our part" of any interaction. Anger and resentment, even when justified, blocks the channel to spirit and keeps the hero cut off from the energy and love of God. The old self's behavior would be to stew in resentment, damming up this energy. This type of action leads to trouble, though, as the saying goes, "Resentment is like taking poison, hoping the other person dies." But by staying humble and being willing to look at her part of the interaction, and by becoming willing to make amends for this, the will of God is allowed to flow through the hero, healing the hurt and resolving the conflict. This practical part of the inventory process also gives the hero insight and direction to help her avoid these situations in the future.

In addition, the inventory process fosters a deepening reliance and surrender to this healing energy, which helps the hero adopt a new life philosophy. In describing Step Ten, the Big Book reminds the hero that she has "ceased fighting anything or anyone."[4] Only through the cessation of conflict can continued peace and contentment be cultivated, and this means constant surrender and careful introspection though the Tenth Step inventory process. By talking to God each night and submitting to this unlimited source of Power to relieve her of the character defects that threaten to block the channel, the hero strengthens her newly reborn self.

Once the character defects have been identified and turned over, and once a course of amends has been determined, the next step in the inventory process is for the hero to identify how she might have acted better in the situation and what to do if the situation is encountered again. The sponsor directs the hero to use the power of visualization to go through the situation again, this time seeing herself acting as she wished she would have, or how she perceives God would have her act. This visualization is important for the development of the new soul and creates a working blueprint for better actions the next time the same fears, feelings, or situations come up, as they inevitably will.

A pitfall to be on the lookout for at this stage is to avoid allowing the ego to use the inventory process to beat up on the new self. Alcoholics are quick to dwell on their own faults, and self-loathing is a serious character defect. This is another ploy the ego uses to isolate and denigrate the self, thereby making it easy to continue to act out. If the hero feels bad about herself, it's easy to continue acting out, to continue to sabotage herself, and once she's at a bottom again, the ego has won because it's easy to have a slip and drink: After all, she reasons, she deserves it. She deserves to be bad and to fail. This self-condemnation is the ego coming in the back door, and the hero is encouraged to be vigilant for this kind of old thinking. Because of this, it is also an important part of the inventory process to acknowledge not only the faults but also where she acted in attunement with her new self. Upon careful inspection, there will be many situations where the hero has carried the spirit of the program into her affairs, and these need to be recognized and encouraged. Giving thanks to God for right behavior is just as important as finding and correcting behavior that needs to change.

As such, the last part of the Tenth Step inventory process always ends by making a list of the things the hero did well. Focusing on, acknowledging, and reinforcing the parts of the personality that are growing and changing for the better are essential to continuing to grow along spiritual lines. Where was she helpful? When was she patient? Where and when did she act as she would like to see herself acting? By identifying the good, orderly direction (G.O.D.) of her life and the influence of spirit, the hero keeps the channel to her Higher Power open, thereby furthering her spiritual development.

The process of a daily inventory, coupled with the continuing amends process, not only helps the hero maintain conscious contact with her Higher Power, but it also continues her integration and connection with others. By confronting her own shortcomings daily, and by working to humble the fears and demands of her ego, a new understanding and compassion for herself and for others slowly develops. On her more spiritual days, she realizes that other people are, for the most part, acting out of the same illusion of duality and separateness from spirit as she once did, and their actions are often motivated by the same fears and defects of character she is trying to overcome. This understanding cultivates empathy, which, in turn, helps her develop the willingness to understand, forgive, and trust others.

By connecting with people more openly in this way, the hero sees past the last vestiges of duality and the illusion of good and bad in others, especially others in the program, and by seeing the power of spirit as it flows through all people, she comes to the realization that each person she meets has the power to heal. Each person she comes in contact with has the power of the protecting father, and each and any one of them has the power to not only redeem but to heal one another. Anyone in the rooms of recovery, for example, at any time, has the power to save her life by helping her stay sober another day. Regardless of their seeming differences in social standing, religious affiliations, political standing, or race, anyone can transcend these opposites to arrive at a common purpose: to follow the path of recovery and become a channel for God's love. This is the commonality of us all. When the hero has reached this realization, she has indeed entered the world of the spirit and the time for the apotheosis is near.

The Tenth Step inventory is the process that enables this realization and growth to expand. The regular activity of identifying and correcting where the old self and ego have tried to reassert themselves is the key to continued spiritual development. Inside the hero the opposites of fear and faith, illusion and the truth, continue to do battle, and it is only by constantly feeding the new self that she is able to stay on the path to spiritual enlightenment. There is a Native American tale that speaks of these two opposing forces in each of us, known as the power of the light wolf and the dark wolf.

In each of us are two wolves: the light wolf and the dark wolf. The light wolf is the wolf of hope and faith, of optimism, and of helpfulness to others. We feed this wolf by constantly thinking about others and what we can bring into their lives. We feed this wolf by looking for the positives in our lives, and finding and acknowledging the beauty in this world. We feed this wolf by staying close to our Creator, to the source of redemption and strength that lives within us all. This is the power of the light wolf, the power of truth.

But there is a dark wolf inside us as well. This is the wolf of fear, selfishness, and illusion. We feed this wolf by isolating and cutting ourselves off from our Creator. We feed this wolf by seeking out the dark and ugly things in this world, by looking for, finding, and reinforcing the negative. We feed this wolf by ignoring the needs of others and only thinking about ourselves. This is the power of the darkness, the power of the lie.

When a chief told this tale to a youth in the village, the youth asked, "Which wolf holds the most power in a person's life?" The chief replied, "The wolf that you feed the most."

When a hero begins to feed the truth, a realization comes: It takes much less energy to feed the light wolf and feel better than it does to feed the dark wolf and feel discontented. Once the hero focuses on connecting and helping others, she begins to feel better almost immediately. The power of truth, love, and spirit is that strong. On the other hand, it often takes days or weeks of feeding the dark wolf before a state of despair and disconnection settles in. The moral of this tale is that it takes much more energy to suppress the truth than it does to reveal it, much more energy to hide the light than to let it out.

Maintaining the channel to God by doing a daily Tenth Step allows the light to flow into the new self, and as His Spirit fills the hero, she becomes more and more God conscious. As she becomes more attuned with God, the vision of His will for the hero becomes a daily, working reality, and her thoughts become: "How can I best serve Thee—Thy will (not mine) be done."[5] As the hero moves further into this selfless state of surrender and service, she moves closer to the apotheosis. The next Step in recovery is for the hero to improve her conscious contact with God, seeking only for the knowledge and power to more fully do His will. This is the purpose of Step Eleven.

Step Eleven: Apotheosis

"Now and then we may be granted a glimpse of that ultimate reality which is God's kingdom. And we will be comforted and assured that our own destiny in that realm will be secure for so long as we try, however falteringly, to find and do the will of our own Creator."
—*Twelve and Twelve*[6]

Step Eleven, "Sought through prayer and meditation to improve our conscious contact with God as we understood Him, praying only for knowledge of His will for us and the power to carry that out," represents the ongoing immersion of the hero into the realm of the spirit. The daily practice of prayer (talking to God) and meditation (listening for God's will and guidance) now serve as the primary tools of the new self. When these tools are combined with the Tenth Step inventory, the hero expands the channel to God, helping him to stay focused on his primary purpose: to understand and gain the strength to become of more complete service to others and to the world. The daily practice of the Tenth and Eleventh Steps allows the seeds of good to flower in the hero and continues the ongoing development of the reborn self by improving and expanding his conscious contact with God.

This transcended state of consciousness is in obvious, sharp contrast to His Majesty the Baby, who began the journey and symbolizes the state of apotheosis that the hero will fall in and out of throughout the rest of his journey of recovery. At its best, the most complete working of Step Eleven allows the hero to transcend the world of illusory wants and strivings, keeping him focused on the reality of eternity beyond the appearances of the world. This glimpse of the divine state is achieved through the direct actions of working with others, helping out at meetings, and other times of selfless thought and action in service to others. To achieve this elevated state, the first goal, as always, is to evade the continued call and demands of the both the old self and ego, and instead seek the source and direction of his Higher Power. This is the spirit and direction of Step Eleven.

While still being new to asking for and listening for God's will, it can be difficult at first to differentiate between his own well-meaning will and the will of his Higher Power. The first temptation, for example, is to pray for a specific result, as the hero is still convinced in some instances that he knows what the specific result for his life (and others') should be. Sometimes it seems obvious that the cure of a physical ailment or the resolution of a family matter is surely God's will, and praying earnestly for such a result seems natural. In instances such as these, however, the hero is reminded of the exact direction of Step Eleven, which is to pray only for the knowledge of God's will and the power to carry that out. Resisting the temptation to outline what he thinks the result should be is paramount, for when he does he is simply imposing his will by masking God's will with his own. Doing so creates a back door for the ego to sneak back in, and it soon becomes easy to assume that what he thinks would be the right outcome for himself would and should also be God's will.

The fallacy of this misguided thinking is born out in the hero's life over and over again. There have been times when seemingly disastrous events have led to wondrous, life-changing opportunities. Hitting a bottom and beginning the recovery journey is a fine example. What at first seemed like the end of the world—quitting drinking and using, and attending recovery meetings—often turns out to be one of the most wonderful gifts the hero has ever been given. Remembering events such as these helps the hero cultivate the belief that God's will, despite its mystery, and despite being in contrast with his own best thinking, will always be better than his own. At this stage, it helps to remember a saying from earlier in the journey: "God has just three answers to any prayer—Yes; Yes, but not now; and No, because I have something better for you." This simple wisdom often gives the hero the proper perspective.

The hero should also not assume he knows what God's will is for others, especially those close to him that he knows and loves the most. As before, the hero must avoid this temptation because when he prays for an outcome he believes is right for someone else, he is again masquerading his own will as God's will. The essential problem is that he is interfering with the learning and development the other person would gain from an experience, and this is rarely justified. It is the very definition of playing God. Another helpful saying in recovery reminds the hero to ask himself: "Are you doing God's job or God's will?"

Moreover, by trying to save someone from what he thinks are mistakes, he is also denying them from seeking and developing their own relationship and faith in their Higher Power. The sponsor often reminds the hero that it was only after repeated mistakes and bottoms that he himself developed the willingness to seek his own Higher Power.

This new guiding principle of seeking God's will above his own takes repeated, patient practice, but it is the surest way to broaden the channel of the spirit and to improve conscious contact with God. This new way of living becomes the most important part of the hero's spiritual tool kit, and is needed frequently as the pressures and illusions of life continue to activate his character defects of fear, anger, and resentment. At these times especially, the hurt self wants to revert to its ego-based defenses, thereby choking the channel to wisdom, healing, and help. Pausing at moments like these, and asking for the direction and strength of the will of God, is the answer that restores the hero to both emotional and spiritual balance. Once restored to the proper understanding, the hero again enters the realm of the spirit and experiences the state of the apotheosis.

Working the Eleventh Step starts in the morning and continues throughout the day, and very specific direction is offered in the Big Book to help the hero in recovery establish a daily routine focused on asking for and receiving God's will. On pages eighty-six through eighty-eight, a description of this practice is laid out, beginning with how to start the day, and what to do if the channel or connection is lost during the course of the day. On awakening, it reminds the hero to start by asking God to direct his thinking. It is vital to ask for this direction at the beginning of the day before self-seeking, dishonest, or fear-based motives take over. Once relieved of the bondage of self in this way, the hero is free to seek out opportunities to be of service and to use his will to help others.

In starting his day, direction is also given to think solely about the twenty-four hours ahead. For the still self-obsessed alcoholic, this suggestion is critically important. Oftentimes, upon awakening, the hero is not thinking about the twenty-four hours ahead as much as he is thinking about the next twenty-four days or years ahead. And the moment he leaves the present, he has also left the Presence of God. God, his sponsor reminds him, is only in the present, where he is now. This means that God's help, wisdom, and peace are only available in the here and now. Each time he ventures from the present, either to the past or into the future, he has abandoned God, and he is alone with either regret or fear. This is when his character defects come into play and, left to himself and his ego, his life quickly becomes unmanageable. Reminding the hero to think only about today, and teaching him to start by asking God to direct his thinking, clears his mind of wrong motives and keeps him open to receiving God's strength and guidance, and to doing God's will.

The next suggestion given is how to handle indecision and doubt throughout the day when faced with new or difficult situations. Once again the hero is directed to turn to his Higher Power for inspiration or for an intuitive thought or direction. The hero is advised not to struggle against life as it presents itself, but rather to relax and take it easy. This is once again in sharp contrast to how his ego tried to control people and situations, and it underlies the new wisdom and direction in his life. By turning to God, the hero cultivates a new way of thinking and acting, and as long as he keeps his ego out of things and keeps the channel to God open, the proper direction and inspiration will come. By relying on the will of God in these situations, in place of his own reactions, the hero develops the vital sixth sense of inspiration that comes from asking for and receiving divine guidance. Consistent and patient practice of this way of living moves the hero further into the realm of the spirit, where the knowledge of God's will becomes a more active part of his daily life and thinking.

In concluding the morning meditation, the hero is encouraged to ask for continued guidance throughout the day and the strength, resources, and help to handle life on life's terms. He is reminded to continue to rely on the grace and power of his Higher Power rather than on his own self-will. Praying for himself, or for a specific outcome, is discouraged as this is the path to isolation and ego. He can, however, pray for himself if it be in the service of helping others. This is the proper use of the will, and a simple prayer here can be "God, help me, to help you, to help others." Once the hero is centered, and his thought life is on an elevated plane, he can begin his day with the proper purpose of being of maximum service.

While this idealized state is one the hero strives to attain, maintaining perfect adherence to it can be a struggle. Life on life's terms may sound simple, but it is rarely easy to practice. Agitation and doubt can arise as soon as the hero pulls out of the driveway and enters traffic, or as soon as his spouse or kids become disagreeable. The Big Book lists the litany of emotions that can trigger the ego throughout the day: "excitement, fear, anger, worry, self-pity, or foolish decisions,"[7] to name a few. Any of these reactions can quickly choke the channel to spirit, causing the hero to become defensive and further distancing him from the peace of his Higher Power. A humbling reminder that he is no longer running the show is helpful in arresting the ego and restoring the willingness to reestablish the connection. The immediate direction is to pause when any of these emotions are recognized, and to realign himself with God by asking for the knowledge of His will and the power to carry that out.

By developing a daily practice of living and relying on the grace of God, the hero becomes God conscious, and the more time he spends seeking to do God's will, the more he experiences the state of apotheosis. The stasis of this state is a fragile thing, and the enlightenment that comes with this alignment is rarely an enduring experience. The hero is constantly reminded, though, that it is progress, not perfection, he is seeking. If he continues to seek, then he will find, even briefly, those moments of the eternal love and peace of God. Working with others gets him close to this state, as he soon stops thinking about himself when he is of service to others. The ego, however, will forever keep him tethered to the world, and things will continue to happen—life happens. When he falls from the grace of the moment, as humans and alcoholics surely will, what is important is how he reacts. By not acting out, he makes progress, and by turning back to the source, he approaches perfection. The daily practice of the Eleventh Step keeps the hero on the path of spiritual development, ever reminding him of his true role and purpose: to be a channel of God's love and will.

As the hero continues practicing living in and returning to the source, he glimpses, ever more, the perfect kingdom of the Creator. During these moments, an overwhelming awareness of belonging comes to him, and he feels at one with the spirit of the universe and with his fellows. In these moments, he senses with awe the splendor and truth of God's will, the beauty in the divine. His frightened feeling of people, places, and things—and even of death—leaves him as he attunes with the eternal truth that pervades everything. As his ego dissolves over and over by turning to God's will, he continues to annihilate in the perfect peace and order of eternity. And it is here, in God's realm, that he begins to see the true order that emerges out of the seeming chaos of life. It is here that he sees the truth that lies beyond injustice, the love that lies beyond hostility, and the faith that readily overtakes his fear. These are the moments of true apotheosis —the moments of nirvana when the ineffable splendor of the spirit is all there is—and in these moments the hero finally comes to rest and becomes one with his Creator.

The Eleventh Step Prayer

The Eleventh Step prayer, as it is often called in the recovery program, is the prayer of St. Francis, and it is the epitome of the spiritual transformation the hero has undergone. The prayer, with its emphasis on self-forgetting and service, points to the perfect state of apotheosis the hero is striving to attain. From its opening line, "Lord, make me a channel of thy peace," it is clear that the selfish, self-seeking self is gone, replaced by a complete willingness to act solely as a channel and instrument of God's love and will. Each line offers direction for spiritual service, leading to the ultimate sacrifice and spiritual rebirth.

> THE ELEVENTH STEP PRAYER (THE PRAYER OF ST. FRANCIS)
>
> Lord, make me a channel of thy peace;
> that where there is hatred, I may bring love;
> that where there is wrong, I may bring the spirit of forgiveness;

that where there is discord, I may bring harmony;
that where there is error, I may bring truth;
that where there is doubt, I may bring faith;
that where there are shadows, I may bring light;
that where there is sadness, I may bring joy;
Lord, grant that I may seek rather to comfort, than to be comforted;
to understand, than to be understood;
To love, than to be loved.
For it is by self-forgetting that one finds.
It is by forgiving that one is forgiven.
It is by dying that one awakens to Eternal Life.

The death of the hero's separate self has resulted in his rebirth to the larger community, and he now lives, and lives on, through the contribution he makes to others. This ultimate spiritual revelation awakens the hero to the fact that by himself he is merely dust and ashes. To achieve immortality it matters not what the hero gains for himself, but rather what he gives away to others. By becoming a channel for spirit, the hero touches the lives of countless others, and in this way his contribution and memory live on forever. By submitting to his new reality of purpose, the hero is ready for the final phase of the journey: to return to his community and deliver the boon—the gifts of wisdom the journey has given him. By returning, the hero not only completes his journey, but he completes the circle of the life energy itself, finally allowing the spirit of God to flow through him to heal the world.

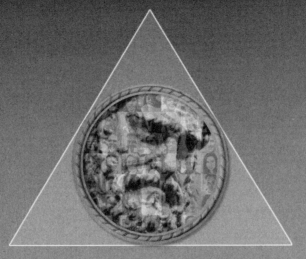

PART THREE
RETURN

STEP TWELVE

The Return

> "Heroism is a matter of integrity—
> becoming more and more,
> at each step, ourselves."
> —*Joseph Campbell*

WHEN THE HERO ANSWERED the call, he departed from the known world and braved to enter an unknown landscape that led him beyond the boundaries of his own consciousness. As he journeyed through the abyss of self, he finally pierced the source zones of spiritual energy and saw past the duality and illusion of the world. Enlightened, the hero now understands and accepts everything for what it is: the endless renewing and infinite manifestation of the one ineffable void. This eternal truth now points the hero toward his final task: to become the bridge between these two worlds. The ultimate boon for the hero, and the ultimate goal of the journey itself, is to remember and teach others that these two kingdoms are, in reality, the same.

Thus the goal of the journey has always been to prepare the hero for this solemn task. By dying to the individual ego, the hero was reborn to a universal representation of the cosmic force itself, and now, devoid of self, he is capable of being a channel for the perpetual, life-giving energy of spirit. Transfigured in this way, the hero is an agent capable of great change, healing, and guidance, and his final journey is to return to the world to deliver the boon of his experience, to enlighten those still in darkness, and to deliver the lessons of a life renewed.

The boon includes the gifts and new insights gained from the journey, and by returning and sharing these with the community, the hero helps to renew society itself. As Prometheus did when he brought fire back to humankind, the hero contributes the boon to the world, enriching it and helping it to expand and grow. Throughout history, the world has been blessed by the spiritual boons brought back by Gautama Buddha, Moses, and Jesus, and the world literature and myth is rich with examples of returning heroes: some returning with a magical sword, a sleeping princess, or a golden fleece. Everyday examples abound of heroes who return with a seemingly simple, yet profound rearrangement of attitude or awareness. The reintegration with society is the last necessary step for the hero to ensure the continuous flow of spiritual energy back into the world, and indeed, the journey would not be complete if the hero did not return.

Returning to and rejoining society completes the journey for wholeness the hero sought in the beginning. This coming full circle is symbolized by the universal symbol of the mandala—itself a representation of wholeness and completeness. Inside the mandala, seemingly disparate parts connect and are integral to the whole design, just as the illusion of opposites also combine and are needed to make up the whole of eternal, cosmic expression. By returning to his community, the hero's journey, and often the sacrifice of the long withdrawal, is validated as the hero now contributes to the whole of life, offering as the boon his experiences, both good and bad, and lending knowledge, resources, and meaning to the group. By contributing to life that which he has found, the hero completes the cycle of healing both he and the world need.

Step Twelve:
The Return of the Hero in Recovery

> "He has been granted a gift which amounts to a new state of consciousness and being."
> —*Twelve Steps and Twelve Traditions*[1]

The hero in recovery began his journey with a great surrender, which launched him on an adventure, leading him from his ordinary world into a strange new world of meetings, sobriety, and Steps. During this journey, he was restored to sanity as he journeyed to the zone of magnified power and found a Power greater than himself. By turning his will and life over to this Power, his ego was deflated and he was transformed, becoming a channel for spiritual energy, with the final task of returning and releasing this transformative energy back into the world. This is the final Step, Step Twelve, in recovery: "Having had a spiritual awakening as the result of these steps, we tried to carry this message to alcoholics, and to practice these principles in all of our affairs."

The journey through the Steps has enabled the hero to recover from the disease of alcoholism and addiction, and he is now in the unique position to help others recover from it as well. By continuing to attend recovery meetings, the hero not only receives the support and guidance he needs to maintain his new spiritual condition, but he is also in constant contact with others who need his assistance as well. Understanding the alcoholic's unique world as other outsiders can't—their feelings of fear and self-loathing, coupled with their grandiose state of self-centeredness—the transformed hero in recovery is able to quickly gain their trust and has the tools and experience to help them in ways that friends, family members, and others can't. It is said that the program of recovery is carried by one alcoholic talking with another, and this is how the miracle is passed on.

The hero, who has forged an awareness of a Power greater than himself, helps others on the journey by sharing his experience, strength, and hope. These are the boon of his journey. By working closely with another alcoholic, the hero becomes the channel for spiritual energy, and through this pure act of giving, the Power flows from the source zones through one alcoholic to another, healing both. It is commonly said in the program that the only way to keep recovery is to give it away, and in this miraculous exchange of energy, hope, and healing, both heroes move toward enlightenment.

This wondrous exchange of energy also helps heal the world as well. By practicing spiritual principles in all his affairs, the hero brings the gifts of forgiveness, understanding, and tolerance to a world still under the illusion of ego and fear. Learning how to live life on life's terms and knowing how to intuitively handle situations that used to baffle him are just some of the gifts the hero brings back to complete his journey. Directing the spirit of God back into the world is the ultimate goal of the journey, and the hero in recovery, now at the crest of the Twelfth Step return, is poised to bring this healing force with him.

Refusal of the Return

But there are dangers and difficulties for the hero who contemplates the return, and the obstacles he faces sometimes persuade him to remain outside the world of illusion and attachment. How, for example, is the hero to maintain his perspective of the eternal truth in the face of daily, earthly desires, illusions, and realities? How is he to remain in the realm of the divine amid the immediate and real pains and joys—the opposites—of the world? During the apotheosis, the hero rose above the temporal change and death that tie men to this world and saw them for what they are: the unending renewal of the one eternal form. Once returned to the world of the senses, however, the impending and persistent illusion will tempt, distract, and impose itself, backed by the cries of thousands of human voices declaring its reality. Staying centered in truth and spirit amid this constant dissent, and finding a way to unite these two worlds, is the immense challenge of the return.

Another danger the hero faces during the return is the sometimes aggressive refusal of the world to acknowledge a truth that is beyond its immediate capacity to comprehend. To a world built on the delusion of completeness and self-sufficiency, the mere mention of an ethereal reality of which they are but a fractional part is a message often too much for many to accept. Guided by their egos and by their own hard-won truths, resistance to the message of the gods has regularly been fortified with elaborate, reasoned arguments, with hard science or soft intelligence, and often through hostile disagreements, resentments, and even wars. Who cares to abandon the truth of the enlightened state to return to the dark denial of a defensive world still unaware?

Before his return, and in the seven days leading up to his enlightenment, Gautama (the future Buddha) had to overcome the desires and illusions of the world, and his ultimate challenge came from the many obstacles and temptations thrust upon him by Kama-Mara, the god of love, desire, and death. Mara knew that if Gautama was to rise above the pleasures and pains that keep the human spirit chained to the world, then his own hold over humanity would be lost. Raising a horrific army to accompany him, the treacherous god traveled to the sacred tree and appeared before Gautama on a majestic elephant. Mara carried weapons in his thousand hands, and his terrifying army filled the land, stretching beyond the horizon. So threatening was his presence that even the protecting deities of the universe withdrew, leaving Gautama alone to face the onslaught.

Seeing the future Buddha unmoved and deep in contemplation, Mara raised a piercing battle cry and began a massive assault meant to break his concentration. Mara's army unleashed a whirlwind of thunder and flame, and attacked by hurling weapons of burning coals, and blistering sands, rocks, and other projectiles with razor-sharp edges, and the sky blackened to a fourfold darkness while hot ashes descended, lighting the pitch-black hell like tiny demons sent on a rampage to destroy the one who sat unguarded beneath a simple tree. Unmoved by the terrifying threats, the missiles were transformed into celestial flowers and ointments by Gautama's power and perfection.

Startled that the fury of fear had no impact on him, Mara next tried to distract Gautama with the sensual beauty of his daughters: Desire,

Longing, and Lust. Accompanied by their sensual and enchanting attendants, they sang and danced and pranced provocatively around him, but the mind of the Great Being remained unmoved. Finally they withdrew, and Mara, now frustrated and furious by the seeming ease with which the future Buddha resisted his assaults, tried to distract Gautama with logic and the sense of duty and honor that kept men and nations chained to the world of arbitrary alliances.

"Gautama, you are a prince and your duty, indeed, the obligation of the lineage of all your ancestors, are commanded to serve your people. You have no right to seek liberation." Even these words, though, had no effect on the deep contemplation of the future Buddha, and with a humble act of truth, he simply reached out his hand and touched his fingertips to the soft soil, and asked the mother goddess Earth to confirm his right to be where he was. In response to this simple request, she filled the air with a hundred thousand roars of acquiescence, and upon hearing the thundering sound, Mara's elephant fell to its knees, and the frightful army disappeared.

With the defeat of Mara, Gautama withdrew deeper into meditation, reviewing, contemplating, and finally transcending the concepts of life and death. Now the Buddha understood the meaning of rebirth and became one with the eternal law of karma. As Gautama arrived at the final release, the sun shone on a new morning, and he experienced the perfect state of enlightenment. For seven weeks, the Buddha sat and basked in a state of Nirvana, free from the pain, illusion, and impermanence of the physical world. Nearing the end of this period, a raging storm swept around him, but he was shielded by a giant cobra who emerged from the roots of the tree and made a seat out of his body and a canopy by expanding its neck into a protective hood. It was here, while the Buddha enjoyed the sweetness of liberation, that Mara saw a final chance to sway the Enlightened One by appealing to his heightened sense of reason.

Mara approached the Buddha one last time and spoke the words that had danced at the corners of his new consciousness. "The state of awareness to which you have arrived is far beyond the capacity of man to understand, and even in their world of endless desires, the desire for this truth is rarely sought," he tempted. "How can people who mistake the evidence of their senses as the final reality begin to pierce their veil of illusion and even begin to comprehend what has taken you years of searching and self-sacrifice to find? Why bother to teach the unteachable? Why not leave mankind chained to the banal world of passion, for those who have no interest nor capacity to accept the transcendental bliss you have found will reject you and your truth, and your reward will be scorn and resentment. Retain the wisdom you have found and slip at once into the nirvana you have earned."

The Buddha paused and felt the sting of truth in these words. In his experience, people were slow to recognize wisdom and were distrustful when presented with honest truth. Why labor under a seemingly impossible burden when it would be so easy to enjoy the ecstasy of an eternal state? As the Buddha hesitated, the Hindu gods appeared and pleaded with him to remain in the world and save humanity from the pain of attachment and the sin of ignorance. "You alone hold the key to freedom, and it is up to you to teach the gods and men the path of liberation and peace," they implored. In an instant, the Buddha was restored to his purpose, and in that moment he resolved to complete his journey by returning to the world to share the ultimate boon of the knowledge of the Way.

By deciding to return, the Buddha, as with all heroes, became the bearer of an elixir that had the power to transform the world, just as he had been transformed. This treasure or blessing is the ultimate boon bestowed on the hero, and often mirrors the thing that was most missing in his own life and experience. For some it is true love or perfect knowledge, or the meaning of life or the experience of immortality. Because the hero has achieved an illuminated state, or has gained an awareness of the eternal truth that transcends physical reality, it is up to him to convey, as best he can, the knowledge of this timeless, immortal state to the ordinary world to which he returns.

Refusal of the Return in Recovery

But not every hero is ready to return, and sometimes they balk at the thought of leaving the safety, understanding, and comfort of the recovery program environment to fully engage with the ordinary world. To some, the idea of returning to a world still enmeshed in ego and illusion, driven less by spiritual principles than the competitive, dog-eat-dog mentality, often discourages them. Other heroes in recovery have difficulty fitting in with their families and find it hard to practice their own spiritual principles in situations where other family members are still bitter or not willing to understand or embrace a spiritual life. In some of these families, or other relationships, grave harm, abuse, or negligence is still being perpetrated. For these heroes, the thought of maintaining their spiritual condition and bringing their hard-won lessons of love and tolerance to an unaccepting and sometimes suspicious world seems like a thankless and futile task. Why must they go out and try to enlighten a world unaware, a world seemingly not even interested in the spiritual awareness and values they bring? Why must they always be the ones to take the high road when wrongs are still imposed on them? Others aren't doing a daily Tenth Step inventory and looking at their part, so why should they bother?

Instead, some reluctant heroes prefer to spend the majority of their free time attending meetings or joining in with fellowship before and after meetings. Some who are unemployed might choose to attend two or three meetings a day rather than looking for work, and claim the accomplishment of another day sober as victory enough for themselves and the world. Others, still struggling with character defects such as selfishness or isolation, aren't yet comfortable interacting with or revealing these flaws to others outside the rooms and choose instead to work on and share these shortcomings in meetings where they are met with understanding and acceptance. These thoughts, fears, and real dilemmas that tempt the hero to remain in the "pink cloud" of recovery can become dangerous though, and if they lead to a refusal of the return, they can eventually pose as much of a risk to his newfound sobriety and peace of mind as alcohol did in the beginning.

Other heroes suffer from a different form of refusal, one that prevents them from sharing the boon they have already received with others in the program itself. They question whether they have achieved the kind of spiritual awakening sufficient for their return to help others by sponsoring or being of help in other ways. For some, the idea of having something as elusive or profound as a spiritual experience is difficult to grasp, and, fearing they haven't had one, they choose to keep taking from the program rather than giving back to others the gifts they have already found. The way the Big Book defines a spiritual experience, however, shows that the experience isn't as elusive or mystical as it seems. If a hero is willing to carefully examine the changes in attitudes and actions he has undergone, he sees that the spiritual highway is broad indeed, and that there are as many different types of spiritual experiences as there are those who have them.

While Bill W., the cofounder of A.A., had a dramatic, "burning bush" kind of spiritual awakening in Towns Hospital, this is not what happens for most people. Instead, for the majority of heroes, the spiritual experience comes more gradually and occurs through what William James, in *The Varieties of Religious Experiences*, calls the "educational variety." In this way, a series of subtle yet fundamental shifts in thinking and feeling occur slowly, resulting in a similar change in awareness as a more dramatic or profound experience. The end result is the same, and in alignment with Carl Jung's description of "vital spiritual experiences,"[2] manifested as profound changes in outlook and perception. The Big Book, in Appendix II, also equates a spiritual experience with this type of change in personality, coupled with an awareness of a Power greater than oneself. Seen in this light, most heroes in recovery can point to their vastly altered reactions to life, their change in awareness, and their reliance on spiritual principles, concluding that they, indeed, have had some kind of spiritual awakening.

As the reluctant hero grapples with the perceived burden of his new responsibilities, it soon becomes clear that if he does not return, he will face the same spiritual sickness as before: the sure consequences that come from damming up the flow of spiritual energy. This energy *must* flow to others or it will surely destroy the sober hero. The Big Book makes it clear that returning to work with other alcoholics is the surest way to insure immunity from a relapse back into the darkness of drinking. If heroes don't begin working with others, and practicing these principles in all their affairs, then their chances of keeping sobriety and their new way of life are in serious jeopardy. They will either drink again or they run the risk of living life "dry": not drinking, but not living a life that is happy, joyous, and free. By not returning to practice and share the boon, the hero can begin harboring secrets and resentments, opening the door for ego to once again choke the channel to God.

While the solution for continued recovery of the hero is to keep attending meetings and working the Steps in his life, especially the daily Tenth and Eleventh Steps, the key to ensuring his long-term sobriety and contentment is to bring this solution back to his everyday world. The great challenge, then, becomes living in both worlds without being swallowed by either, traveling easily between them and bringing the eternal truth and awareness of spirit without being distracted or tainted by the misunderstandings and illusions of the world at large. This balancing act—keeping his emotional and spiritual sobriety in the face of both his ever-threatening ego and the challenges and temptations of the world—becomes the final trial of the recovered hero. Once he is ready to attempt, again and again, this eternal undertaking, then, and only then, is he able to become the great renewer of life, the perpetual agent for the enlightenment and change in the world.

Most heroes in the program do choose to return, however, and the first people they carry the message of recovery to are other heroes on the Twelve Step journey. By choosing to share their spiritual boon with others on the path, the hero comes full circle and completes the cosmic cycle. Armed with the experience of both worlds—the darkness of drinking and using, and the light of recovery—the hero has truly incorporated both worlds. Thus, he has the unique ability to ferry another from the abyss and hell of self, through the spiritual journey of the Twelve Steps, as no one else is able to do. Speaking to newcomers at meetings, joining in and sharing during fellowship, and working closely with others as a sponsor are just some of the ways the hero allows the flow of spirit and the miracle of recovery to pass through himself to others. Twelve Step work releases wondrous, transformative energy, and through this selfless service, each hero becomes the channel of eternal change and healing.

Giving in this way, without expecting anything in return, is the hallmark of all Twelve Step programs, and the ultimate boon of the recovered hero thus becomes "the kind of love that has no price tag."[3] By passing along the gifts of recovery, which were so freely given to him, he in turn receives a gift: seeing the miracle of recovery happen for others as they transform their broken lives, reunite with their families, and restore their standing in the community. Being the vehicle through which this spiritual awakening takes place for others, and then witnessing them become another channel through which the message of hope and healing is carried, is the ultimate goal of the Twelfth Step and the most powerful boon bestowed by the returning hero.

The Ultimate Boon

The return thus represents the crossing of another threshold—this time from the mystical realm back into the common, known world. Having resolved the two worlds and holding on to the newly discovered truth that the spiritual world is simply a forgotten dimension of the world to which he returns, the hero is free to live and pass freely between the two realms. This final awareness enables the hero to act as the renewing presence for the changing world, passing on to the next hero the knowledge of life imperishable.

In the movie *Groundhog Day*, Phil Connors lives for years in the realm of eternity, experiencing a twisted kind of immortality. As he struggles in the timeless abyss of self, it is only his total surrender of ego that leads to the transfiguration, making his return possible. Acting through his new self, Phil prepares to cross the threshold back into the world by acting in a way that earns him the karma to return as a hero. Day after day, Phil now spends his time helping the people of Punxsutawney, doing things such as jacking up a car to change a flat tire, catching a boy falling from a tree, and saving a choking man's life by performing the Heimlich maneuver on him. Once Phil has atoned with each person or situation he had either taken advantage of or ignored, he becomes the master of both worlds, moving freely between them. For Phil, the stage is set for his return to the land of time, and when he does, he is met with a hero's welcome.

At the charity party near the end of the film, Phil enters a grand ballroom filled with the people he knows and has come to love. As he dances with the woman of his dreams, Rita, the beneficiaries of his redemption and transformation parade before him to express their heartfelt gratitude. Phil accepts their thanks with the true humility of a hero, and his display of sincere selflessness inspires Rita to wipe out her bank account to bid on him at the bachelor auction. In return, Phil sculpts her face in ice, a symbolic gesture, showing that in his hands her body is now a means of creative expression rather than a tool of physical pleasure. He offers this sculpture back to her as a gift, revealing the selfless and giving nature of the ultimate boon he has received.

Phil has acquired a true understanding of the meaning of life. Before the journey, his reckless, childish ego sought gratification and meaning through the baser things he could acquire or conquer. After his rebirth, however, he discovers that giving to others offers the true path to meaning, and the ultimate boon he is given is the boon of kindness, selflessness, and acceptance. He brings this new awareness and appreciation back with him, and it is clear that he will now contribute these things to the world. Phil has become a channel through which flows the understanding and healing energy of the spirit. Transfigured, his presence now serves the world, helping it grow and evolve by bestowing the lessons learned in an eternity spent in a timeless day.

Sometimes the hero needs help to return, and during these times there is a rescue from without, some kind of special assistance that is given to the hero so he can complete his journey. For Luke Skywalker in *Star Wars: Episode IV—A New Hope*, this occurs during the final battle scene when he is being chased by Darth Vader as he attempts to fire the missiles into the core of the Death Star. One by one, Luke's accompanying fighters are either damaged or destroyed leaving him defenseless with Darth and two other Empire fighters closing in for the kill. Just as Darth prepares to fire and things look grim for Luke, Han Solo appears from without and rescues him by firing on the enemy fighters. The Empire fighters are destroyed, and with Darth's ship now floundering, Luke is able to rely on assistance from another source outside himself, the Force, to complete his task.

Luke's return to the Rebel base is inspiring. In the final scene, there is a victory celebration at Yavin 4, and here we see the former young moisture farmer march down the colonnade of rebel forces to receive the recognition of his accomplishment and acts of heroism.

Transformed into a man, the ultimate boon Luke bestows on his new community is the spirit of cooperation, selflessness of service, and commitment to a larger cause than just himself. These are the qualities Luke needed most when he began his journey, and these are what is needed most by the rebel army as they continue the battle to win their freedom. Being at one now with the Force and one with his new community, Luke is a master of both worlds and can now set about rebuilding the Jedi.

Sometimes the rescue from without comes from a supernatural source the hero has discovered in the zone of magnified power, and the assistance it provides is essential to her return. Dorothy, in *The Wizard of Oz*, receives such help just when her last hope seems to float away. This happens when Dorothy has at last been offered a way home by the Wizard, but he loses control of the hot air balloon he was using to ferry her back to the world. As the crowd watches him float away without her, Dorothy is overwhelmed with despair, convinced that she and Toto will now be stuck in Oz forever. Just when all seems lost, Glinda, the Good Witch of the North, offers the rescue Dorothy needs.

In a theme common to many hero myths, Glinda teaches Dorothy that what she has seemingly lacked and searched for during the journey—a way back home—she has carried within her all along. Glinda instructs Dorothy to look down at the magical ruby red slippers and to click her heels three times while repeating, "There's no place like home." Dorothy holds Toto close and repeats the spell, and in a whirling moment reminiscent of the tornado that launched her on the adventure, she is transported back to the world.

When Dorothy awakens from her journey, she finds herself back in her bed, surrounded by her family and by the farm hands and even the Wizard himself, all transformed back into their everyday appearance. Her return home is a powerful reminder of the ethereal nature of the everyday world (along with its endless manifestations and forms), and the ultimate boon she brings with her is an enduring awareness and acceptance of this seemingly simple, yet profound truth. In the faces of those she once saw past, she now recognizes the eternal bonds of family and friends, and in the known world into which she awakes, she is also awakened to the unknown presence of the spiritual realm. Aware of both worlds now, Dorothy can live a life free from the fear of the future and at peace with both the past and the present.

The hero's transcendence and return go beyond the awakened state she has accessed and points to her heroic purpose: to help those in the world break through their own illusion to glimpse their connection to what is eternal. With new eyes, she sees all things and people not only as they appear, but also what they can and will become in this and countless incarnations. The hero, as an agent now of great change, becomes a facilitator helping others progress in awareness and grow in consciousness.

Acting as a channel for the flow of spiritual energy, Sister Ignatia spent her adult life helping alcoholics transform their lives. She had the boon of seeing past the way men and women temporarily were, to where they could be, providing they were willing to answer their call to get sober and take the journey of the Twelve Steps. In her later years, Sister Ignatia was sought out by the larger community outside the alcoholic wards she had helped create, and her return to the general public served to spread the message of hope and recovery to the world. In acknowledgment of her service, she received the Catherine of Siena Medal in 1954, and later that year she was approached by Hollywood with the notion of bringing her life and efforts to the big screen. Several years later, even President John F. Kennedy acknowledged the work she had done to help those suffering from alcoholism.

Sister Ignatia remained humble throughout and was never interested in promoting herself (and quickly declined the Hollywood offer). She always focused her attention on what God was able to do through her and others. In a high-profile radio interview with one of the most famous female personalities of the time, Dorothy Fuldheim, Ignatia once again deflected praise for her own efforts, insisting that she was merely a small part in a larger spiritual solution:

Ignatia: Pardon me, I *do* want to say that I couldn't do this alone!

Fuldheim: I know, but...

Ignatia: Sometimes we're a bit overcrowded at Rosary Hall. We have only sixteen beds—fourteen for men and two for women—now how would I be able to take care of that group?

Fuldheim: Well...

Ignatia: I say that I turn the key, but it's these wonderful people who have dedicated their lives *and* their free time to come in and help others. We have a group visiting there *every* day.[4]

As a hero, Sister Ignatia transcended her individual identity and served others by helping unlock and open the door to the realm of the spirit. Through recovery, she introduced and initiated thousands of men and women to a life reborn. By becoming a channel through which the healing energy of God could flow, Sister Ignatia became the great facilitator of the endlessly shifting and changing expression of the life force itself. She embodied the hero archetype as Joseph

Campbell described it: "The hero is the champion of things becoming, not of things become, because he *is*."[5] Sister Ignatia brought back the ultimate boon of selfless service and humility, and as a tireless renewer of life, her efforts helped create and sustain a movement that transforms countless lives even today—that of Alcoholics Anonymous.

Of all the gifts the hero brings back to society, the most important of them all is the boon of unconditional love. Love, in its purest sense, accepts the limitations of others, forgives the shortcomings caused by fear and illusion, and is tolerant of the path and the process others go through as they find their way. Tolerance of others and respect for their journey—answered or not—is what gives the hero the ultimate power of redemption and healing. For Harry Potter, the ultimate boon he brings back is the expression of this kind of perfect love.

From the very beginning of the Harry Potter series, Harry is the beneficiary of unconditional love. His parents, Lily and James, loved Harry enough to sacrifice themselves to protect him, and this enduring love acts as a protective charm shielding Harry throughout much of his journey. Even though Harry is the recipient of this kind of love, he is unable to incorporate or use its power, often acting instead from the character defects of ego such as fear, self-righteousness, and revenge. It takes the heroic journey for Harry to finally transform, and in his last act of sacrificing himself to Voldemort, Harry finally acts out of love by protecting the wizarding world from Voldemort, the same way Lily's sacrifice of love protected him. During his time with Dumbeldore, Harry receives the understanding and awareness that lead to his enlightenment. It is here that Harry embodies the power of love, and his decision to return to the wizarding and common world is the ultimate expression of this unconditional love.

When Harry crosses the threshold back to the world and returns to his body, he is in possession of the ultimate boon: the wisdom, forgiveness, and tolerance of love. Having transcended the duality of good and evil, his first act of redemption is directed at Voldemort. Locked in a duel to the death, Harry refuses to use a killing curse on Voldemort and instead even encourages him to feel remorse—one way to restore Voldemort's shattered soul. Defending himself with a disarming charm, however, causes Voldemort's curse to rebound, killing him. After the victory, the Death Eaters lose their hold over the Ministry of Magic, and the power of love Harry has returned with helps to restore balance to the world, bringing peace and understanding between the opposites of good and evil, and the wizarding and Muggle worlds as well. Nineteen years after this event, we see that Harry has been granted the freedom to live a happily married life, sharing and enjoying the love of his own family.

The journey completed, the hero has fulfilled the ultimate goal of the adventure: to pierce through the primordial source of spiritual energy, and return to release the flow of this vital life force back into the world. Having achieved this wondrous state, the hero becomes the master of these two realms, able to access and move between the causal zones of raw energy, and their material manifestations. The heightened perception this awareness brings allows the hero to see past the flickering, shifting forms of the world, freeing her from attachment to its limitations, ambitions, hopes, and fears. Liberated in this way, she is now able to help others win their freedom as well.

Like Sister Ignatia, who comprehended the whole of the disease of alcoholism—from the resistance of the alcoholic, to the misunderstanding and rejection of the world to it, as well as the great path to freedom it represented—her new awareness allowed her to accept it all. The disease and the cure are all one: one morphing, changing manifestation of the life force being alternately chained and freed accordingly. The knowledge of this eternal truth sets the hero free and allows her to live in this world, but not of it. Instead, she now lives in the world of spiritual truth and order, free to journey between the two, bridging, repairing, and ferrying the healing power of love to the world unaware.

Freed at last from the fear of death itself, the hero achieves the sublime state of watching, without attachment or judgment, each moment arrive and then pass. Expecting nothing and accepting everything, the hero uses the realizations and gifts of enlightenment to keep his spirit and consciousness centered in the eternal now. Grounded in the present with the presence, and witness now to life's ever-changing, ever-evolving manifestation of life, the hero's grand appreciation for the timeless void and ever present now are merged, surrendered to, and honored as all there is. This freedom of awareness allows the hero to live the temporal existence of his life now, knowing that he lives not only in the hearts and minds of those he touches, but he lives forever as one part of the grand, ever recreating cosmic dance. He was, is, and always will be a part of the universal soul.

The Ultimate Boon in Recovery

In addition to the ultimate boon of love and the spirit of selfless giving the hero in recovery returns with, he also brings and contributes the valuable lessons in living he has learned, and the practical spiritual tools he developed by successfully working the Twelve Steps. These principles of recovery led to his transformation, and they become the boon of wisdom and experience he passes on to others. Each Step offers a specific principle the hero used to help him navigate life back into the world, and, taken together, they form the boon the hero uses to keep the flow of spirit moving through himself to his community and the world.

In Step One, the hero heard the call of recovery, and the gift he needed to answer that call was *honesty*. Only by honestly admitting to his innermost self that he was an alcoholic, and that years of denial and justification have led him to this jumping off point, is the hero ready to surrender to and answer the call that begins his journey. And he will soon find that this quality of rigorous honesty will be needed throughout the journey to keep him moving forward through the unknown world of trials and transformation that lies ahead.

Step Two offered the hero a new *hope* that his future could be different and that he might not have to take the journey alone. By developing hope that a Power greater than himself could restore him to sanity, the hero glimpsed an unexpected resource—a resource that would provide all the power he did not, by himself, possess. He also sees the miracle of recovery unfolding in those around him and, for the first time in years, entertains the hope that perhaps his life can improve as well.

At Step Three, he sees that only by surrendering his will and his life over to the care of God as he understands Him, will he have the power to transform his life. He learns that his will and his life are his thoughts and his actions, and that both have to be dramatically altered if he is to make any progress. This gift of *surrender* is the first crack in the almighty ego, and this precious quality will be tested, relied on, and eventually treasured as the path to ongoing peace and contentment. Once this great surrender is made, the hero is ready to enter the abyss of self.

In Step Four, the hero learns that only by developing *courage* will he have the strength to begin the disintegration of an ego firmly entrenched in self-righteous denial. The precious gift of courage will enable him to conduct a searching and fearless moral inventory, looking past the perceived wrongs and harms done to him, allowing him to identify and focus on his part. Taking responsibility for his side of the street gives him the ability to finally change things, and the courage to do so will remain an ongoing tool in his spiritual tool kit as he ventures further along the road of trials ahead.

In Step Five, the hero works toward achieving *integrity* with himself, another person, and with his Higher Power. By admitting his faults to himself and to another, the hero achieves the first honest integration of the disparate parts of himself and his rapacious ego. At this point, the hero is fully exposed, and the principle of integration becomes the full focus of the remaining Steps.

With the ego and the old self laid bare, the hero desperately needs to remain *willing* to do the important work ahead in Step Six: to become entirely willing to have God remove his defects of character. How free, how recovered does the hero want to be? How willing is the hero to truly let go of the defects of character that keep him chained to his old self? In answering these questions, the hero relies on the early gifts of the gathering boon: honesty, surrender, courage, and others. These principles come to his aid, and together, they help the hero become more open to abandoning his personal objectives in favor of God's will and direction.

In Step Seven, the hero acquires the great gift of *humility*. Through this foundation principle, the hero becomes willing to have God remove his shortcomings, and thus relies on the gifts of strength, courage, and faith to help him deal with the inevitable adversity these shortcomings have caused in his life. True humility, he finds, is a strength, not a weakness, and by practicing it he is given admission into a new life and the tools to uniquely help another. In addition, humility will become an all-enduring quality, one much needed for the disclosure and amends Steps ahead.

Step Eight, made a list of all persons the hero has harmed and become willing to make amends to them all, requires the gift of *love*—love for his own duality, as well as the love of others. The hero is asked at this point to transcend the hurts and resentments of his past, and he is offered the only key that will set him and others free: forgiveness both of himself for his part and from those he has harmed. Love is the gift that will allow the hero to trudge through this Step and on to the supreme ordeal that lies ahead.

As the ultimate test for the new self—the adult who is to return to the society of his fellows—*responsibility* is the defining quality that is both required and that will be bestowed in Step Nine. As the hero now approaches those he has harmed, and been harmed by, and offers sincere amends for his part, he is taking responsibility for himself fully, sometimes for the first time in his life. Having assumed the crown of the father figure here, the hero will emerge from this Step as the adult he not only needs to be but that the world requires him to be as well.

Step Ten is the daily maintenance Step needed to keep the hero acting in accordance with the new self he has become. *Discipline* is the key here: discipline to remain rigorously honest, humble, and willing to admit when and where he was wrong, and then to have the continuous courage to set things right. By remaining vigilant throughout his day, the hero is able to check his motives and correct his actions, all in alignment with the new self he has become.

In Step Eleven, the hero continues his integration with his Higher Power, finally recognizing his true purpose: to be of maximum service to others. *Awareness* of this central fact, as well as awareness of the constant presence and will of his Higher Power, is the quality that is not only sought in this Step but also deepened during prayer and meditation, which are the hallmarks of Step Eleven.

In Step Twelve, the hero completes the circle of his journey by returning to be of *service* to others and to the world. Transformed, the hero returns as a channel for spiritual truth and wisdom. Through constant *service*, the hero allows the healing energy of God to flow through him, renewing and enlightening the world.

The principles of recovery taken together are:

Step One = Honesty

Step Two = Hope

Step Three = Surrender

Step Four = Courage

Step Five = Integrity

Step Six = Willingness

Step Seven = Humility

Step Eight = Love

Step Nine = Responsibility

Step Ten = Discipline

Step Eleven = Awareness

Step Twelve = Service

These principles, along with the many other qualities and gifts from his journey, form the ultimate boon he returns with. The full treasure of this boon is ultimately measured by what he gives away, and the prize that the hero in recovery sought the most—control over his drinking and using and an escape from the troubles it brought him—becomes just a small part of the overall gifts he has been granted. His new awareness of the transcendent reality of spirit, manifested as the living consciousness of the Presence of God, and his ability to bring this awareness into all of his affairs, has awakened the hero to the realization of his eternal self. This awakening, and the sense of ease and comfort of living it brings, is embodied by his new attitude and outlook on life and becomes one of the greatest gifts he has to bestow.

As the hero now moves through life, he brings this new sense of freedom and acceptance to the world. Having access to the Power of the spiritual realm, as well as the experience of living through and solving the problems of living using a set of spiritual tools, the hero in recovery is at last comfortable in his own skin. By continuing to lessen his attachment to the results demanded by his ego, he now has the freedom to live beyond the temporary situations and results of life. When in complete acceptance to what is, he is able to release expectations, and by surrendering the illusion of control, he is contented to let one perfect moment fade into the next. Instead of fighting and struggling, the hero lets go and lets God take over. Instead of willfully trying to arrange life to fit his needs, he prays for the knowledge of God's will and the Power to carry that out. By releasing the demands of his own will, he is liberated; by accepting what is and taking the next indicated action, he is empowered; by living in accordance to spiritual principles, he has access to the eternal bliss of being.

In theory, the spiritual life is simple, but it is not always easy to practice. Life, with its multitude of demands, personalities, desires, and fears, always threatens the perfect peace that is occasionally glimpsed yet rarely attained. When the hero travels too far from his spiritual center, he runs the risk of being pulled back into the disillusionment and demands of the world. To remain on the spiritual beam, he is encouraged, again and again, to see past the illusion and labels of good and bad experiences. By seeing how even calamities offer great lessons, and how, by successfully dealing with them with the strength and courage of faith, the hero remembers that even the darkest times can be transformed into boons to help others. This is the recurring miracle of the spiritual awakening of recovery.

The Big Book is filled with individual stories of heroes who have been transformed by the journey of recovery, and the last two thirds of the Big Book consists of a collection of forty-two personal stories beginning on page 165 of the text Alcoholics Anonymous, Fourth Edition. The stories are structured in the hero journey pattern of separation, initiation, and return. In recovery this structure is called "What it was like, what happened, and what it's like now." Each story is inspiring and offers a different view of the same miracle of recovery unfolding in a hero's life. While each experience is unique, the collective boons of acceptance, surrender, faith, humility, honesty, and more permeate the stories, weaving the spirit of God through each journey. The result of each story is ultimately the same: Each hero has been awakened to the presence of a loving God and becomes a channel through which the message of hope and recovery flows to the next alcoholic. In this way, the modern hero's journey continues to renew and heal the lives of countless people throughout the world.

At its essence, the journey of the hero has always been about unlocking the spiritual energy that is trapped in the labyrinth of self. The universal call to adventure—in classic myth, traditional stories, and modern recovery—is the very call of the spiritual energy of life itself, and in answering this call, each hero becomes an individual vehicle through which this energy finds freedom and expression. As the hero comes full circle, she completes the quest for wholeness by achieving the integration of spirit and self. She becomes what she has always been, an archetype of God.

Having died to her personal ego, the hero is reborn to the larger, universal self. The program of recovery leads the hero to this state of nonbeing (a worker among workers), to a state of anonymity where the qualities of love, tolerance, and selfless giving now define her. Freed from the bondage of both self and the world, the hero is at last free to live from her own mythmaking process, fully present in the various roles she plays. Acting at times as a guardian, helper, or mentor, she participates and contributes to the lives of others, alternately aiding or guiding them in their own journey to freedom and enlightenment. Moving fluidly through each role, like the energy of spirit itself, she *becomes* the miracle of recovery.

Growing in awareness and experience, the hero now uses the journey's stages to make better decisions and more easily solve the problems of daily living. By seeing difficult situations as personal points of passage, and by embracing the lessons and significance they offer, each life experience opens the doors to greater knowledge, and each challenge becomes a potential boon for others. Freed from the limited perspective of self, the hero realizes that no struggles are hers alone to bear. Likewise, each victory is shared with and kept by society and humanity forever. During each new adventure of life, the hero now focuses on the energy of spirit, where it is going, and what she can do to help it get there.

From this transformed perspective, life shifts from something that needs to be controlled or feared to a series of miraculous moments that continually unfold to reveal the power, purpose, and magic of spiritual energy on the earthly plane. Instead of trying to control or twist life to suit herself, her task becomes, as Browning put it, "to set free the imprisoned splendor," and to witness, with indescribable joy, the wonder of life. Free now to live in the sunshine of the spirit, the hero is at last able to fulfill her destiny as a link in the eternal chain of the universal source.

Appendix

Preface

1. Joseph Campbell, *The Hero with a Thousand Faces,* second edition (Princeton, NJ: Princeton University Press, 1968), p. 3.

2. When most people hear the word *myth*, they usually think of Roman or Greek gods like Zeus, the king of the gods, or Aphrodite, the goddess of love, or tales of heroes fighting monsters and dragons, or of King Arthur's search for the Holy Grail. Depending on what part of the world they are from, they may think of the great trickster, Maui, who fished the Hawaiian Islands from the sea, or of Odin, the one-eyed ruler of the Norse gods who traded his other eye for a drink at Mimir's well of wisdom. To this day, two ravens are said to fly around the world gathering knowledge for him. While the world of myth may at first seem ancient and bewildering in its breadth and complexity, understanding myth is actually easier, and more important, than you think.

   There is nothing mysterious about myth. Derived from the Greek *mythos* or *mythus,* the word *myth* simply means "story" or "word," and humans have been telling stories as long as we've been alive. The earliest remnants of the Neanderthals' graves tell a story of how they prepared their dead for another life in the hereafter. Hunting tools, weapons, and the bones of sacrificed animals all suggest a future life, and we can imagine the kinds of stories they may have told one another around countless fires during the preparation for this new life. In fact, this attempt to explain the unexplainable gives us insight into the very meaning and purpose of myth.

In hundreds of prehistoric caves dating as far back as 40,000 years, we find humans telling stories, this time painting animals and tales of hunts, giving us access into the thoughts and experiences of our past, and the trials and rituals of early man. In the province of Santa Cruz, Argentina, there is the Cueva de las Manos (Spanish for "cave of the hands"), a cave filled with paintings of not only animals, but also human beings, geometric shapes and patterns, and many, many hands. Most of the hands are small and thought to be of thirteen- to fourteen-year-old boys, and one theory is that they marked their passage into manhood by stamping their hands on the walls of the cave. Myths and stories are as old as the imagination and are an expression of a creative process of making sense of the universe, of our place in it, and what it means to be alive.

Think about how our stories expanded as man began creating civilizations. Think of the Egyptian pharaohs and their pantheon of nine gods. The many myths of these gods not only explained the creation of the world and the underworld but also created codes of conduct that ruled every facet of everyday life. The laws of the god Osiris, for example, explain many of the elaborate burial and preparation ceremonies found in pyramids throughout Egypt.

Osiris was a god who ruled Egypt as a king in a time when death was unknown to the world. The people lived in perfect peace and prosperity as Osiris taught them to farm the desert through the gift of irrigation. Osiris's evil brother, Set, ruled the lifeless desert and grew resentful as the people encroached on his barren kingdom. He killed Osiris, not once but twice, and Osiris's soul went to the land of the dead where he became the king of the underworld and the Great Judge of men's souls.

Osiris created the laws that governed the land of the dead and the rules of judgment. At death, part of a man's spirit, his "ka" spirit, continues to live and awaits the body, which is preserved by mummification. If a man's ka, or soul, is judged favorably, then it can take possession of the body once again and live forever in bliss. This is the reason Egyptian tombs were filled with food and personal possessions accompanying the mummified bodies. Like the Neanderthals, the Egyptians told stories and used myths to explain the passage of life and death.

In its search for a deeper meaning or understanding of life, myth differs from the other kinds of stories we tell. While folklore, for example, is a collection of fictional tales often describing how the characters cope with the events of everyday life, myth attempts to explain the grander mysteries of life such as the origins of the world or a people, or to interpret supernatural events or cultural traditions.

While legends are stories based on a purported historical fact, like Robin Hood or Blackbeard the Pirate, myths, instead, often deal with the sacred and willingly involve gods or creatures to represent reality in dramatic ways. And although fairy tales may involve many of the same creatures, like giants, dragons, or fairies, to teach children lessons of life experience, myths often force us to go beyond our experience and help prepare us to do things we have never done before, like making the transition into the afterlife.

Myths also help us feel connected to the cosmos and to ourselves, and they help us understand our place in the timeless universe. The stories we develop and tell help us make sense of the infinite and allow us to glimpse an underlying pattern of a life that can seem, at times, mysterious or threatening. Myths calm us, soothe us, and give us answers to questions that have no answers. Myths tell a collective narrative of events that are universal in human experience and yet personal at the same time.

Because myths seek to answer our deepest questions and so tell a bigger tale, the themes that myths deal with are timeless and are found across cultures and across centuries. The questions we ask cross all boundaries, and our need to understand and make sense of our lives is universal. Our collective myths deal with recurring themes such as creation, tales of morality and mortality, love and betrayal, floods, the underworld, and many others. And all these stories are far more similar than they are different. Take for example the myth of the Great Flood.

Many people are familiar with the biblical story of Noah's Ark and the flood that lasted for forty days and forty nights. God instructed Noah to build a great ship and then to collect animals of each kind—seven clean and two unclean—and was told to board the ship before the flood waters covered the Earth. The waters soon swelled and covered the highest mountains for a hundred and fifty days, and all things of the flesh perished.

At the end of forty days, Noah opened a porthole in the ark and sent out a raven to see if the waters had receded, and then he sent out a dove, but the dove found nowhere to land and so returned to him. Noah waited another seven days and once again sent the dove out. This time, the dove returned to him in the evening with an olive branch in its beak. Noah waited seven more days and once again sent out the dove. This time it didn't return, and Noah knew that the waters were finally receding and soon he found the ground was dry.

Some people might be surprised to learn of a Babylonian character, Utnapishtim, who related a strikingly similar flood story, in 2,900 BC, to Gilgamesh, the hero of the epic poem from Mesopotamia. In this story, the gods also instructed Utnapishtim to build a great ship in anticipation of a terrible flood. He was told to collect his family, animals of every kind, both male and female, as well as provisions, including gold, silver, and jewelry.

Once the ship was completed, the skies opened and it began to rain in torrents. The flood became so fierce that even the gods, including Ea, the god of the waters who had sent the terrible flood, became frightened. Yet after six days and nights, a great wind blew the flood away and the weather calmed. As Utnapishtim watched the waters subside, he wept as he saw that all the creatures on Earth had perished. After seven days, Utnapishtim first sent a dove and then a swallow to search for land, but each returned having found nowhere to land. After seven more days, Utnapishtim sent a raven that did not return, and he knew it was time to leave the ship.

Because our myths and stories draw from the collective unconscious, it isn't surprising to find this same flood motif occurring in countless other cultures as well. There is the Greek story of Deucalion, son of Prometheus, who gathered his wife into a large wooden chest to survive a great flood that covered all but two mountain tops and destroyed the rest of the world. There are similar flood myths from the Incas, the Egyptians, Native American Indians, and many other cultures.

The themes of myth tell the worldwide narrative of man and not only seek to explain our place in the world but have defined our cultures and our very values. Our collective stories evolved into our literature, shaped our philosophies, and began our religions. They taught us about one another and ourselves, gave meaning to our experiences, and helped us shape our societies. From these stories we learn and grow, and in this way myths have been teaching us how to live and how to become ourselves for thousands of years.

Myths are metaphors, not history. The great storytellers were more concerned with the meaning of an event and the implications of that meaning rather than if the event happened. In this way, myths didn't depend on facts but relied on something more important—truth. Jesus's parables are good examples of fictional stories that carry great truths. The reason we connect with myth is that we see parts of ourselves in the lives and situations the great heroes have endured. This is why myths are told over and over again and why they still move us today.

Myths teach us to look deep within ourselves, where the real answers are, where the magic is, where the place of change and transformation occurs. This is the place where myths come alive and move us with their timeless truth. When we align ourselves with this truth, we discover an ancient power to grow and become more ourselves.

The magic of myth is that it calls to us, encouraging us to live more fully and to cherish the experience of being alive. It is one thing to read the old myths and be enthralled by their stories, but it is another thing altogether to engage with their stories and use them as guides to change the course and meaning of our own lives. When we do, we are given the tools to grow and change in a deep and fundamental way, and this in turn gives us the ability to transform ourselves and our world. As we honor the wisdom in the old myths, we give them life, and they give life to us.

Because myths are so essential to the essence of who we have been, who we are, and who we are always becoming, it is fascinating to watch them change and evolve as man himself evolves. The stories of early hunters focused on honoring and trying to make sense of the endless cycle of life and death. They created powerful ceremonies around the hunt, developing rituals of sacrifice to appease the great animal masters on the other side, hoping to coax the animals into returning again, thus guaranteeing a successful hunt. In this way, the mundane event of the hunt was turned into a collaborative narrative that united the whole tribe, the animals, and the mysterious afterlife.

As man moved from hunting to planting with the advent of agriculture, his stories changed, too. Man lived in harmony with the seasons of growing and harvesting, and the seed now became the magic symbol of the endless cycle of life and death. As the plant died and was buried, its seed sprouted and was born again. This symbol of death begetting life gave birth to countless stories of creation. Man created important rituals of sacrifice that once again helped him understand his place in the flow of life, and his connection to the cycles and seasons of life.

As our societies grew and changed, so did our stories. The Egyptians, Greeks, and Romans, among other cultures, all expanded their myths and created an ever-growing cast of characters—gods, heroes, mythical animals—to interpret their new situations. The pantheon of the twelve Roman gods who lived on Mt. Olympus served the purpose of creating new myths to explain their mysterious and ever-changing world. From these gods, new rules were put in place to help define events and to create new meaning from new experiences.

The themes from our collective mythology recur over millennia and continue to give meaning to the familiar journey and challenges we face today. While our modern stories are often told through different media like films, books, and blogs, we find that human nature and the human condition hasn't changed much. The themes of redemption, transformation, morality, and our need to explain life still burst through the surface of our modern stories.

I remember watching the first Harry Potter movie *The Chamber of Secrets* and being struck on an unconscious level by the familiar themes and images I was seeing. At the end of the story, when Harry descends into the abyss of the castle, he and the other characters are confronted by a large, three-headed creature who is guarding the trap door. This monster's name is Fluffy, and I thought immediately of another three-headed monster from another era and another myth.

Some of you may remember the fearsome creature Cerberus from Greek mythology. Cerberus was also a three-headed dog that guarded the gates of the underworld, preventing those who had crossed the river Styx from ever escaping. The twelfth labor of Heracles was to capture Cerberus without using weapons and to return the "hellhound" to the Styx's shore.

Throughout history we have instinctively referred back to our mythology and reinterpreted our stories to make them fit our new situations. Whether it's the story of the transformation of the character Tony Stark in *Iron Man*, from that of a destitute soul to redemption as a superhero, or the enduring power of how love triumphs over all in Harry Potter, the timeless tales of myth and their truths speak, direct, and continue to give our lives meaning.

The more we examine our shared stories, the more we come to see how human nature doesn't change that much, and we learn how much our myths, created in societies and times that could not be more different from our own, still help us deal with our most enduring fears and desires today.

3. The word *monomyth* is from James Joyce, *Finnegans Wake* (New York: Viking Press, Inc., 1939), p. 581.

Scholars and theorists began studying the hero's journey myth and discovering consistent patterns and plots back in 1863, when English anthropologist Edward Tylor found that many hero myths followed the same structure: The hero is born vulnerable and exposed, is rescued by other people or animals of the forest, and then goes on to triumph and become a national hero. In examining these early hero myths, Tylor was interested in the common structure of these stories and identified what he called underlying "imaginative processes" within man's psyche that were responsible for them. He wrote:

> The treatment of similar myths from different regions, by arranging them in large, compared groups, makes it possible to trace in mythology the operation of imaginative processes recurring with the evident regularity of mental law; and thus stories of which a single instance would have been a mere isolated curiosity, take their place among well marked and consistent structures of the human mind.
> ["Wild Men and Beast-Children," *The Anthropological Review*, 1, no. 1(May 1863)]

The "consistent structures" Tylor writes about describe the archetypes that Dr. Carl Jung, the noted Swiss psychoanalyst, identified nearly thirty years later. In agreeing further with Tylor, Jung wrote that archetypes did indeed exhibit "a kind of readiness to produce over and over again the same or similar mythical ideas."

In 1876, Austrian scholar Johann Georg van Hahn examined fourteen "Aryan" hero tales and defined a more cohesive "exposure and return pattern." Once again, the hero was abandoned and left exposed, rescued by animals, raised by poor peasants, and then went through adventures of war before triumphantly returning to defeat his enemies and free his mother. Likewise, in 1928, Vladimir Propp, a Russian folklorist, showed how Russian fairy tales followed the common pattern of the hero who leaves his village, undertakes a series of adventures, and then returns and weds a bride and ascends the throne. Like Tylor, both von Hahn and Propp were more interested in comparing and identifying the common themes and patterns they found in these stories than they were in interpreting the meaning and implications of the hero's journey pattern.

The first in-depth attempt to interpret and analyze the meaning and purpose of the hero's journey was made by Otto Rank in his work *Myth and the Birth of the Hero*. In keeping with his psychoanalytic training, Rank identified the common pattern of the hero myth as the manifest pattern that he then interpreted into latent Freudian terms. In Freud's conflict model of the psyche, problems originate from fixated or unresolved issues with either the parents or instincts. Indeed, the myths and patterns Rank examined mostly dealt with the hero's first half of life and with instinctual drives and oedipal relationships.

As much as Freud focuses on the first half of life, however, the emphasis of Jungian psychology focuses on the second half. Moreover, according to Jung, the journey of the second half of life is to connect individual consciousness with the collective unconsciousness, thereby forging a bridge for spiritual energy to flow from the individual into the community. And it is through this Jungian lens that Joseph Campbell interprets and thereby reveals the true significance of the hero's journey archetype.

4. *The Rite of Passage and the Hero's Journey*

When we look at the numerous rituals and ceremonies that tribes, societies, and cultures use to mark the transition of the child into an adult, we see the rite of passage as a symbolic death and rebirth: the death of the dependent, ego-centered child, and the rebirth of a responsible adult member of the community. The ritual taught the child that he needed to learn, think, and act in a new way, and this emotional change was often marked by a physical change, such as tattooing, circumcision, or scarring. The purpose of these elaborate and often severe rituals was to effect a permanent change in both the conscious and unconscious life of the initiate.

As such, the rite of passage has three distinct stages: separation, initiation, and return. In the separation phase, initiates (usually adolescent boys in tribal communities) are separated, or sometimes literally dragged, from their mothers and their communities, and forced to undergo an initiation process designed to transform them into adults. The separation phase acts to strip the initiate away from their familiar support and framework that maintained the old self—the self that was about to die.

During the initiation phase, the initiate undergoes a long and elaborate process of initiation and transformation. This is an intense process of death and rebirth where initiates might enter a cave or cavern where the initiation ceremonies are performed. Initiates might be buried alive or placed in a tomb, or told by a shaman they are about to be ripped apart by a monster or devoured by a spirit. Australian Aborigine boys complete a "walkabout," where they are forced to survive walking across a desert with only a spear and the survival skills they have learned.

During the weeks or months of this often severe and intensive process, the minds of the initiates are radically separated from the attitudes and attachments of the life stage being left behind. So intense and traumatic is this experience that an internal reorganization is often the result, and this process changes the initiate forever. The successful transformation in this phase turns a boy into a man and helps harmonize the individual's growth with the needs and values of the community.

Once this threshold of transformation has been crossed, the initiate returns to the community or village as an adult. Having undergone the mental and emotional adjustments needed to take on the vital tasks of protecting and sustaining his society, a welcome ceremony acknowledges the new roles of the initiate by according him the rights and respect of adulthood. This rejoining and merging of the individual with his society instills wholeness to the group that strengthens and promotes healing for both.

Rites of passage rituals like this occurring in caves like Cueva de las Manos and around the world gave birth to a new myth: that of the hero's journey. All cultures have a similar mythology around the heroic quest, and this journey follows the same pattern of separation, initiation, and return. Like the rite of passage, the hero's journey is a pattern for growth and change. It involves the essential element of transformation of the childish or self-centered individual into a mature person who is initiated into the group or returns to it with life lessons and wisdom, which enriches the society. Ultimately, it is a journey of growth from individual ego concerns to awareness of and concern for others.

Introduction

1. https://silkworth.net/alcoholics-anonymous/god-as-we-understood-him/

    Sam Shoemaker's saying, "Turn as much of yourself over to as much of God as you understand Him."

Part One: Separation

Step One: The Call to Recovery

1. *Alcoholics Anonymous,* fourth edition (New York, NY: Alcoholics Anonymous World Services, Inc., 2001), p. 547.

2. King Minos was one of three sons from the union of the beautiful mortal woman Europa and the god Zeus. In a theme that would soon repeat itself, Zeus seduced Europa as he appeared to her in the form of a mighty bull that she could not resist. The three sons were adopted by King Asterius of Crete when he married Europa, and when he died many years later, the three brothers challenged one another for the throne. To gain the advantage, the industrious Minos built a great altar to the god of the sea, Poseidon, and beseeched him to send a great white bull that would symbolize the power and confidence of the gods and prove that they favored him. He promised Poseidon that once he had secured the throne, he would sacrifice the great bull in deference to the gods.

    Poseidon heard Minos's prayers and reacted immediately by conjuring up a powerful wave covered in sea foam, from which emerged a great white bull. Minos became king and dutifully made plans to sacrifice the great bull on behalf of his people. As he watched the majestic animal in the stable, however, he began to have reservations. *How could an animal this beautiful, this perfect be sacrificed?* he thought. *I know what I'll do. I will take my own best bull, almost as lovely, and I will sacrifice him instead. This one, I will keep as a permanent symbol of my power.* Thinking that Poseidon wouldn't notice the switch, he sacrificed his own bull and hid the great white bull in his herd. But Poseidon did notice. Angered and armed with the patience of eternity, Poseidon waited and plotted his revenge.

Years later, as King Minos's empire expanded and his wealth and reputation grew, he fell in love with the beautiful Pasiphae, the daughter of the Sun itself, and married her in a spectacular ceremony. Poseidon now saw his chance and created in Pasiphae a passion for the bull so strong that she was nearly driven mad with desire. She finally sought out the greatest craftsman and inventor in the kingdom, Daedalus, and ordered him to find a way, and soon, so that she could finally satisfy her lust for the bull. The two came up with a plan. Using all his skill, the great artist Daedalus constructed the most realistic cow made from the finest woods and covered it with cowhide. He created an opening for Pasiphae to enter, and wheeled the decoy cow into the center of the herd. The great white bull was immediately intrigued, and at the sight of him Pasiphae began making the most longing mooing noises she could. The great bull approached, and finally she was able to satisfy her passion.

Nine months later, Pasiphae gave birth to a monster. The hideous baby had the body of a man and the head of a bull. Shocked by shame and a terrible knowing, the king at once seized upon what had happened. When the child grew, he became known as Minos's bull, or the Minotaur (Taurus means *bull*). As if this horror wasn't enough, shortly after the birth of the Minotaur, the white bull escaped from the herd and wreaked havoc on the land and the people. It destroyed everything in its path and no one could contain or capture it. The beast became a daily reminder of King Minos's betrayal of the gods and of the trust the public had put in him.

Minos now had two problems: The first was trying to avoid the scandal and public humiliation that would ensue if anyone found out about the Minotaur, and the second was the ravaging white bull. Minos desperately sought advice from an oracle who advised him to construct a labyrinth in which to hide the Minotaur. The king, unaware of the role Daedalus had played in the conceiving of the Minotaur, commanded the great inventor to design and construct a labyrinth so complex that none could escape it. Daedalus set to work on it immediately.

It took several months to complete, but the labyrinth was so magnificent, so elaborate that Daedalus himself could barely find his way out once it was finished. Minos imprisoned the Minotaur deep within the labyrinth and, with the monster out of sight, thought he had solved at least one of his problems. Unfortunately for Minos however, this created a new problem. Once the Minotaur was hidden away, the creature demanded periodic sacrifices resulting in the deaths of many of Crete's—and soon to be Greece's—youths in order to satisfy the beast.

Things continued to go badly for King Minos. He soon lost his son, Androgeus, during an athletic contest in Athens, prompting him to attack and conquer that city in revenge. He mandated that Athens send fourteen youths to be sacrificed to the Minotaur every ninth year, and this only increased the resentment and hatred toward him and his kingdom. Sometime later, a Greek named Theseus agreed to travel to Crete to slay the Minotaur and end the sacrifice. He was able to accomplish this task with the help of Minos's daughter, Ariadne, who had fallen in love with him. He promised to marry her and take her away if she would help him accomplish this task.

Ariadne pleaded with Daedalus to help, and he invented a magical ball of thread that Theseus used to get into the center of the labyrinth, slay the Minotaur, and find his way back. He then sailed back to Athens with Ariadne but had second thoughts about marrying her along the way. When the ship landed on a small island, the god Dionysus appeared to him and told him that Ariadne would only bring misfortune to the people of Athens. Dionysus promised to look after her if Theseus were to abandon her on the island, which he did. Things didn't go well for Theseus after this. He was so filled with grief for having left Ariadne that he forgot that he agreed with his father that he would change the sails on his ship from black sails to white if he had been successful in slaying the Minotaur. His father, Aegeus, watching for Theseus from his castle on the cliffs, thought Theseus was dead when he saw the black sails, and was so brokenhearted that he threw himself into the sea. Theseus, thinking he was returning in triumph, returned to tragedy instead.

The myth of King Minos is a perfect example of the kind of ongoing and elaborate trouble the hero creates when he refuses the call and tries to have it his own way. Just as the traditional rites of passage taught the individual to die to the old self and be reborn as part of the group, so did the ceremonies of public office divest the king of his individual identity and make him responsible and of service to the people. The Minotaur was the ultimate symbol of shame for Minos's refusal, and the labyrinth is an appropriate symbol for the convoluted wreckage a hero creates when he avoids or refuses his call.

3. *Alcoholics Anonymous*, fourth edition (New York, NY: Alcoholics Anonymous World Services, Inc., 2001), p. 82.

4. *Alcoholics Anonymous*, fourth edition (New York, NY: Alcoholics Anonymous World Services, Inc., 2001), p. 30.

5. *Alcoholics Anonymous,* fourth edition (New York, NY: Alcoholics Anonymous World Services, Inc., 2001), p. 151.

6. Joseph Campbell, *The Hero with a Thousand Faces,* second edition (Princeton, NJ: Princeton University Press, 1968), p. 16.

Step Two: Meeting the Mentor

1. Joseph Campbell, *The Hero with a Thousand Faces,* second edition (Princeton, NJ: Princeton University Press, 1968), p. 25.

2. As Odysseus was preparing to leave for the battle of Troy, he knew it would be many years before he would return home and see his son, Telemachus, again. Odysseus was an attentive parent, and the thought of his son growing up without the attention of a father to guide and shape him into the leader Odysseus envisioned Odysseus to be tore at him night and day. Finally, the king asked an old trusted family friend named Mentor to look after his son. Mentor spent much time with Telemachus over the ensuing years, helping him learn, grow, and mature into a capable young man.

3. Sometimes the mentor provides a psychological "anchor" for the hero, as Forrest does for Jenny in the film *Forrest Gump.* Although Forrest doesn't see Jenny much, when he does, his presence and practical down-to-earth wisdom gives Jenny a standard by which she measures her own progress and frames her own desolation. Other times, mentors provide a magical presence, helping to protect and guide the hero to his destiny, as Merlin did for King Arthur.

Often, the mentor acts as a shaman or channel through which the energy of spirit flows into the world, such as Rafiki does for Simba in the film, *The Lion King.* Rafiki leads Simba on a journey to find his father and takes him to the deepest part of the jungle, to a quiet pool that reflects Simba's fragmented consciousness. When Rafiki stirs the water, Simba finally sees his image begin to reassemble and sees his father looking back at him through his own reflection. Through Rafiki's guidance, Simba atones with his father and gains the strength to reclaim his proper place as the true king of Pride Rock.

4. At the beginning of Harry Potter's journey, he also receives a mentor, two actually, who provide Harry with the amulets, magical potions, hexes, and charms, he needs throughout his journey. When he departs from his known world, he enters the foreign world of Hogwarts School of Magic, where he learns to use these tools and charms both to survive and grow as a wizard. At the beginning of his journey, Hagrid, his first mentor, takes him to a street in London called Diagon Alley, where there are specialty stores and shops offering amulets, talismans, and other objects needed to make a successful transition into life at Hogwarts. There is Flourish and Blotts, which sells the textbooks needed for courses at Hogwarts, including a section dedicated to divination with books like *Predicting the Unpredictable* and *Death Omens: What to Do When You Know the Worst Is Coming*. There is the Eeylops Owl Emporium, where Hagrid buys Harry's snowy owl, Hedwig, which allows him to communicate with other wizards. As Harry goes from store to store, he accumulates the charms, tools, and other amulets needed to help keep him safe and that allow him to develop the skills and knowledge to meet and overcome the strange new challenges ahead.

When Harry arrives at Hogwarts, his next mentor, Albus Dumbledore, the headmaster of Hogwarts, provides Harry with other amulets, such as his Cloak of Invisibility, as well as knowledge and secrets that help him survive his adventures and prepare him for his ultimate destiny of defeating Voldemort. Dumbledore tells Harry about the secret of the Mirror of Erised, and enchants the mirror so it hides the Philosopher's Stone. At the end of *Harry*

Potter and the Philosopher's Stone, it is Dumbledore who reveals to Harry that his mother's love is what protected him from Voldemort, and this knowledge acts as an (perhaps his most) important talisman protecting Harry throughout the tests and trials on the road ahead. Harry also acquires and uses a variety of spells and charms from his courses at Hogwarts, including the Four-Point Spell during the Triwizard Maze, which he uses to keep himself walking in the right direction. This maze recalls Daedalus's labyrinth, and, like the thread of Ariadne that brought Theseus safely through it, this spell helps guide Harry through his.

Another significant charm that Harry uses to escape imprisonment and spiritual death by the Dementors is the Expecto Patronum charm. This is known as the Patronus Charm, which conjures a silvery phantom shape, usually that of an animal, that embodies positive energy used to drive away the soul sucking Dementors. Harry uses this several times, most importantly when he faces a large group of Dementors who are trying to attack Sirius Black during the adventure of *Harry Potter and the Prisoner of Azkaban*. In a neat twist, the Patronus that he sees charging across the lake to protect him, which at first he thinks is sent by someone else, is actually cast by himself from the other shore during the use of another spell that allows him to time travel. Whether it's Expelliarmus, the disarming charm, or the Aparecium charm, which reveals invisible ink, or the Impervius charm used to repel anything from fire or water, the various amulets, talismans, charms, and spells Harry acquires are essential for his successful passage from one stage of the adventure to the next.

5. *Alcoholics Anonymous,* fourth edition (New York, NY: Alcoholics Anonymous World Services, Inc., 2001), p. 132.

6. *Alcoholics Anonymous,* fourth edition (New York, NY: Alcoholics Anonymous World Services, Inc., 2001), p. 58.

7. Joseph Campbell, *The Hero with a Thousand Faces,* second edition (Princeton, NJ: Princeton University Press, 1968), p. 71.

8. In the film *Star Wars: Episode IV—A New Hope,* Obi-Wan "Ben" Kenobi becomes Luke Skywalker's first mentor, and his protection, guidance, and wisdom are invaluable in helping Luke both start and navigate the journey. In the beginning, it is Ben who first rescues Luke after he is attacked by the Sand People, and while in his dwelling, Ben gives Luke the lightsaber owned by his father, a famous Jedi Knight, and tells Luke of his father's courage and skill, and also how he died at the hands of Darth Vader. Ben tells Luke about the history of the Jedi Knights and about the dark times and rise of the evil empire, and how Darth was once his friend and a Jedi Knight as well, but also how he was seduced by the dark side of the Force. This is the first time Luke hears about the Force, and it is Ben who now introduces Luke to this supernatural aid that he describes as "The Force is what gives a Jedi his powers. It's an energy field created by all living things; it surrounds us, penetrates us, binds the galaxy together." Ben also activates the message from the princess in distress, Leia, who calls him into the adventure to Aldernaan to save her and the rebellion forces from the dark side. "You must learn the ways of the Force if you're to come with me to Aldernaan." In this way, it is Ben who introduces and invites Luke to answer the call to the adventure.

Once Luke arrives home, he finds that his aunt and uncle have been killed by the Imperial Stormtroopers, and when he comes back to meet with Ben, he accepts his call and tells him that he is ready to learn the ways of the Force, and that he's ready to become a Jedi like his father. As they start the adventure, Ben acts as a protecting force by saving Luke again, this time from the Imperial troops who question him about the droids at the entrance to the Mos Eisley Spaceport. It is during this encounter that Luke sees Ben use the power of the Force for the first time, influencing the troops by tricking them into believing that they are not the ones they are looking for. Next Ben saves Luke from a bully at the bar who is about to attack him. Ben first tries to deal with the bully but then has to resort to his old skills as a Jedi Knight by pulling out his lightsaber and cutting off the man's arm. Ben then introduces Luke to Han Solo and Chewbacca—who become two of his most trusted companions on the journey—and the adventure then takes off in the Millennium Falcon spaceship.

Once onboard, Ben uses his experience as a Jedi Master to begin the initiation of Luke into the Jedi tradition, by teaching him to use his father's lightsaber, and by learning to rely on a source of power beyond himself—the Force. All the skills, experience, and guidance that Ben provides to Luke help him navigate and survive the early part of the journey, and Ben's spiritual presence and wisdom continue to support and guide him even after Ben has died a physical death, as he speaks to him through the Force during the last battle with the Death Star. During the second film in the Star Wars series, *The Empire Strikes Back*, Luke gets a new mentor who is a combination of the archetypes of the wise old medicine man living in a primitive forest and a magical being. This character, of course, is Yoda, and he continues Luke's development as a Jedi Knight, and tries to guide and keep Luke on the hero's path.

9. *Twelve Steps and Twelve Traditions,* paperback edition, nineteenth printing (New York, NY: Alcoholics Anonymous World Services, Inc., 1995), p. 26.

10. *Twelve Steps and Twelve Traditions*, paperback edition, nineteenth printing (New York, NY: Alcoholics Anonymous World Services, Inc., 1995), p. 26.

Step Three: Crossing the First Threshold

1. Joseph Campbell, *The Hero with a Thousand Faces*, second edition (Princeton, NJ: Princeton University Press, 1968), p. 82.
2. Joseph Campbell, *The Hero with a Thousand Faces*, second edition (Princeton, NJ: Princeton University Press, 1968), p. 77.
3. The epic Greek poem, "The Odyssey," focuses on the journey of the hero, Odysseus, as he tries for ten long years to return home from the Trojan War to reassert his place as the rightful king of Ithaca. Many threshold guardians appear and challenge Odysseus and his men, including the wicked north winds that blow his twelve ships off course after the raid on Ismaros. The ships arrive in a land dominated by a race of men called the Lotus-eaters, who eat food that comes from wild lotus flowers that populate the island. The Lotus-eaters befriend the men and urge them to try the lotus flowers themselves. So delicious are the flowers that the men soon find they cannot stop eating them, and worse, while under the spell of the lotus they lose all interest in continuing their journey for home. Odysseus, seeing the state that has descended upon his men, realizes the great danger they are under, and so begins to herd and carry men back to their boats on the shore. The men, thoroughly under the influence and resistant to the call to return, weep bitterly as Odysseus and other men from the ship force them into the boats to carry them back onboard the ship.

Another threshold guardian that tests both the will and skill of Odysseus and his men is Polyphemus, the Cyclops. When Odysseus lands on the island of the one-eyed giants, he and his men take refuge with their provisions in a cave. Soon the giant Polyphemus returns from a hunt and discovers and attacks Odysseus's men, capturing and eating two of them and trapping the rest of them by blocking the entrance of the cave with a huge boulder. The next morning the giant kills and eats two more men and then leaves the cave's entrance to graze his sheep. Before he leaves he asks who is in charge of the men, and Odysseus gives his name as "Nobody." The giant laughs a terrible and threatening laugh and promises to eat this Nobody last.

Things don't get better that evening when the giant returns and immediately kills and eats another two men. Odysseus uses his skill and trickery at this point by offering Polyphemus the powerful wine given him earlier on his journey. The giant soon falls into a drunken stupor, and Odysseus seizes his advantage. While the giant was away earlier that day, Odysseus had sharpened a solid stake and hardened it in fire. Using this weapon, he charges the giant, plunging it into his eye and blinding him. As the giant calls out for help to the other giants on the island, they ask who has attacked him, and he calls out the name Nobody. Thinking him possessed by a divine power, they tell him to pray for help from the gods and refuse to come to his aid.

The next day the blind giant awakes in a terrible mood. Infuriated and determined to keep the men trapped, he carefully feels the backs of his sheep as he lets them out to graze, making sure the men are not using them to escape. Odysseus, once again more resourceful, has his men tie themselves to the undersides of the animals where they pass undetected to the open fields and

Appendix

hurriedly make their way back to their ship. By outwitting and passing yet another threshold guardian, Odysseus proves himself capable of continuing his journey to return home.

4. Another famous example of a threshold guardian in myth appears in the ancient Babylonian "Epic of Gilgamesh." Gilgamesh was the powerful and ruggedly handsome king of Uruk, who was two-thirds god and one-third mortal. Gilgamesh was hated throughout his kingdom for the very unpopular custom he instituted of sleeping with every new bride on the night of her wedding. Gilgamesh had many great adventures with his friend, Enkidu, until his friend's death by the gods for retribution of him killing the Bull of Heaven. This loss awakens in Gilgamesh his hidden fear of dying and his hatred of his own mortality. Growing increasingly agitated and discontented, Gilgamesh finally answers his call to the great adventure of searching the Earth to find the secret of eternal life.

Once he sets out on his journey, Gilgamesh is immediately challenged by threshold guardians who appear as two threatening Scorpion Men guarding the way to the underground tunnel used by the sun to reach the other side of the Earth. After interrogating Gilgamesh, they recognize his semidivine nature and allow him to pass. On the other side of the tunnel, Gilgamesh eventually meets with Utnapishtim, the survivor of the great flood. Utnapishtim and his wife have been granted eternal life by the gods for their participation in the flood, and Gilgamesh begs him for the secret to this same gift as well. Utnapishtim, acting as a threshold guardian, sets up a test for Gilgamesh: If he can stay awake for six days and seven nights, he will provide him with the immortality he searches for. Gilgamesh falls asleep almost immediately, and

Utnapishtim has his wife bake a loaf of bread on each of the days he is asleep so he can't deny his inability to stay awake. When Gilgamesh wakes up, Utnapishtim tells him that he's not ready to overcome death if he can't even conquer sleep.

Distraught, Gilgamesh prepares to leave, and as he does Utnapishtim's wife urges her husband to provide him with hope in the form of a parting gift. Utnapishtim tells Gilgamesh of the fabled boxthorn-like plant at the bottom of the sea that, once eaten, will restore his youth. Gilgamesh finds the location of the plant and ties large stones around his feet so he'll sink to the bottom long enough to harvest the plant. Once he has it, he plans to test it on an old man when he returns to Uruk. On his journey home though, Gilgamesh comes upon a stream and decides to stop and refresh himself by bathing. Disrobing and carefully putting the plant down next to his clothes, he wades out into the water, keeping a close lookout for anyone who might come upon his treasure. When Gilgamesh returns to his clothes, he is shocked to discover the plant is gone. As he searches wildly for it, he finds that a snake has eaten the plant and sees the evidence that the plant has indeed renewed its life, as all that is left of the snake is its old, shed skin. Great tears fall from his cheeks as he weeps at losing his last chance for immortality, and he returns home to make peace with his mortality and spends the rest of his days as all men do, searching for meaning in his humanity.

5. *Alcoholics Anonymous,* fourth edition (New York, NY: Alcoholics Anonymous World Services, Inc., 2001), p. 62.

6. *Alcoholics Anonymous,* fourth edition (New York, NY: Alcoholics Anonymous World Services, Inc., 2001), p. 62.

7. *Alcoholics Anonymous,* fourth edition (New York, NY: Alcoholics Anonymous World Services, Inc., 2001), p. 60.

8. *Twelve Steps and Twelve Traditions,* paperback edition, nineteenth printing (New York, NY: Alcoholics Anonymous World Services, Inc., 1995), p. 37.

9. Dorothy meets many other threshold guardians early in her adventure, and while running away from home with Toto, she meets the next one, the traveling salesman and psychic, Professor Marvel. The professor, who has traveled extensively and knows the dangers of the world well, recognizes immediately that Dorothy has impetuously run away from home and is not at all prepared for the adventure she is on. Using his sales and manipulation skills, he gets Dorothy to reveal where she is from and who is responsible for her. Playing with a crystal ball, he then tricks the naïve Dorothy into believing that he "sees" a sick Aunt Em, and so gets her to quit the adventure and turn back home. Dorothy hurries back to the farm only to find that she is too late; the journey she began seems to have a life of its own, and she is locked out of the safety of the tornado shelter.

Dorothy is then launched into the journey by the tornado and arrives in the unknown Land of Oz. Everything is strange and different here, and she immediately finds that she is treated as a hero by a village of little people, called the Munchkins, because her house lands on and kills the Wicked Witch of the East. Dorothy soon learns that she has freed them from the witch's oppression, and just as a celebration begins, the Wicked Witch of the West appears and angrily threatens Dorothy for killing her sister. Dorothy needs instant protection, and luckily her mentor,

Glinda, the Good Witch of the North, transfers the ruby slippers (amulets) onto Dorothy's feet, protecting her from the Wicked Witch. Glinda tells Dorothy that she must journey down the Yellow Brick Road to meet with the Wizard if she wants to get back home, and this is when the Wicked Witch acts as the next threshold guardian, threatening Dorothy and Toto to watch their backs should they attempt the adventure. Dorothy must make the hero's decision here and she does, choosing to attempt the journey regardless of the dangers ahead.

Sometimes threshold guardians serve the dual role of not only testing and challenging the hero's resolve, but, once passed, they join the hero on the adventure and become trusted friends and valuable allies. This happens next for Dorothy as she and her new companions, the Scarecrow and Tin Man, are marching and singing their way down the Yellow Brick Road. Suddenly, the Cowardly Lion jumps out on the road, roaring, threatening, and scaring everyone. While the Cowardly Lion bullies the Scarecrow and the Tin Man, Dorothy hides behind a big tree. When Toto barks at him, he turns around and attempts to bite him, and this is when Dorothy shows her first measure of growth. Instead of backing down, Dorothy charges forth, snatches Toto from the Lion, and punches him in the nose, rebuking him for threatening such a small and harmless dog. The Cowardly Lion, instantly ashamed and defeated, shrinks at the attack and breaks down whimpering and crying. In this moment, he reveals his own inner call, the need to grow and develop courage, and joins them on the hero path. By standing up to the Lion, Dorothy has not only passed the latest threshold guardian, but she is now surrounded by the helpers and companions she needs to complete her journey.

10. *Alcoholics Anonymous,* fourth edition (New York, NY: Alcoholics Anonymous World Services, Inc., 2001), p. 55.

11. Joseph Campbell, *The Hero with a Thousand Faces,* second edition (Princeton, NJ: Princeton University Press, 1968), p. 77.

12. Joseph Campbell, *The Hero with a Thousand Faces,* second edition (Princeton, NJ: Princeton University Press, 1968), p. 81.

13. *Pass It On, the Story of Bill Wilson and How the A.A. Message Reached the World* (New York, NY: Alcoholics Anonymous World Services, Inc., 1984), p. 120.

14. *Alcoholics Anonymous,* fourth edition (New York, NY: Alcoholics Anonymous World Services, Inc., 2001), p. 47.

15. *Twelve Steps and Twelve Traditions,* paperback edition, nineteenth printing (New York, NY: Alcoholics Anonymous World Services, Inc., 1995), p. 41.

16. *Alcoholics Anonymous,* fourth edition (New York, NY: Alcoholics Anonymous World Services, Inc., 2001), p. 63.

17. *Alcoholics Anonymous,* fourth edition (New York, NY: Alcoholics Anonymous World Services, Inc., 2001), p. 63.

18. *Twelve Steps and Twelve Traditions,* paperback edition, nineteenth printing (New York, NY: Alcoholics Anonymous World Services, Inc., 1995), p. 53.

Part Two: Initiation

Step Four: Into the Abyss

1. The motif of the whale's role in the collective imagination has its origins in the Greek mythological story of Andromeda and the sea monster Cetus. The story begins with a boast by the

arrogant and vain queen Cassiopeia (the wife of king Cepheus of Aethiopia) that her daughter, Andromeda, is more beautiful than the Nereids (sea nymphs) who surround Poseidon, the god of the sea. Poseidon is at once offended, and his wrath is quickly manifested by the huge sea monster Cetus who is sent to attack Aethiopia. Appalled and quickly overwhelmed, Cepheus and Cassiopeia consult a wise oracle who tell them the only way to pacify Poseidon is to sacrifice Andromeda to Cetus.

Reluctantly, they order Andromeda to be chained to a rock near the ocean so that Cetus can swallow and devour her. As she shivers chained to the rock, Andromeda becomes more and more terrified with each wave that washes over her. Sure that the next wave will bring the monster to her, she is on the verge of fainting when Perseus arrives to rescue her. In one version of the story, Perseus drives his sword deep into Cetus's back killing him, and in another, he uses Medusa's head to turn Cetus to stone. Today Cetus is known as "the whale" and is a constellation located in the same region of the sky that contains other water-related constellations such as Aquarius, Pisces, and Eridanus.

2. The concept of being dismembered and put back together is the central theme in all initiation rites of passage, and the practice of scarring, tattooing, or circumcising the young initiates all symbolize the dismemberment of the inner personality structure and consciousness. In tribal societies and smaller groups, the shaman is responsible for conducting the initiation ceremony of transformation, and a description of this elaborate process is captured in the book, *Serpent in the Sky*, by John Anthony West. Here the ceremony of the initiation of a shaman of the eastern Siberian Yakout tribe is revealed:

> "A Yakout shaman, Sofron Zatayev, affirms that customarily the future shaman dies and spends three days without food and drink. Formerly one was subjected to a thrice-performed ceremony during which he was cut in pieces. Another shaman, Pyorty Ivanov, told us about this ceremony in detail: 'the members of the candidate were detached and separated with an iron hook, the bones were cleaned, the flesh scraped, the body liquids thrown away and the eyes torn out of their sockets. After this operation the bones were reassembled and joined with iron. According to another shaman, the dismembering ceremony lasted three to seven days: during this time the candidate remained in suspended animation, like a corpse, in a solitary place.'"
>
> —West, from Robert Lafont, in Encyclopedies des Mystiques, p. 146

This symbolic description of ritual dismemberment signifies that the complete death of the old self is but the beginning of the process to prepare oneself for the reintegration and rebirth that is to come. During this process of dismemberment, the core pieces of the old self, symbolized here as the physical being (the bones, flesh, and bodily liquids) represent the deeper reaches of the personal unconscious, complete with the unrealized fears and suppressed or disowned qualities of the conscious self—the shadow. Each of these pieces of the psyche threatens to take back control and keep the shaman chained to the old way of life, and so each must be exposed and cut out as coldly as with an iron hook. Only from this purged place can they then be put back together to form a new spiritual whole.

3. *Alcoholics Anonymous*, fourth edition (New York, NY: Alcoholics Anonymous World Services, Inc., 2001), p. 215.

4. Many popular examples illuminate the transformation that takes place in the belly of the whale, such as when Pinocchio is swallowed by the whale Monstro while trying to rescue his father, Geppetto. They escape by setting a fire in the belly that forces the whale to sneeze them out, but as they try to get away, Monstro destroys Geppetto's raft. It is in this moment that Pinocchio reveals the change he has gone through by making the supreme sacrifice of saving Geppetto at the cost of his own life. Pinocchio has died to his old self of wanting to remain a child and so is transformed from a puppet and reborn as a real live boy.

5. *Twelve Steps and Twelve Traditions,* paperback edition, nineteenth printing (New York, NY: Alcoholics Anonymous World Services, Inc., 1995), p. 48.

6. *Alcoholics Anonymous,* fourth edition (New York, NY: Alcoholics Anonymous World Services, Inc., 2001), p. 64

7. *Alcoholics Anonymous,* fourth edition (New York, NY: Alcoholics Anonymous World Services, Inc., 2001), p. 67.

8. The concept of dismemberment, regeneration, and rebirth is nearly as old as the concept of storytelling itself. Between the first and fifth dynasty of Egypt, the myth of Osiris, referred to as both the king of the living and as the ruler of the dead, tells the story of the Egyptian god and king who was killed and dismembered by his brother, Set. Osiris was the oldest son of the earth god Geb, and sky goddess Nut, and was an ancient and revered king who brought many of the arts of civilization to the Egyptians, including agriculture. He married his sister, Isis, and together they ruled over a largely peaceful and prosperous Egypt.

In one version of the myth, Set grew increasingly jealous of his brother's popularity, and along with his wife, Nephthys (sister of

Isis), plotted to kill Osiris and usurp his power. Set held a banquet to honor Osiris and invited seventy-two others who had conspired to take part in the assignation. Set waited until Osiris was fully in the spirit of the party, and then he announced a challenge. Set rolled out a beautifully designed and richly adorned casket and announced to all that it would be awarded to whomever it fitted. Each guest had a try in the casket, but no one was a fit. Not until Osiris tried it. Unbeknownst to Osiris, Set had taken his measurements some months ago and had the casket made to his exact specifications. Once Osiris was inside, Set immediately slammed the lid closed, nailed it shut, and poured molten lead on the edges, sealing it securely. With the help of the others, the coffin was then carried and thrown into the Nile.

Devastated yet determined, Isis searched for the casket throughout Egypt and then overseas. Finally, she discovered the casket on the Phoenician coast where it had become embedded in a tamarind tree trunk that had been turned into a pillar holding up the roof of a palace in Byblos. When Isis managed to free the casket from the pillar and open it, she found that her beloved king was indeed dead. Heartbroken yet again, she returned the casket to Egypt for an appropriate burial ceremony but had to hide it in the marshes of the Nile for fear that Set would find and destroy it.

Unfortunately for Isis, Set was out hunting one day when his men came across the familiar looking casket. The moment Set saw it, he flew into a rage and tore the body of Osiris out of the casket, chopping it up into fourteen pieces. He then ordered his men to take the pieces to the far ends of the land, and to scatter them indiscriminately. Upon hearing of this latest atrocity, the faithful Isis once again set about searching and collecting the pieces of her dismembered king. Isis was able to collect all the pieces save one—the phallus, which had been eaten by a catfish—and she wrapped them all, mummy style, back together for the proper ceremonies and burial.

Before Isis buried Osiris, however, she magically breathed life into him and together they conceived a child, Horus (no small feat, even for a god, considering his missing piece!). Horus went on to battle his uncle Set, attempting to avenge his father's death. No clear victory was ever achieved, and the gods eventually resurrected Osiris as the god of the underworld while declaring Horus the king of the living and Set the ruler of the deserts and the god of chaos and evil. Because of his death and resurrection, Osiris was forever linked with the flooding and retreating of the Nile and with the fate of the crops along the Nile valley.

Today, the area most closely associated with the worship of Osiris remains the Giza Plateau, and the most sacred temples used are the Giza pyramids and the underground complexes beneath them. Much has been written and studied about the purpose and use of the pyramids, and one theory is that they were constructed for the elaborate and secret ceremonies used in the transformation and rebirth of a human being into a living god. These important rites of passage emulate the stories of Osiris: the preparation and mummification, etc., being brought back to life by Isis and then the resurrection and transformation into the god of the underworld.

9. Mary C. Darrah, *Sister Ignatia, Angel of Alcoholics Anonymous*, second edition (Center City, MN: Hazelden, 2001), pp. 77–78.
10. Mary C. Darrah, *Sister Ignatia, Angel of Alcoholics Anonymous*, second edition (Center City, MN: Hazelden, 2001), p. 80.

11. Joseph Campbell, *The Hero with a Thousand Faces*, second edition (Princeton, NJ: Princeton University Press, 1968), p. 25.

12. *Alcoholics Anonymous*, fourth edition (New York, NY: Alcoholics Anonymous World Services, Inc., 2001), p. 27.

13. *Alcoholics Anonymous*, fourth edition (New York, NY: Alcoholics Anonymous World Services, Inc., 2001), p. 68.

Step Five: Initiation
The Road of Trials

1. Joseph Campbell, *The Hero with a Thousand Faces*, second edition (Princeton, NJ: Princeton University Press, 1968), p. 16.

2. Initiation rites and ceremonies are found throughout cultures around the world, each helping the hero transition into his new station in life, as well as connecting him with the power of spirit. There are coming of age initiations like the walkabout Australian aborigines go through during adolescence, where initiates journey into the wilderness for up to six months. During this adventure, they follow dreaming tracks, also called songlines, which help them trace the paths their ancestors took. The paths of the songlines are recorded in the songs and stories of the culture, and one of the trials for the initiate is to use the songs' lyrics to help him navigate the unfamiliar and uncharted landscape of the Outback. As the adolescent follows the path taken by the ancient heroes who have gone before him, he learns to survive, grows in ability, and prepares himself to return to his village as a man. There are religious and spiritual initiations, too, like the Native American ceremony of the vision quest. Here initiates spend several days and nights secluded in nature, intensely focusing on spiritual communication and transcendence. The goal

is to receive the spiritual guidance necessary to help them identify their purpose and life direction. Many rituals and amulets are used as well, such as sweat lodges, hallucinogenic drugs, fasting, sleep deprivation, and other methods and tools. Each of these is used to open the channel to spirit and connect the initiate with the wisdom of the supernatural world.

3. The adventures that heroes go on during the initiation phase, and throughout the road of trials that punctuate this phase, make up the bulk of stories that are associated with the journey of the hero. The rich tapestry of myth, fairy tales, and modern story telling weave entertaining and insightful stories of the danger, opportunity, and growth that occur during this phase. Many ancient stories still stir the collective imagination and are retold even today. The Labors of Heracles are a great example of the road of trials, as Heracles relies on both helpers and companions, as well as reliance on help from the gods. Heracles also grows stronger through each trial, using the tools and skills he gains through each one to become more competent in facing the next, more difficult, challenge ahead. In Greek mythology, Heracles was the son of the god Zeus and the mortal woman Alcmene, and was considered a divine hero. (The Romans' version of Heracles is Hercules, the name known mostly in the modern West.) Heracles had extraordinary strength and the courage to match, and his sexual ravenousness was unbounded, consuming both males and females. In overcoming obstacles, Heracles used his brute strength, though his wit and ingenuity was also legendary. For example, during his eleventh labor, when Heracles had agreed to taking on the burden of the world while Atlas gathered the golden apples for him, he lured a reluctant Atlas into taking

the world back onto his shoulders by asking him to reassume the burden for a moment so he could rearrange his cloak as padding on his shoulders. Once Atlas did, Heracles quickly escaped, leaving Atlas to forever carry the heavens on his shoulders.

The trials that Heracles was forced to undergo were in the form of twelve labors sentenced him by his archenemy, Eurystheus, the man who became king in Heracles's place. Heracles, driven mad by Hera, the jealous wife of Zeus, had slain his own wife and children, and when he regained his sanity, the devastated Heracles traveled to the oracle of Delphi to seek advice on redemption by the priestess Pythia. She advised him that the only way to pay for his horrible crime was to serve the king and perform any task demanded of him for ten years. She told him that if he was able to successfully complete these labors, he would not only be forgiven but would also achieve immortality and take his rightful place among the gods. The trials that Eurystheus and Hera laid out were calculated to finally thwart even someone as strong and cunning as Heracles, for they involved seemingly impossible tasks such as slaying the invincible Nemean lion, whose claws were sharper than mortals' swords and whose golden fur was impervious to attack. Given the eleven other labors (originally there were ten labors, but two were discounted by Eurystheus because Heracles received help, and thus did not accomplish them himself), the road ahead of Heracles represented trials of truly epic proportion.

The first labor of Heracles was to slay the vicious Nemean Lion. This ferocious beast was the son of the monsters Typhon (known as the "Father of All Monsters" and with a hundred dragon heads was the deadliest monster in Greek mythology) and Echidna (the

"Mother of All Monsters," halfwoman and half serpent), and was brother of the Theban Sphinx. The monstrous lion terrorized the valley of Nemea by capturing women from the village and then luring warriors to his cave by imitating the injured women and crying out for help. As the warriors rushed into the lair, they discovered the trap too late as the lion quickly transformed back into the raging monster and attacked the warriors. The warriors fought bravely at first but soon realized that their swords and arrows were useless against the lion's impenetrable fur. As they turned to run, the lion pounced and easily ripped them to shreds with its vicious claws. Once the furious yet short struggle was over, the lion feasted on the flesh of the remains and then made an offering of the bones to Hades, god of the underworld.

Heracles, not knowing of the lion's pelt of invincibility, and confident in his own enormous strength, hunted the lion, intending to kill the monster with an arrow from his mighty bow. Heracles tracked the lion to an open field and stalked close enough to take careful aim at the great beast. Heracles drew back his bow with the full force of the heavens and let the deadly arrow fly. The force of the arrow was such that it shook the air as it flew, causing a terrible shrill as it hurtled toward the lion. When it hit the thigh of the monster it harmlessly bounced off, and the lion, now alerted to Heracles's presence, turned and charged. Shocked but not deterred, Heracles reverted to his ingenuity and carefully lured the lion back to its lair.

Unbeknownst to the lion, Heracles had scouted out the cave earlier in the day and blocked the main entrance, one of only two ways into the cave. When the lion returned, its only option was to enter through a dark and narrow passageway, a dangerous route because of its tight quarters. Heracles had taken up position in the darkest part of this hallway, and he lay well hidden and prepared to ambush the lion as he approached. Once the lion passed him, Heracles emerged from his ambush and surprised the lion with the swiftness of his perfectly timed attack. Heracles drew back his powerful club and charged the lion, delivering a thunderous blow that stunned and temporarily dazed the lion. He then leapt upon the monster and, with his immense strength, seized the beast's neck and strangled it to death.

As the lion lay lifeless in its lair, Heracles knelt down and attempted to skin the mighty pelt as proof of the impossible first task accomplished. Just as his arrow had, though, his razor-sharp knife bounced off the impenetrable, golden fur. Unable to find a solution, Heracles sought help from the gods, and Athena, the goddess of wisdom and courage, intervened and suggested that Heracles use the lion's own claws to the skin the fur. Following this supernatural advice, he carefully used one of the claws and was able to cut away the entire coat intact. Once done, Heracles donned the coat and carried the carcass of the lion on his shoulders back to King Eurystheus. The king was terrified when he saw the fearsome figure of Heracles dressed in the lion's monstrous pelt. He hid behind his palace guards and warned Heracles that each of the next tasks would grow in complexity and danger. So frightened was Eurystheus that he ordered Heracles to leave any future trophies outside the city's gates, and then he dispatched Heracles to his next trial, which was to destroy the Lernaean Hydra. After Heracles left the palace, the king commanded that a large, bronze jar be built and buried deep within the earth of the castle. From then on, whenever he received word of Hercules's approach, the king hid in this jar and communicated with the hero through messenger only.

As is typical with the trials that heroes face, each task does grow harder for Heracles, and they require him to continue to grow in both skill and ingenuity, as well as rely on supernatural guardianship and assistance from companions he meets along the way. With each successive trial, Heracles becomes even more capable, leveraging the lessons learned and using the resources he accumulates to help prepare him for the ever more dangerous trials to come. From his first trial, Heracles has use of the lion's invincible pelt as a protective layer that he uses to shield him during the labors ahead. And while the trials force the hero to grow his skills and awareness, they also move him closer to his new ideal self.

For Heracles's second labor, he faced a beast that was a sibling of the Nemean lion, but even more deadly, as the Lernean Hydra was a monstrous dragon/snake-like creature that had nine poisonous heads, one of which was immortal. Hera herself had carefully raised the Hydra to one day slay Heracles, and as such, she made the monster invincible by giving the Hydra the grotesque ability grow two new heads as soon as one was cut off. The Hydra was so dangerous, in fact, that even its breath was poisonous, and its blood so corrosive that its tracks left a deadly stain that would kill on contact. The Hydra lurked in the murky waters of the marshes and swamps of a place called Lerna, and this is where Heracles journeyed next to complete his trial.

Sensing the nearly impossible task ahead of him, Heracles wisely sets off on the hunt with his nephew, Iolaus, as his companion and helper. After searching the gloomy swamps for days, they finally discover the lair of the monster but keep clear of it at first as a poisonous stench emanates from the dark patch of boiling water. Heracles makes his plan with Iolaus and approaches it slowly, covering both his mouth and nose with a thick cloth to protect himself from the fumes. Drawing back his mighty bow, Heracles shoots flaming arrows into its den to lure the creature to the surface, and once it raises its heads out of the water, he seizes one of them and begins to pound it with his powerful club. The monster has been waiting for this moment, though, and swiftly winds one of its coils around Heracles's legs to trap him, and then calls on a companion of its own, a huge crab, to begin viciously biting the trapped foot of the hero. So adept is Heracles with his club, that he instantly smashes the crab, and then raises it to deliver a fatal blow to one of the heads. As soon as he does, however, two more appear in its place, and the menacing monster only grows stronger with each seeming defeat.

As Heracles struggles to defend himself, he calls on Iolaus for help. Receiving guidance from the god, Athena, Iolaus comes up with the idea to scorch each of the stumps of the heads and uses a firebrand to cauterize each one that Heracles smashes. This works, and as Heracles destroys each poisonous head, there remains the one immortal head that still has the power to defeat him. Relying on the supernatural protection of Athena yet again, Heracles produces a golden sword she has given him that has the power to kill even the immortal. Heracles raises the mighty sword and delivers a mortal blow at the base of the neck, and it slices the head off cleanly. Heracles quickly gathers the head which is still alive and writhing on the ground, and he buries it under a great rock. Before he does, however, he dips his arrows in its poisonous blood, further strengthening himself for the trials ahead. Hera, seeing the battle lost, grows inconsolable by Heracles's latest victory and puts the remains of the beasts in the sky to immortalize them, where they stand even today as the Constellation Hydra and the crab as the Constellation Cancer.

Once again Heracles not only survives another trial but he grows wiser, stronger, and more confident as a result. In addition, Heracles does what all heroes do during the adventure: He makes use of the amulets and talismans he is given; he relies on the help and assistance of companions; and, most of all, he draws continued strength and guidance from the supernatural guardianship provided by the gods. All of these resources combine with the new tools he gains along the way—the impenetrable skin of the lion and his arrows dipped in the poison from the Hydra—which prepare him for the increasing difficulties he faces in the remaining labors. Heroes pass through innumerable tests and trials during the initiation phase, and many of them target the weakest parts of their new personality, the parts that need the most growth and development. With each successful passage, the hero transitions into a more cohesive whole, becoming one with his new self, and finally capable of facing the ultimate conflict that looms at the end of the road of trials.

4. In one adventure, Harry, along with his companions Ron and Hermione, descend through a trap door into the abyss of the castle to keep Voldemort from stealing the Sorcerer's Stone, the only stone from which the elixir of life can be extracted. The first trial in this series is to get past the modern-day Cerberus, Fluffy,

the vicious three-headed dog who is guarding the entrance. Fluffy is a formidable threshold guardian, and Harry must rely on knowledge and guidance he received from one of the most important helpers on his journey, Hagrid. Hagrid told Harry earlier that music puts Fluffy to sleep, so when they face Fluffy, Harry is prepared with a flute that was a Christmas present from Hagrid the previous year. The power of this amulet works well, and once the monster is asleep, the heroes lift the trapdoor and descend into the labyrinth of the castle.

On their way to the Sorcerer's Stone, they face a series of ever more threatening trials, and the only way Harry ultimately succeeds is by relying on special skills and knowledge he does not yet possess, but that each of his companions separately do. Once through the trapdoor, they immediately land in a slimy pit that is covered by the dangerous plant, Devil's Snare. As its tentacles coil around each of them, they become trapped and dangerously close to being suffocated. Fortunately, Hermione recognizes what it is, and also the way out, which is to resist struggling and simply relax. Although easier than it sounds, both Hermione and Harry are eventually able to do this and are released, but Ron continues to struggle and grows increasingly entwined. Once again, Hermione comes to the rescue by remembering that there is another way out of the Devil's Snare, and she uses her wand to cast the Lumos Solem spell that lets in the light, forcing the plant to recoil, thus freeing Ron.

The next obstacle is a magical set of giant chess pieces that block the door to the next chamber. Chess is one of Ron's strengths, and Harry and Hermione rely on his skill and courage this time to get past this challenge. Ron directs both Harry and Hermione to take the place of black chess pieces, Harry a bishop and Hermione the queen, while he jumps on the back of one of the knights and plays from this role. Ron then conducts the game brilliantly until he sets up an opportunity for checkmate—made possible only through a sacrifice of his own piece and himself. While both Harry and Hermione argue with him to avoid this move, he convinces them it is the only way to get Harry past the white king and through to the next room. Ron then makes the sacrifice, and Harry is able to move into a checkmate, thus winning the game and allowing him to advance to the next obstacle that lies beyond the door.

In the next chamber there are flying keys, only one of which will allow Harry to continue. Here Harry uses his own magic broom and his new skills as a Quidditch Seeker to capture the right one. In the final chamber, Harry is able to transfer the Sorcerer's Stone into his pocket by the enchanted spell of Harry's supernatural protector, Dumbledore, and Harry survives because of the power of love his mother bestowed on him when she sacrificed herself for him. Harry's growth through the initiations and adventures of this part of his journey is impressive, and through the following books in the series, and the ever-increasing tests and trials they offer, Harry continues to grow up and grow into his true self. The culmination of his new skills and his new self as a wizard is tested in his final trial and supreme ordeal: his showdown with Lord Voldemort in *Harry Potter and the Deathly Hallows—Part 2*.

5. *Twelve Steps and Twelve Traditions,* paperback edition, nineteenth printing (New York, NY: Alcoholics Anonymous World Services, Inc, 1995), p. 58.

6. *Twelve Steps and Twelve Traditions,* paperback edition, nineteenth printing (New York, NY: Alcoholics Anonymous World Services, Inc., 1995), p. 57.

7. Luke's naiveté and self-will are continually tested by Yoda, and when he fails a test, he is slow to learn from the experience. The next trial comes when Luke feels a cold presence outside a cave and says, "There's something not right here. I feel cold." Yoda points to the cave and says, "That place is strong with the dark side of the Force. A domain of evil, it is. And you must go." "What's in there?" Luke asks. "Only what you take with you," he says. As Luke marches off to the cave, he grabs his lightsaber belt, and Yoda warns, "Your weapons, you will not need them." Once again Luke chooses to disregard Yoda's advice and instead enters the cave relying on himself and his weapons.

As he descends into the darkness of the cave, he enters the darkness within himself, and in this abyss he is given the hero's choice of surrendering to the light of the Force or of choosing his own power yet again, a power driven by the ego's resentment and fear—the exact qualities that will lead him to the dark side. Continuing deeper into the gloomy cavern, a giant shadow suddenly appears from around a corner, and Luke sees that it is the epitome of evil, Darth Vader. Luke raises his lightsaber and duels with Vader and soon strikes a gruesome blow that decapitates him. As Vader's head rolls on the ground, the mask explodes and exposes the face within: the face of Luke himself. Looking into his own face, Luke's deepest fears of succumbing to the dark side have materialized. Luke has failed to learn the lesson that only the light of the Force can destroy evil, and that by carrying his hatred and darkness into the cave ("Only the things you take with you"), Luke perpetuates the evil in the world and becomes more vulnerable to giving in to it. If he had not carried his weapons into the cave and instead taken Yoda's advice and gone in with the power of the Force, he would have passed this test and grown in wisdom and power. Unfortunately, Luke emerges from the cave still fueled by self-righteous rage, and this self-will leads him into the next trial, which turns out even worse for him because he falls right into a trap set by Darth Vader.

During the intensive training with Yoda that follows, Luke has a premonition that Han and Leia are suffering, and he impetuously decides to leave against his mentor's advice. Yoda is afraid that Luke is still not ready to resist the pull of the dark side, and this will be severely tested as Darth Vader is holding Han and Leia as bait in the Cloud City run by Lando Calrissian. When Luke arrives, he once again confronts Vader, only this time it is for real. As they duel with lightsabers over the city's central air shaft, Luke learns a truth he is not quite ready to accept: that Vader didn't kill his father, but rather that Darth Vader *is* his father. At this moment Luke is offered another choice: to give in to his anger and resentment and turn to the dark side to rule the galaxy as father and son, or to turn away and follow a greater truth. This intense trial once again challenges the internal obstacles still blocking Luke's growth, and his progress in the journey depends upon how he responds, if he survives, and what he learns. As with all heroes, the external tests mirror his inner needs to grow, and the passage of each trial leads to the discovery and integration of his true self.

Steps Six and Seven: Revelation
The Curiously Fluid Stage

1. Joseph Campbell, *The Hero with a Thousand Faces*, second edition (Princeton, NJ: Princeton University Press, 1968), p. 8.

2. Joseph Campbell, *The Hero with a Thousand Faces*, second edition (Princeton, NJ: Princeton University Press, 1968), p. 97.

3. Ritual purification has always been a common part of religious and spiritual practice and can be traced throughout the cultures and history of the world. Practices including bathing or washing in water, such as a river or stream, fasting or prolonged meditation, or even more extreme means such as bloodletting, flagellation, or other forms of self-mortification all serve to ritually cleanse the body or spirit, preparing the initiate for elaborate religious ceremonies and practices. Baptism is a common form of ritual purification for several religions, and for Roman Catholics and other faiths, confession is required to purge and receive absolution from sin, especially as a preparation for receiving the Eucharist. In Hinduism, ritual purification is achieved by bathing the entire body, especially in holy rivers such as the Ganges, prior to sacred festivals, and even after the death of someone close as a way to maintain purity.

Many North American Indian tribes use sweat lodges as a means of ritual purification, and during the eighteen and nineteenth centuries, they developed elaborate rituals to protect and cleanse their spirits from the increasing corruption of early European culture. Sweat lodges traditionally serve as a way back to the wisdom and power of the spirit, and each part of the ceremony follows strict rituals, starting with the placement of the lodge. The entrance often faces the East, toward Father Sun, because this is considered the source of life and wisdom. There is often a sacred pit of fire just beyond the entrance and its flame symbolizes the eternal light of the world, as well as the renewed spiritual experience sought in the sweat ceremony. In some traditions, tobacco is offered to participants through either a pipe or as loose tobacco to be thrown on the fire. The tobacco smoke is thought to carry prayers or requests to the Great Spirit.

Retreating into the darkness of the sweat lodge is like going back into the mother's womb, returning to the place of purity and innocence. This is a place where one can be close to the Creator of all life and where healing and rebirth takes place. A talking stick is sometimes passed around, giving each person the chance to ask for guidance or pray for forgiveness for any misdeeds. Mirroring the four directions—West, North, East, and South—a sweat can last for four, thirty-minute rounds. In the first round, the sun goes down into the black West and participants can ask for a spirit guide for the journey ahead. In the second round, respect is paid to the white North, and a request for courage, cleanliness, and honesty is made to this direction of strength. Next, reverence and prayers go out to the East and the daybreak star so that one might share in the wisdom and guidance of the new day. The yellow South symbolizes growth and healing, and in this round the emphasis is on spiritual growth and renewal.

By following the spiritual guides from the West, and borrowing honesty, humility, and courage from the North, and using the wisdom and knowledge from the East, the participant journeys the full circle to the South to complete his quest for growth and renewal. Healing comes as the result of this process of purification, and the rebirth of the participant symbolizes the spiritual renewal of the tribe.

Many other cultures, including Scandinavian, Baltic, and some Eastern European cultures, also use sweat lodges as a means of ritual purification. Evidence of rudimentary sweat lodges have been found as far back as the fifth century BC by the Scythians, the early Iranian equestrian tribes who inhabited the central Eurasian steppes. When Finnish immigrants settled in America in the seventeenth century, they, too, brought their practice of sauna with them and were known to the local Delaware natives as "sweat lodge men." This affinity with the local practice of the sweat lodge formed a bond with the native Indians, and as such, some Finnish settlements were spared the burning and looting during the ongoing French and Indian Wars during that time.

In addition to tobacco, many herbs are used during the sweat ceremony and often bundled together to form smudge sticks that are then burned to cleanse the area of any evil presence. Of all the herbs used, sage, particularly ceremonial white sage, is most frequently used in purifying rituals. The use of sage is an ancient tradition, used by both the Druids and early Celts to help them acquire wisdom and for protection and healing. Today, the burning of sage as a cleansing and purifying ritual for new homes and dwellings continues the ancient use of this herb.

4. For centuries, myths have symbolized this descent into the unexplored and feared region of the unconscious with tales of a journey into the underworld. As far back as 4000 BC, in ancient Mesopotamia, the story of two very different sisters, Inanna and Ereshkigal, tells of such a descent and how the interaction of opposites created the conditions for the eternal change in seasons. Inanna was the goddess of love, fertility, and warfare, the goddess of the grains of the earth and people of this world. Her sister,

Ereshkigal, lived in the darkness of the underworld and was the queen of the dead and fallen heroes and ordinary people alike, and her power was so fearful that even the gods and goddesses respected and revered her. When Ereshkigal's husband, Gudgalana, died, Ereshkigal's cries of anguish and despair rose from the depths of the buried darkness, and Inanna could no longer ignore or deny her own unacknowledged feelings of shame and abandonment over her estranged sister. Inanna knew she would have to descend into the underworld to face at last her disavowed self that was embodied by her sister. Against the wishes of her husband and many of her advisors, Inanna decided to enter the land of the dead to attend the funeral rites of Gudgalana. Because of the rules of the underworld, whereby no one who enters the darkness shall ever return to the living (except specific messengers), Inanna, supremely confident in her earthly power, nonetheless takes precautions by instructing her handmaid, Ninshubur, to pray to the deities Enlil, Nanna, and Enki to come to her aid should she be prevented from crossing back.

In preparation for the journey, Inanna gathers seven symbols of life and civilization and transforms them into powerful amulets of protective clothing and jewelry, including her stunning "pala dress" adorned with rich beads, her lapis lazuli necklace, and full turban and wig. Anointing her left hand is a giant golden ring, and in the other hand she carries the sacred lapis lazuli measuring rod that has the power to measure the thread of life allotted to each person. So appointed, Inanna confidently approaches the outer gate of the underworld and announces to Neti, the guardian of the entrance, that she has come to witness the funeral rites of her sister's husband. Suspicious of her attire and attitude, Neti quickly sends a message to his queen, Ereshkigal, telling her of the glorious Inanna, draped in the ostentatious allure of feminine power and sexuality. Ereshkigal quickly becomes enraged. She instructs Neti to let Inanna pass but to lock the doors of the seven gates of the underworld behind her, and to require Inanna to remove one of her garments at each gate in order to pass. As she approaches the first gate, a guardian stops her and demands that she surrender her crown if she wishes to pass. Indignant, yet eager to enter, Inanna asks why such a sacrifice is needed, and she is simply told, "Quiet Inanna, the ways of the Underworld are perfect. They may not be questioned."

As Inanna arrives at each additional gate, she encounters the same, sordid ritual: The gate opens but a crack, and as the hot breath of death escapes each chamber, she is ferried through while another piece of jewelry or clothing is stripped from her. As she journeys deeper into the abyss, she abandons more and more of her power, until finally, at the bottommost cavern, she arrives naked and bowed over, completely surrendered and at the mercy of her furious sister. In the dark throne room of the underworld, Ereshkigal unleashes her full wrath and calls in the seven judges of the damned to pass their sentence. The judges look down upon Inanna with the dark look of disgust they reserve for the dead and dying, and, after measuring her guilt, they pronounce their judgment with the fury of the righteous and condemn Inanna to death. She is instantly turned into a corpse of rotting flesh and hung from a hook on the wall of the chamber.

After three anxious days, Inanna's faithful servant, Ninshubur, suspects the worst and turns to the temples of each of the deities pleading that they intercede and rescue Inanna. Both Enlil, Inanna's paternal grandfather, and Nanna, Inanna's father, refuse to help, both still angry that she has taken a path apart from what they had chosen for her. But Enki, Inanna's maternal grandfather, understands the importance of the journey she has undertaken, and becomes compassionate, vowing to do what he can to help. While Enlil and Nanna sleep, Enki collects dirt from under their fingernails and creates two beguiling, asexual figures, galatur and kurgarra, to enchant and distract Ereshkigal. They descend to the underworld disguised as flies so as not to be detected, and once in the chamber throne, they reappear as beguiling figures and win Ereshkigal over with their combination of compassion for her pain at losing her other half, her sister, while they enchant her with their wanton sexuality. While under their trance, they get Ereshkigal to turn over to them Inanna's corpse, which they revive by sprinkling it with the food and water of life.

Once alive again, Inanna races through the decaying catacombs of the underworld, desperate to reach the surface of life again. In her frantic escape, she is alternately assisted and chased by demons that Ereshkigal has dispatched—such is the nature of her complex feelings—to both help her sister return and block her way. When Inanna finally reaches the threshold of the living again, she understands the great lesson of her journey: that for her to complete her rebirth, she must not forget nor neglect her abandoned sister, the dark side of herself. And the only way for her to keep the passageway between the consciousness of light and the unconsciousness of darkness open is for someone to take her place in the underworld. At first the demons demand that Ninshubur be sacrificed, but Inanna refuses to hand over her faithful servant. They next try other servants close to Inanna, but all of them are deep in mourning, and Inanna can't help but plead to the demons to spare them, too. Finally, the demons find Dumuzi, Inanna's husband, who they come across resting under a tree in his most exquisite clothes. Seemingly unbothered by his wife's disappearance and rumored death, Inanna becomes infuriated and condemns him with the power and fury that she herself had received just days before. Shaken and terrified, Dumuzi is led away by the demons. Dumuzi calls on the deities to come to his aid and his loyal sister, so distraught by his disappearance, demands to take his place. To appease them both, the deities decide to have the two split the time in the underworld, each spending six months so enslaved.

As a result of Inanna's descent into the underworld, and her union with the dark side of her sister, she finds that she has emerged with a peculiar power of Ereshkigal's: the power of death. During the six months while her husband is away, Inanna falls into grief during which the plants of the field die away. When her husband returns for six months, her powers of fertility once again take over and the fields become alive and full. Inanna's journey into the underworld has allowed her to accept and assimilate the dark power of her neglected self, her sister, and in doing so, she finally understands that in the darkness there lies a vital power capable of sustaining and even creating life anew.

5. *Twelve Steps and Twelve Traditions,* paperback edition, nineteenth printing (New York, NY: Alcoholics Anonymous World Services, Inc., 1995), p. 73.

6. *Twelve Steps and Twelve Traditions,* paperback edition, nineteenth printing (New York, NY: Alcoholics Anonymous World Services, Inc., 1995), p. 63.

7. *Alcoholics Anonymous,* fourth edition (New York, NY: Alcoholics

Anonymous World Services, Inc., 2001), p. 27.

8. *Twelve Steps and Twelve Traditions*, paperback edition, nineteenth printing (New York, NY: Alcoholics Anonymous World Services, Inc., 1995), p. 90.

9. *Alcoholics Anonymous*, fourth edition (New York, NY: Alcoholics Anonymous World Services, Inc., 2001), p. 76.

10. *Alcoholics Anonymous*, fourth edition (New York, NY: Alcoholics Anonymous World Services, Inc., 2001), p. 124.

Steps Eight and Nine: Atonement

1. The first hint Harry has of his destiny is in the book, *The Prisoner of Azkaban*. When Harry is on the shore, the Dementors attack, and he is about to be overwhelmed by them until he sees a figure on the other side, casting the Expecto Patronum spell. He thinks this is his father who has come to save him, and it is only later that he comes to understand that it is his future self instead. Harry grows past his old self in this moment when he realizes that he alone has the power to overcome the Dementors and, perhaps, the power to do something his father couldn't do—defeat Voldemort. It is Harry's commitment to assuming his father's path by facing and defeating Voldemort that serves as his final atonement. Voldemort remains the one figure that holds supreme power over him, and only by accepting the responsibility of facing him does Harry finally cross the ultimate threshold and transcend his past. In the last book, *Harry Potter and the Deathly Hallows*, Harry not only completes his father's task by facing and defeating Voldemort, but he surpasses his father by showing tolerance and understanding, and by offering Voldemort the chance of redemption. He does this by refusing to kill him, thus offering

Voldemort a way out of his own darkness. In this final scene, Harry atones with both his father and with Voldemort, passing them both in development and consciousness. His journey comes full circle by the end of the series as Harry becomes a father himself, thus completing his transformation from the child he was in the beginning to the adult he has become at the end.

2. In Japan, a tale is told of a Zen monk who was accused of raping a local village girl. The girl cried with angry tears that the monk, who had publicly ignored her, had one day turned around and raped her. As his captors arrested him, they demanded what he had to say for himself. "Is that so?" was all he said. The ensuing trial was stormy and quick. On the stand, the girl cried even more and pointed at the accused who sat with quiet detachment during the charges. When it was his turn on the stand, the crowd who gathered to hear his defense was disappointed as he answered each accusing question with the same, "Is that so?" By neither denying nor confirming the charges, the verdict was quickly delivered—guilty!

The monk was transferred to the local prison where he went about his daily schedule in much the same way he had done during his freedom. He woke and prayed and meditated till noon, took his afternoon meal, and prayed once again. At the end of the day he studied the spiritual texts and gave the guards no trouble when it was time to sleep. When taunted and tormented by the other inmates as a child molester, they, too, demanded an explanation. "Is that so?" was all they received.

Months later, the child's parents went to the authorities with shocking news. Upon meeting with the prosecutor, the crying daughter in tow, they professed their shame and regret: The daughter had lied. The monk, the daughter said through sobs, had done nothing but ignore her. To get back at him and teach him a lesson, she had made up the whole story. Upon hearing the truth, the judge was summoned, and he pronounced that a great injustice had been done and ordered the immediate release of the monk.

In the following days, a new storm brewed about the sham trial and sentencing of an innocent man. The local news and reporters clamored for an interview with the monk but he refused to comment. Finally, the judge himself summoned the monk to his office and, with the prosecutor in attendance, called for a news conference. As the reporters gathered, they waited anxiously to hear the indignant statement from the wrongly accused man. Amid a flurry of questions of what he thought the punishment of the girl should be, to what he thought of the justice system, to how he felt now that his standing in the community was ruined, he answered softly, "Is that so?" Realizing they would get nothing more from this man who could say so much, they eventually dispersed, and the monk went home to his evening prayers.

3. *Twelve Steps and Twelve Traditions,* paperback edition, nineteenth printing (New York, NY: Alcoholics Anonymous World Services, Inc., 1995), p. 83.

4. *Alcoholics Anonymous,* fourth edition (New York, NY: Alcoholics Anonymous World Services, Inc., 2001), pp. 83–84.

Steps Ten and Eleven: Attunement

1. Joseph Campbell, *The Hero with a Thousand Faces,* second edition (Princeton, NJ: Princeton University Press, 1968), p. 167.

2. *Alcoholics Anonymous,* fourth edition (New York, NY: Alcoholics

Appendix

Anonymous World Services, Inc., 2001), p. 88.

3. *Twelve Steps and Twelve Traditions,* paperback edition, nineteenth printing (New York, NY: Alcoholics Anonymous World Services, Inc., 1995), p. 90.

4. *Alcoholics Anonymous,* fourth edition (New York, NY: Alcoholics Anonymous World Services, Inc., 2001), p. 84.

5. *Alcoholics Anonymous,* fourth edition (New York, NY: Alcoholics Anonymous World Services, Inc., 2001), p. 85.

6. *Twelve Steps and Twelve Traditions,* paperback edition, nineteenth printing (New York, NY: Alcoholics Anonymous World Services, Inc., 1995), p. 98.

7. *Alcoholics Anonymous,* fourth edition (New York, NY: Alcoholics Anonymous World Services, Inc., 2001), p. 88.

Part Three: Return

Step Twelve: The Return

1. *Twelve Steps and Twelve Traditions,* paperback edition, nineteenth printing (New York, NY: Alcoholics Anonymous World Services, Inc., 1995), p. 107.

2. *Alcoholics Anonymous,* fourth edition (New York, NY: Alcoholics Anonymous World Services, Inc., 2001), p. 27.

3. *Twelve Steps and Twelve Traditions,* paperback edition, nineteenth printing (New York, NY: Alcoholics Anonymous World Services, Inc., 1995), p. 106.

4. Mary C. Darrah, *Sister Ignatia, Angel of Alcoholics Anonymous,* second edition (Center City, MN: Hazelden, 2001), p. 240.

5. Joseph Campbell, *The Hero with a Thousand Faces*, second edition (Princeton, NJ: Princeton University Press, 1968), p. 243.